Anna Sanina

PATRIOTIC EDUCATION IN CONTEMPORARY RUSSIA

Sociological Studies in the Making
of the Post-Soviet Citizen

With a foreword by Anna Oldfield

ibidem-Verlag
Stuttgart

Bibliografische Information der Deutschen Nationalbibliothek
Die Deutsche Nationalbibliothek verzeichnet diese Publikation in der Deutschen Nationalbibliografie; detaillierte bibliografische Daten sind im Internet über http://dnb.d-nb.de abrufbar.

Bibliographic information published by the Deutsche Nationalbibliothek
Die Deutsche Nationalbibliothek lists this publication in the Deutsche Nationalbibliografie; detailed bibliographic data are available in the Internet at http://dnb.d-nb.de.

Cover picture: © copyright 2017 by Anna Polyanskaya

∞
Gedruckt auf alterungsbeständigem, säurefreien Papier
Printed on acid-free paper

ISSN: 1614-3515

ISBN-13: 978-3-8382-0993-7

© *ibidem*-Verlag
Stuttgart 2017

Alle Rechte vorbehalten

Das Werk einschließlich aller seiner Teile ist urheberrechtlich geschützt. Jede Verwertung außerhalb der engen Grenzen des Urheberrechtsgesetzes ist ohne Zustimmung des Verlages unzulässig und strafbar. Dies gilt insbesondere für Vervielfältigungen, Übersetzungen, Mikroverfilmungen und elektronische Speicherformen sowie die Einspeicherung und Verarbeitung in elektronischen Systemen.

All rights reserved. No part of this publication may be reproduced, stored in or introduced into a retrieval system, or transmitted, in any form, or by any means (electronic, mechanical, photocopying, recording or otherwise) without the prior written permission of the publisher. Any person who does any unauthorized act in relation to this publication may be liable to criminal prosecution and civil claims for damages.

Printed in the EU

Soviet and Post-Soviet Politics and Society (SPPS)
ISSN 1614-3515

General Editor: Andreas Umland,
Institute for Euro-Atlantic Cooperation, Kyiv. umland@stanfordalumni.org

Commissioning Editor: Max Jakob Horstmann,
London, mjh@ibidem.eu

EDITORIAL COMMITTEE*

DOMESTIC & COMPARATIVE POLITICS
Prof. **Ellen Bos**, *Andrássy University of Budapest*
Dr. **Ingmar Bredies**, *FH Bund, Brühl*
Dr. **Andrey Kazantsev**, *MGIMO (U) MID RF, Moscow*
Prof. **Heiko Pleines**, *University of Bremen*
Prof. **Richard Sakwa**, *University of Kent at Canterbury*
Dr. **Sarah Whitmore**, *Oxford Brookes University*
Dr. **Harald Wydra**, *University of Cambridge*

SOCIETY, CLASS & ETHNICITY
Col. **David Glantz**, *"Journal of Slavic Military Studies"*
Dr. **Marlène Laruelle**, *George Washington University*
Dr. **Stephen Shulman**, *Southern Illinois University*
Prof. **Stefan Troebst**, *University of Leipzig*

POLITICAL ECONOMY & PUBLIC POLICY
Prof. em. **Marshall Goldman**, *Wellesley College, Mass.*
Dr. **Andreas Goldthau**, *Central European University*
Dr. **Robert Kravchuk**, *University of North Carolina*
Dr. **David Lane**, *University of Cambridge*
Dr. **Carol Leonard**, *Higher School of Economics, Moscow*
Dr. **Maria Popova**, *McGill University, Montreal*

FOREIGN POLICY & INTERNATIONAL AFFAIRS
Dr. **Peter Duncan**, *University College London*
Prof. **Andreas Heinemann-Grüder**, *University of Bonn*
Dr. **Taras Kuzio**, *Johns Hopkins University*
Prof. **Gerhard Mangott**, *University of Innsbruck*
Dr. **Diana Schmidt-Pfister**, *University of Konstanz*
Dr. **Lisbeth Tarlow**, *Harvard University, Cambridge*
Dr. **Christian Wipperfürth**, *N-Ost Network, Berlin*
Dr. **William Zimmerman**, *University of Michigan*

HISTORY, CULTURE & THOUGHT
Dr. **Catherine Andreyev**, *University of Oxford*
Prof. **Mark Bassin**, *Södertörn University*
Prof. **Karsten Brüggemann**, *Tallinn University*
Dr. **Alexander Etkind**, *University of Cambridge*
Dr. **Gasan Gusejnov**, *Moscow State University*
Prof. em. **Walter Laqueur**, *Georgetown University*
Prof. **Leonid Luks**, *Catholic University of Eichstaett*
Dr. **Olga Malinova**, *Russian Academy of Sciences*
Prof. **Andrei Rogatchevski**, *University of Tromsø*
Dr. **Mark Tauger**, *West Virginia University*

ADVISORY BOARD*

Prof. **Dominique Arel**, *University of Ottawa*
Prof. **Jörg Baberowski**, *Humboldt University of Berlin*
Prof. **Margarita Balmaceda**, *Seton Hall University*
Dr. **John Barber**, *University of Cambridge*
Prof. **Timm Beichelt**, *European University Viadrina*
Dr. **Katrin Boeckh**, *University of Munich*
Prof. em. **Archie Brown**, *University of Oxford*
Dr. **Vyacheslav Bryukhovetsky**, *Kyiv-Mohyla Academy*
Prof. **Timothy Colton**, *Harvard University, Cambridge*
Prof. **Paul D'Anieri**, *University of Florida*
Dr. **Heike Dörrenbächer**, *Friedrich Naumann Foundation*
Prof. **John Dunlop**, *Hoover Institution, Stanford, California*
Dr. **Sabine Fischer**, *SWP, Berlin*
Dr. **Geir Flikke**, *NUPI, Oslo*
Prof. **David Galbreath**, *University of Aberdeen*
Prof. **Alexander Galkin**, *Russian Academy of Sciences*
Prof. **Frank Golczewski**, *University of Hamburg*
Dr. **Nikolas Gvosdev**, *Naval War College, Newport, RI*
Prof. **Mark von Hagen**, *Arizona State University*
Dr. **Guido Hausmann**, *University of Munich*
Prof. **Dale Herspring**, *Kansas State University*
Dr. **Stefani Hoffman**, *Hebrew University of Jerusalem*
Prof. **Mikhail Ilyin**, *MGIMO (U) MID RF, Moscow*
Prof. **Vladimir Kantor**, *Higher School of Economics*
Dr. **Ivan Katchanovski**, *University of Ottawa*
Prof. em. **Andrzej Korbonski**, *University of California*
Dr. **Iris Kempe**, *"Caucasus Analytical Digest"*
Prof. **Herbert Küpper**, *Institut für Ostrecht Regensburg*
Dr. **Rainer Lindner**, *CEEER, Berlin*
Dr. **Vladimir Malakhov**, *Russian Academy of Sciences*

Dr. **Luke March**, *University of Edinburgh*
Prof. **Michael McFaul**, *Stanford University, Palo Alto*
Prof. **Birgit Menzel**, *University of Mainz-Germersheim*
Prof. **Valery Mikhailenko**, *The Urals State University*
Prof. **Emil Pain**, *Higher School of Economics, Moscow*
Dr. **Oleg Podvintsev**, *Russian Academy of Sciences*
Prof. **Olga Popova**, *St. Petersburg State University*
Dr. **Alex Pravda**, *University of Oxford*
Dr. **Erik van Ree**, *University of Amsterdam*
Dr. **Joachim Rogall**, *Robert Bosch Foundation Stuttgart*
Prof. **Peter Rutland**, *Wesleyan University, Middletown*
Prof. **Marat Salikov**, *The Urals State Law Academy*
Dr. **Gwendolyn Sasse**, *University of Oxford*
Prof. **Jutta Scherrer**, *EHESS, Paris*
Prof. **Robert Service**, *University of Oxford*
Mr. **James Sherr**, *RIIA Chatham House London*
Dr. **Oxana Shevel**, *Tufts University, Medford*
Prof. **Eberhard Schneider**, *University of Siegen*
Prof. **Olexander Shnyrkov**, *Shevchenko University, Kyiv*
Prof. **Hans-Henning Schröder**, *SWP, Berlin*
Prof. **Yuri Shapoval**, *Ukrainian Academy of Sciences*
Prof. **Viktor Shnirelman**, *Russian Academy of Sciences*
Dr. **Lisa Sundstrom**, *University of British Columbia*
Dr. **Philip Walters**, *"Religion, State and Society", Oxford*
Dr. **Zenon Wasyliw**, *Ithaca College, New York State*
Dr. **Lucan Way**, *University of Toronto*
Dr. **Markus Wehner**, *"Frankfurter Allgemeine Zeitung"*
Dr. **Andrew Wilson**, *University College London*
Prof. **Jan Zielonka**, *University of Oxford*
Prof. **Andrei Zorin**, *University of Oxford*

* While the Editorial Committee and Advisory Board support the General Editor in the choice and improvement of manuscripts for publication, responsibility for remaining errors and misinterpretations in the series' volumes lies with the books' authors.

Soviet and Post-Soviet Politics and Society (SPPS)
ISSN 1614-3515

Founded in 2004 and refereed since 2007, SPPS makes available affordable English-, German-, and Russian-language studies on the history of the countries of the former Soviet bloc from the late Tsarist period to today. It publishes between 5 and 20 volumes per year and focuses on issues in transitions to and from democracy such as economic crisis, identity formation, civil society development, and constitutional reform in CEE and the NIS. SPPS also aims to highlight so far understudied themes in East European studies such as right-wing radicalism, religious life, higher education, or human rights protection. The authors and titles of all previously published volumes are listed at the end of this book. For a full description of the series and reviews of its books, see
www.ibidem-verlag.de/red/spps.

Editorial correspondence & manuscripts should be sent to: Dr. Andreas Umland, Institute for Euro-Atlantic Cooperation, vul. Volodymyrska 42, off. 21, UA-01030 Kyiv, Ukraine

Business correspondence & review copy requests should be sent to: *ibidem* Press, Leuschnerstr. 40, 30457 Hannover, Germany; tel.: +49 511 2622200; fax: +49 511 2622201; spps@ibidem.eu.

Authors, reviewers, referees, and editors for (as well as all other persons sympathetic to) SPPS are invited to join its networks at
www.facebook.com/group.php?gid=52638198614
www.linkedin.com/groups?about=&gid=103012
www.xing.com/net/spps-ibidem-verlag/

Recent Volumes

160 Mieste Hotopp-Riecke
Die Tataren der Krim zwischen Assimilation und Selbstbehauptung
Der Aufbau des krimtatarischen Bildungswesens nach Deportation und Heimkehr (1990-2005)
Mit einem Vorwort von Swetlana Czerwonnaja
ISBN 978-3-89821-940-2

161 Olga Bertelsen (ed.)
Revolution and War in Contemporary Ukraine
The Challenge of Change
ISBN 978-3-8382-1016-2

162 Natalya Ryabinska
Ukraine's Post-Communist Mass Media
Between Capture and Commercialization
With a foreword by Marta Dyczok
ISBN 978-3-8382-1011-7

163 Alexandra Cotofana, James M. Nyce (eds.)
Religion and Magic in Socialist and Post-Socialist Contexts I
Historic and Ethnographic Case Studies of Orthodoxy, Heterodoxy, and Alternative Spirituality
With a foreword by Patrick L. Michelson
ISBN 978-3-8382-0989-0

164 Nozima Akhrarkhodjaeva
The Instrumentalisation of Mass Media in Electoral Authoritarian Regimes
Evidence from Russia's Presidential Election Campaigns of 2000 and 2008
ISBN 978-3-8382-1013-1

165 Yulia Krasheninnikova
Informal Healthcare in Contemporary Russia
Sociographic Essays on the Post-Soviet Infrastructure for Alternative Healing Practices
ISBN 978-3-8382-0970-8

166 Peter Kaiser
Das Schachbrett der Macht
Die Handlungsspielräume eines sowjetischen Funktionärs unter Stalin am Beispiel des Generalsekretärs des Komsomol Aleksandr Kosarev (1929-1938)
Mit einem Vorwort von Dietmar Neutatz
ISBN 978-3-8382-1052-0

167 Oksana Kim
The Effects and Implications of Kazakhstan's Adoption of International Financial Reporting Standards
A Resource Dependence Perspective
With a foreword by Svetlana Vlady
ISBN 978-3-8382-0987-6

Content

List of tables 7
List of figures 9
List of boxes 11
Foreword 13
Acknowledgements 17

1. Introduction 21
   1.1 The problem 21
   1.2 The approach 26
   1.3 Book structure 30

2. Legislative and Institutional Backgrounds
   of Public Policy for Patriotic Education 33
   2.1 A Brief History of Public Policy on Patriotic Education
       in the USSR and Russia 33
   2.2 Governmental Programming for Patriotic Education
       on the National Level 37
   2.3 Regional and Local Programming for Patriotic Education 55
   2.4 Conclusion 61

3. The Model of Patriotic Education in Schools: USSR to Russia 65
   3.1 The Rise and Fall of Soviet Patriotic Education: 1930s–1980s 68
   3.2 The Decline of Patriotic Education: 1980s–1990s 80
   3.3 The Basics of Succession 84
   3.4 Conclusion 90

4. Historic Elements and Structures
   in Contemporary Patriotic Education 93
   4.1 The Substitution of the Conceptual Basis 94
   4.2 Memorialization 97
   4.3 Youth Organization(s) 102
   4.4 Patriotic Content of School Subjects 116
   4.5 Pedagogical Tools 120
   4.6 Conclusion 134

5. Novel Elements of Patriotic Education in Contemporary Russia ..137
    5.1 New Targets 137
    5.2 New Connotations 142
    5.3 New Agents 158
    5.4 Conclusion 166

6. Conclusions: Social Roots of the Making of Citizens 167

Bibliography 179

List of tables

Table 2.1 – The major characteristics of the four governmental programs in patriotic education in Russia 39

Table 2.2 – Key indicators for patriotic education 2016–2020 48

Table 2.3 – Examples of regional programs on patriotic education 56

Table 4.1 – The Russian Movement of Schoolchildren activity tracks 108

Table 5.1 – Distribution of the manuals on different meanings of patriotic education 156

Table 6.1 – The percentage of answers to the question, "Do you consider yourself a patriot of Russia?" 173

Table 6.2 – The percentage of answers to the question, "How proud are you to be [nationality]?" 173

Table 6.3 – The percentage of answers to the question, "Of course, we all hope that there will not be another war, but if it were to come to that, would you be willing to fight for your country?" 174

List of figures

Figure 2.1 – The number of research papers on patriotic education 52

Figure 2.2 – The percentage of events dedicated to patriotic education implemented by federal authorities in different regions of Russia, relative to those planned………………...54

Figure 3.1 – Number of manuals on the subject of patriotic education, 1965–2015..66

Figure 3.2 – The model of patriotic education and its modification in a) USSR; b) Russia in the 1990s; c) contemporary Russia....................67

Figure 4.1 – School announcement (Pskovskii Region) 101

Figure 4.2 – Soviet and Russian youth organization badges......................112

Figure 4.3 – Youngarmer's Room 113

Figure 4.4 – Symbolic exploration of the "Polite People" image of the Russian Army……….. 114

Figure 4.5 – A child's drawing based on the lesson "Crimea is ours!"..........123

Figure 4.6 – Illustrations from "Basic Military Preparation" (2011) 127

Figure 4.7 – Performance at a Unity Day celebration 131

Figure 5.1 – Covers of the manuals for patriotic education for preschool teachers...138

Figure 5.2 – Google Books Ngram Viewer distribution 148

Figure 5.3 – The cover of the book "Civic-patriotic education in 6–7th grades. Russian statehood: Talks, class meetings, evening gatherings, celebrations, games"……......................................155

Figure 5.4 – A photo from the website of the Department for Charity and Social Service of the Moscow Diocese 160

List of boxes

Box 4.1 – Introductory note to the working plan of the "School Museum" club (for the 2015–2016 academic year, 2 academic hours per week)...99

Box 4.2 – Oath of the Youngarmer 116

Box 4.3 – Class discussion: "Crimea is ours!" 122

Box 4.4 – "Our military trainings," an essay by a student from a rural school 128

Box 5.1 – Fragments of the class "There is such a profession – to defend the Motherland!" for children ages 4–6 139

Box 5.2 – The script of a Victory Day celebration for the younger group (3–4 years old) in a kindergarten 140

Box 5.3 – A message on the website of the Department for Charity and Social Service of the Moscow Diocese 159

Box 5.4 – The message on the website of the Lyskovskaia Diocese (Nizhny Novgorod region) regarding the intellectual game "The spiritual basis of patriotism" 160

Foreword

I first met sociologist Anna Sanina when she gave a talk on Patriotic Education as a visiting Fulbright Scholar at my university. In the beginning, I wasn't quite sure what she meant—the US had scrapped most official "civics" programs before I got to public school, and I was unaccustomed to thinking about patriotism in education. Sanina began with the idea that although Americans tend to think we do not have patriotic education, we do—and as I watched her talk, I realized she was right. Learning to be a US citizen is so ubiquitous in schools that it is almost invisible—and yet, from the pledge of allegiance to the military recruiter to the anthem at the football game, our schools are steeped in what Sanina calls "the patriotism of everything." Thus this monograph, while focusing on patriotic education in Russia, also holds a mirror to other societies where patriotism is created at the crossroads of education and society.

Examining the operations of patriotism can be startling in itself, since patriotism can feel so very natural; as Benedict Anderson wrote, "in the modern world everyone can, should, will 'have' a nationality, as he or she 'has' a gender." (*Imagined Communities*, rev. ed. London: Verso Books, 1991, p. 3.) Love for the nation can feel inborn, and there is a relationship to the "homeland" that is deeply instinctual—a love for the language, architecture, people, even the trees and sky of one's environment. But patriotism, as Sanina points out, is a constructed formation that connects identity, community, country, and state in an emotional complex. Specifically, in this work she questions how that love for the homeland is rerouted "to maintain citizen loyalty not to a *country*, but to a *state* and its authorities." This process of the socialization, as Sanina describes, is produced in educational systems that are embedded in other social structures, from the family to the community to the government. And the story of how these structures have interacted with education in Russia, which has seen such dramatic change since the fall of the Soviet Union in 1991, is a fascinating one.

Sanina's study begins with a mystery: How is it that patriotic education has grown seemingly spontaneously in post-Soviet Russian schools without a strong ideological framework or an effective government supported system? To answer this question, Sanina uses Pierre Bordieau's concept of *habitus* to approach the question as a sociological one, with "its roots in the social values, attitudes and behavior of educational agents and wider society." Combining research from historical archives, sociological data, and personal interviews, Sanina focuses on how multiple factors have contributed to a contemporary patriotic education program that is as rich in emotional power and impact as it is poor on planning and a coherent philosophical framework. Using a multi-faceted approach, this study is a compelling analysis of the everyday enactment of patriotic education that has risen from the ashes of the Soviet Union in an emerging Russia very much in-flux.

The development of Patriotism and Patriotic education has been explored in an interdisciplinary network of fields that coalesce primarily in political studies. Sanina's work draws on important studies that have gone before, such as Marlène Laruelle, Anatoli Rapoport, Jussi Lassila, and Alexei Yurchak. But Sanina is a sociologist, and her grass roots, community centered approach brings new light to the issue. Working in a realm that is ever changing (and where gathering empirical data is difficult and often inconclusive), the author keeps a steady hand in presenting and discussing the connections between inner emotions and social, educational, and political spaces. Her deliberate reliance on interviews and first hand accounts grounds her arguments in lived experience and give the reader a window into the real human situation of a society that has undergone drastic change.

The fall of the USSR and the sudden dismantling of society was dramatic. I remember arriving in Russia in 1993 and finding myself surrounded by the debris of the recently shattered Soviet Union. Improvised flea markets had buckets of 'baby Lenin' pins, schools were still festooned with dusty red and gold banners, and bewildered people showed me their childhood photos in Pioneer uniforms. On Victory day, memorializing the defeat of the Nazis in the Great Patriotic War, veterans marched, proudly wearing medals bestowed by a state that no longer existed. Lenin still lay entombed in Red Square, but I heard an (unsubstantiated) rumor that there was talk of selling him to Spain. The USSR was for sale at every Metro station in Moscow—Soviet uniforms, hats, medals, money, books, and whole sets of Soviet Encyclopedias. An entire way of being in the world was suddenly obsolete, and the new way forward was not yet evident.

Reading Sanina's book, I am finally able to understand what I was seeing: The dismantling of the "patriotism of everything." As Sanina details, patriotic education was taught as a unified, mandatory subject during the Soviet era, backed by a strong ideology and resting on highly emotionalized methods such as the memorialization of historical events and student clubs that kept children involved and invested. Sanina describes the role of "military-patriotic" education, which sought to develop citizens with a love for the country and the willingness to defend it against enemies. Teachers deeply embraced a mission not only to teach subjects, but to develop the whole human being as a healthy, moral, patriotic Soviet citizen. And although the Soviet model was met with growing cynicism in the 1980s, teachers continued to embrace their mission as moral-patriotic guides. In her interviews, Sanina found that teachers would move into the post-Soviet era with this mission intact.

In the post-Soviet era, which saw a period of chaotic change, patriotic education re-formed itself—remarkably, as Sanina describes, not from the top down, but from the ground up, as teachers continued to feel the need to provide patriotic education in communities that expected them to do so. A fascinating aspect of this book is the exploration of how this process, embedded in societal expectations, has both persisted and changed. Without any effective state programming, using those same Soviet structures such as memorialization and student clubs, patriotic education has developed with an emphasis that combines military training, the Orthodox church, and national pride.

This is a highly focused and well-researched monograph that offers cogent analysis of the everyday practice of patriotic education in contemporary Russia. Sanina's work is important for understanding today's Russia, where the changing and often improvised approach to education can take startling turns. She has managed to capture a very confusing moment in time and tease out important elements to make a comprehensible study. Her study also sheds light on the processes of the past twenty years, as various organizations have experienced mixed to no success in creating western-style civil-democratic education in the FSU. I am reminded of Levin in *Anna Karenina,* who argues that European birches don't take well to Russian soil; in other words, American institutions barged in with well meaning plans, but without understanding the deep layers of the society they intended to change. By revealing the underlying processes of patriotic education at work, Sanina sheds light on some of the deep layers of society that have been poorly understood.

Sanina's study has challenging implications not only for Russia but for other societies as well. Her conclusion discusses the implications of an uncontrolled approach to patriotic education, and points out the social divide between those who enact patriotic education and those who would look at it critically. While the processes Sanina describes are specific to Russia, her study ask for a closer look to the ways in which patriotic education functions at the intersections of personal, familial, community, and government structures, a function of social being which it both reflects and reinforces. States have many different ways of constructing citizens, some more organized, others more subtly. In the United States, the "patriotism of everything" has been so diffuse that it has been hard to see until recently, and this study could help to understand why such catastrophic divides in the understanding of patriotism have arisen in different sectors of American society. For no matter how it feels, patriotism is not completely "natural"—it occurs at the intersections of the emotional and the ideologic. Sanina's study gives us more tools to think about how patriotism is constructed, and how that understanding can lead us to an informed future.

Anna Oldfield
Conway, SC USA

Acknowledgements

To be honest, I never planned to write a book about patriotic education. The idea of this study suddenly and discreetly sprang to my mind with the assistance of many people, to whom I am now very grateful and indebted.

It all started with my participation in the Fulbright Visiting Scholar Program, which gave me a fascinating opportunity not only to plunge into the true research environment of Indiana University, but also to travel, to meet many great scholars, and to finally see apparently familiar things from a different angle. I owe my deepest gratitude to Joel Ericson, Elena Shabashova, Cecilia Kocinski-Mulder, and many other people whom I do not know, for managing and coordinating this program and for supporting intercultural communication around the world. I am also grateful to my colleagues from the National Research University Higher School of Economics in Saint Petersburg, Alexander Khodachek, Valentina Kaysarova, Leonid Limonov, and Nadezhda Bebbukina, who supported my decision to participate in this program and made my being away smooth and communicatively lossless.

At Indiana University, I benefited from many candid and frank discussions with Sarah Phillips, Mark and Veronika Trotter, Svitlana Melnik, Miriam Shrager, Maria Shardakova, Roman Zlotin, and other members of the Russian and East European Institute. They not only generously shared their ideas and thoughts, but made me feel at home in the United States. I also want to thank Ashlyn Nelson for her great lectures on Public Program Evaluation that brought a significant governance-related perspective to my study.

I was honored to present the ideas of my research at George Washington University, Coastal Carolina University, and Harvard. I thank Marlène Laruelle, Tripthi Pillai, Stephanie Plant, and Nina Tumarkin for organizing and moderating my talks and for providing an encouraging environment for discussions. I am grateful to all faculty, researchers, and students who attended my lectures. Their comments and questions played a major role in shaping this study. I would like to thank Samantha Proulx and Ashley Canter, students of Coastal Carolina University, for their careful attention and genuine interest in Russian culture, society, and politics.

I extend my gratitude to helpful colleagues and good friends Regina Smyth, Darla Domke-Damonte, Rowenna Baldwin, Alyona Vandysheva, Vlada Baranova, Ivan Kovalyov, and Yanina Grusman, whose valuable ideas, clever recommendations, and relevant information really helped at different stages of initiating, developing, and revising this book. I owe my greatest thanks to Nina Tumarkin, Jussi Lassila, Anna Oldfield, Markku Kangaspuro, Marlène Laruelle, Sarah Phillips, Anatoli Rapoport, Ali Farazmand, Raffaele Gareri, Donata Delfino, and Eugenia Kutergina for critical readings of this manuscript, whether in part or in whole, and for making essential comments and suggestions.

I am grateful to my students, who were sometimes even more interested in this subject than I, for helping me in finding information and gathering and analyzing data: Daria Migunova, Daniil Zuev, Ksenia Lekomtseva, Nurlan Dzhafarli, Oleg Obidovskiy, and Anastasia Kozlova. I'd also like to thank Anna Polyanskaya, who patiently regarded my long explanations and finally painted an excellent picture for the cover of this book.

I am eternally grateful to all the respondents who gave their time, shared their experiences, and allowed me to access information I would never find even in the cleverest books. I am particular grateful to the teachers of Anninskaya school, who were not only the pioneer respondents in the pilot stage of this study, but also gave me a perfect education that in the long run led to this manuscript.

I finally have an opportunity to thank Saint Petersburg State University for bringing me to the wonderful cognitive world of investigations, questions, and puzzles. I am especially grateful to Ludmila Volchkova, Vera Minina, Elena Ostrowskaya, Dmitry Ivanov, and Sergey Damberg, talented teachers and passionate scientists who taught me to write and to think sociologically.

In the end, this book would not have been possible without the participation of Sarah Torbeck, who did a very careful and extensive job proofreading this text. I am grateful not only for her very professional work, but also for her emotional support and for cheering me up. That was very helpful.

I consider it an honor to work with Jakob Horstmann, Andreas Umland, and Valerie Lange from *ibidem* Press. I am grateful for their interest in the topic, for an offer to write a manuscript about patriotic education, and for an excellent collaboration.

My greatest debt incurred in writing this book, as well as all my love, is to my family. They patiently supported me during the intensive, nervous, and significantly underestimated time of contacting, interviewing, writing, and revising the text. My spouse Alexey served in multiple roles as a proponent, a critic, a collaborator, a sounding board, and a shoulder to cry on. I am also grateful to you, Masha, for coming into my life and giving significant meaning to everything I do... but in particular, for those (few) nights that you finally slept, giving your Mommy a chance to write some more pages and to finally drink her morning coffee.

I want to thank my amazing parents Zoya and Georgiy, first of all, for making me a teacher's child who probably unconsciously understood the spirit of the Russian educational system and the nature of teachers' habitus even before going to the nursery. They formed a significant part of my vision and taught me the value of hard work. Without the support and encouragement they have given me throughout my life, I would never have gotten to where I am today.

1. Introduction

1.1 The problem

Discussions about patriotism and patriotic education have arisen in many countries all over the world and in different historical periods. At present, there are plenty of debates about whether or not patriotism should be promoted in schools and how it is related to civic education and nation-building.[1] These discussions are of a very complicated nature because they touch on the issues of civic and national identities, civil rights and civic duties, nation-building, and priorities of raising the younger generation. The focal point of these discussions, the concept of patriotism, is itself ambiguous and ideologically loaded. Whether it is discussed within political, social, or ethnic discourse, patriotism is usually addressed either as something unconditionally necessary for the people or as something almost intolerable and obscene.

At its core, patriotism is a philosophical concept. It reflects emotions of love for a particular place, i.e. a region or a country, and a readiness to support the community of people associated with that place.[2] Years of debate led to the formation of many concepts of patriotism, justifying the distinction between blind and constructive patriotism,[3] active and passive patriotism,[4] and blind and

---

[1] See e.g.: Brent White, "Ritual, Emotion, and Political Belief: The Search for the Constitutional Limit to Patriotic Education in Public Schools," Arizona Legal Studies, 2009; Sigal Ben-Porath, "Civic Virtue Out of Necessity: Patriotism and Democratic Education," *Theory and Research in Education* 5, no. 1 (2007): 41–59; Clinton Allison and Lloyd Williams, "Patriotism: Irrational and Rational P," *The Educational Forum* 35, no. 2 (1971): 235–38.

[2] Charles Blattberg, "We Are All Compatriots," in *Rooted Cosmopolitanism: Canada and the World*, ed. Will Kymlicka and Kathy Walker (Vancouver: UBC Press, 2012), 105–128. P. 105.

[3] Robert T. Schatz, Ervin Staub, and Howard Lavine, "On the Varieties of National Attachment: Blind Versus Constructive Patriotism," *Political Psychology* 20, no. 1 (1999): 151–74.

[4] Joseph Kahne and Ellen Middaugh, "Is Patriotism Good for Democracy? A Study of High School Seniors' Patriotic Commitments," *Phi Delta Kappan* 4 (2006): 600–607.

symbolic patriotism.[5] Despite being constantly criticized and questioned, patriotism nevertheless never disappears from political discourse and public discussions. In spite of globalists' predictions about citizens without citizenship and civilians without patriotism,[6] today's complicated and interconnected world has not reduced the individual's need for identification with a country.[7] In the globalized world, the "mother country" is still a conventional home for many people. It symbolically embodies their belonging to the family, the community, history, and traditions. Feeling connected to a particular country supports the emotional need to come back "home" and ensure that it is safe and sound. This provides an important basis for answering questions about identity and destiny, encourages a sense of security, and enables a mental defense against the incessant threats of a complicated contemporary world.

However, the sophistication of the concept of patriotism, as well as its utilization in the construction of national ideology, is sometimes reflected in misleading terms: The country is associated with the state, or even with the state authorities. In contrast to the support of the community, the merits of state authorities may not be obvious to the people; hence, the perceived necessity of patriotic education, which is most commonly established and developed to maintain citizen loyalty not to a *country*, but to the *state* and its authorities. Patriotic education could be defined as a systematic and state-guided process of establishing the unquestioning and uncritical awareness of certain national values and the behaviors that maintain them. Traditionally, inculcating a spirit of patriotism in the younger generation has been the responsibility of the school, mostly because this educational institution "deals with the socialization

---

5 Christopher Parker, "Symbolic versus Blind Patriotism: Distinction without Difference?", *Political Research Quarterly* 63, no. 1 (2010): 97–114.
6 Nigel Dower and John Williams, eds., *Global Citizenship: A Critical Introduction* (New York: Routledge, 2002); Martha Nussbaum, "Patriotism and Cosmopolitanism," in *For Love of Country?*, ed. Joshua Cohen and Martha C. Nussbaum (Boston: Beacon Press, 2002), 3–20.
7 Bryan Turner, "Cosmopolitan Virtue, Globalization and Patriotism," *Theory, Culture and Society* 19, no. 1–2 (2002): 45–63.

of the young into adults and the differential transmission of the cultural heritage of a society from generation to generation."[8]

In the framework of patriotic education, the concept of patriotism is often embedded in political doctrines and overwhelmed by political meanings. The ruling authorities commonly try to use it for political mobilization and as a tool to signify their position in society. In this respect, patriotism is an overwhelming concept. Any social meanings that may accompany it are buried under its ideological and political tensions. That is why, despite the continual discussions on patriotic education in many corners of the world[9] and its development as an international research subject, it is so complicated to study anything related to patriotism from a sociological point of view.

In some countries, the practice of deploying the ideological dimension of patriotism has become so inherent and historically ingrained that the political and social structures of patriotism are tightly intertwined with each other. The Russian Federation is illustrative of such a situation. Political studies and journalism devoted to understanding patriotism in Russia commonly report that current trends in the development of Russian patriotism suggest ideological reinforcement that aims to disarm any form of criticism, diversity, or officially unapproved distinction, and to promote certain values and attitudes toward the

---

8   Shmuel Eisenstadt, "Social Institutions: The Concept. Comparative Study," in *The International Encyclopedia of the Social Sciences*, ed. David Sills, vol. 14 (New York: Macmillan Publishing Co. and Free Press, 1968), 409–29. P. 409.
9   See e.g.: Joel Westheimer, *Pledging Allegiance: The Politics of Patriotism in America's Schools* (New York and London: Teachers College Press, 2007); Tang Zhiyuan, "Rethinking the Problem of Patriotic Education in the Subject of History in High Schools," *Chinese Education & Society* 32, no. 6 (1999): 78–81; Michael Hand and Joanne Pearce, "Patriotism in British Schools: Teachers' and Students' Perspectives," *Educational Studies* 37, no. 4 (2011): 405–18; Lena Lee and Thomas Misco, "All for One or One for All: An Analysis of the Concepts of Patriotism and Others in Multicultural Korea Through Elementary Moral Education Textbooks," *Asia-Pacific Education Researcher* 23, no. 3 (2014): 727–34; Yusef Waghid, "Patriotism and Democratic Citizenship Education in South Africa: On the (Im)possibility of Reconciliation and Nation Building," *Educational Philosophy and Theory* 41, no. 4 (2009): 39–409; Shinobu Anzai, "Re-Examining Patriotism in Japanese Education: Analysis of Japanese Elementary School Moral Readers," *Educational Review* 67, no. 4 (2015): 436–58; Bruce Haynes, "History Teaching for Patriotic Citizenship in Australia," *Educational Philosophy and Theory* 41, no. 4 (2009): 424–40.

state as well as toward other states perceived as enemies. Expressly or implicitly, they criticize the power elites for ideologizing Russian society and for controlling such an intimate sphere as the education of children. Although this awareness is often justifiable, it is not accurate to attribute all of these tendencies to a master plan of the elites.

Interpretations of patriotism depend not only on the patriotic agenda of the authorities, but also on the cultural and educational experience of the individuals, their family history, culture, and social environment. In other words, the formation of patriotism is played out not only ideologically or politically, but also at the social and even individual level. For some people, patriotism can remain deeply personal throughout their lives, while for others, patriotism is suggestive of ideological manipulation and political violence.[10] In any case, the social meanings of patriotism will differ between "state patriotism"[11] and "state-sponsored patriotism."[12] The concept of patriotism has "extensive use" in society, showing a great adaptability to both individual needs and collective uses.[13] That is why its development in the form of patriotic education "does not necessarily lead to increased engagement in support of the authorities" and "does not guarantee blind faith in the state."[14]

A particular field of patriotism formation is established within the social structure of educational systems and the activity of teachers, school administrators, and local educational authorities. A study of these agents, their attitudes, intentions, and values may uncover the hidden social structures of citizen-raising that are not as obvious as the ideological and political processes.

---

10 Elena Omel'chenko and Hilary Pilkington, eds., *S chego nachinaetsia Rodina: Molodezh' v labirintakh patriotizma* (Ul'ianovsk: Ul'ianovskii State University, 2012). Omel'chenko & Pilkington, 2012. P. 6.
11 Anatoli Rapoport, "Patriotic Education in Russia: Stylistic Move or a Sign of Substantive Counter-Reform?", *The Educational Forum* 73, no. 2 (2009): 141–52.
12 J. Paul Goode, "Russian Patriotism without Patriots? Interviews (in Perm and Tyumen) Reveal the Limitations of Patriotic Education," *PONARS Eurasia Policy Memo*, no. 446 (2016): 1–8, http://www.ponarseurasia.org/memo/russian-patriotism-without-patriots (as of January 10, 2017).
13 Françoise Daucé et al., "Introduction: What Does It Mean to Be a Patriot?", *Europe-Asia Studies* 67, no. 1 (2015): 1–7. P. 4.
14 Ibid. P. 5.

Rowenna Baldwin, referencing Ulf Hannerz,[15] suggests that while the educational system could be considered a facilitator of meaning between the state and citizens, it is still involved in the "wider process of the production, representation and reception of ideas of the nation, both in the present and in the past."[16] This is especially true for Russia, since Russian teachers perceive education as made up of two equally important components: academic education (*obrazovanie*) and upbringing (*vospitanie*). As Anatoli Rapoport highlights,

> Russian pedagogical tradition assumes that both of these components, although practically interdependent, can develop independently through their specific forms and methods. Clearly, academic education is focused on providing students with knowledge and skills, whereas moral education (upbringing) is focused on moral development through teaching values and manners. The Russian term for moral development translates to *spiritual development,* though the expression is almost completely deprived of its religious connotation.[17]

Today, there are 42,500 public schools in Russia, attended by 14.5 million students. In addition, there are about 50,000 public kindergartens, attended by 7 million pupils under 6 years old.[18] Almost all of these children, both in kindergartens and public schools, are included in the process of patriotic education. Compared to Soviet times, these modern processes are fragmentary and poorly integrated into the educational system, but the way in which they are developing is very illustrative. School-based patriotic education in contemporary Russia is an actual example of how specifically social structures can rebuild a political institution. In the 1990s, it seemed as though the historical model of Soviet patriotism would never return; however, in this century, its revival is becoming more and more apparent. It turns out that the model's long-

---

15 Ulf Hannerz, *Transnational Connections: Culture, People, Places* (London and New York: Routledge, 1996).
16 Rowenna Jane Baldwin, "Rethinking Patriotic Education in the Russian Federation" (University of Warwick, 2011).
17 Rapoport, "Patriotic Education in Russia: Stylistic Move or a Sign of Substantive Counter-Reform?"
18 Federal State Statistics Service of the Russian Federation, "Education," available at: http://www.gks.ru/wps/wcm/connect/rosstat_main/rosstat/ru/statistics/population/education/ (as of January 5, 2016).

term preservation within school structures did not require a regulatory framework, clear institutional structure, or money. The Soviet model of patriotic education was preserved by teachers and school administrators, who considered it an indispensable part of their work. Patriotic education, having hidden at the margins of teachers' values and attitudes for the last 20 years, can now easily grow into a giant formal structure. For this to occur requires the assistance of the Russian state, which is already organizing youth movements, establishing all-Russian patriotic lessons, and setting the rules for national celebrations. The initial stage of these processes, however, developed inside the educational institutions.

1.2 The approach

In this research, the sociological perspective is adopted to identify modern patriotic education as a social structure born of the values and attitudes of teachers and school administrators, their experiences of upbringing in the Soviet Union, and a symbolic heritage of memorialization. The tradition of scholarship that influenced this book is based on excellent studies conducted to explain the interconnection of the Soviet trauma with contemporary behavior of the Russian people; the role of schools in educating citizens and broadcasting state-approved knowledge; the peculiarities of the Russian mentality and the national idea relating state, society, and authorities; and the meanings of patriotism and patriotic education in contemporary Russia.[19] These investigations pay very

---

19 Marlène Laruelle, *In the Name of the Nation* (New York: Palgrave Macmillan US, 2009); Daucé et al., "Introduction: What Does It Mean to Be a Patriot?"; Valeria Kasamara and Anna Sorokina, "Post-Soviet Collective Memory: Russian Youths about Soviet Past," *Communist and Post-Communist Studies* 48, no. 2–3 (2015): 137–45. Baldwin, "Rethinking Patriotic Education in the Russian Federation"; Kathy Rousselet, "The Church in the Service of the Fatherland," *Europe-Asia Studies* 67, no. 1 (2015): 49–67; Sergei Oushakine, *The Patriotism of Despair: Nation, War, and Loss in Russia* (New York: Cornell University Press, 2009); Omel'chenko and Pilkington, *S chego nachinaetsia Rodina: Molodezh' v labirintakh patriotizma*; Marlène Laruelle, "Patriotic Youth Clubs in Russia. Professional Niches, Cultural Capital and Narratives of Social Engagement," *Europe-Asia Studies* 67, no. 1 (2015): 8–27; Alexei Yurchak, *Everything Was Forever, Until It Was No More: The Last Soviet Generation* (Princeton: Princeton University Press, 2006).

thoughtful and careful attention to the processes of post-Soviet socialization in its individual, group, and societal dimensions. They help to answer many questions about the peculiarities of the Russian people, Russian society, and the Russian state. However, perhaps more importantly, they also justify the new questions, one of which is: What are the social roots of citizen-raising in contemporary Russia? This question is at the core of this book.

In order to answer the question sociologically, I found the theoretical inspiration for my study in an approach popularized by Pierre Bourdieu and his followers to be an effective method for analyzing social structures and social agents' experience. In the center of this approach lies the *concept of habitus*. Habitus is often described by Bourdieu as a "feel for the game,"[20] referring to the interconnected social and individual processes leading to the formation of structures and contexts. Habitus is a "complex internalized core from which everyday experiences emanate."[21] It is the embodied set of dispositions intuitively generated from practice that determines people's behavioral choices and tastes based on their past experiences.[22] Although perhaps too socially deterministic, this concept provides an opportunity to study phenomena considered to be political, like patriotism formation, from a sociological perspective.

On the one hand, habitus refers to a person's individual history, which forms his or her values, attitudes, and frames for actions and choices. On the other hand, habitus is also connected to the collective history of groups and communities, like family or school, of which the individual is a member,[23] and with historical circumstances, structures, and power arrangements. These internalized layers are reproduced unconsciously and determine individual actions.

---

20 Pierre Bourdieu, *The Logic of Practice* (Stanford: Stanford University Press, 1990). P. 66.
21 Diane Reay, "'It's All Becoming a Habitus': Beyond the Habitual Use of Habitus in Educational Research," *British Journal of Sociology of Education* 25, no. 4 (2004): 431–44. P. 435.
22 Pierre Bourdieu, *Distinction: A Social Critique of the Judgement of Taste* (Cambridge: Harvard University Press, 1984).
23 Pierre Bourdieu, *Sociology in Question* (London: Sage, 1993). P. 86.

As a conceptual and methodological tool, habitus is often used in sociological, cultural, and educational research together with other important concepts like *capital, field,* and *doxa,* which are interconnected and closely linked to habitus. *Capital* represents different forms of resources that individuals use in their practices. These are physical and monetary resources (economic capital), intellectual qualifications (cultural capital), networks and social relations (social capital), and prestige and honor (symbolic capital). *Field* represents a kind of social space with particular rules of the "game," where people perform their social activities, set their social positions, and build social structures. *Doxa* represent fundamental values and discourses, which make a particular field socially unique and different from other fields. These values, attitudes, and discourses are taken for granted by individuals who see them as inherently true and necessary to their existence.[24]

In the present study, I considered the aforementioned concepts as a guiding light for the analysis rather than a firm framing methodology, as my primary interest is a sociological examination of patriotism, not the complicated conceptual labyrinth of the Bourdieurian perspective. Such an approach leads to the creation of a text that is simultaneously theoretically based and still comprehensible to a reader who is not specialized in Social Science or in Russian studies.

Using habitus as a conceptual tool allows for limiting the research focus on social and cultural issues, which is very important for sociological study of such a politicized topic as patriotism and citizenship formation. Viewed in this framework, the model of patriotic education tends to be associated with the attitudes, norms, and values of its major agents: teachers, school directors and deputies of extracurricular activity, local guidance counselors, and regional and federal civil servants involved in the process of patriotism formation. To study them, I used various sources of empirical data, including the texts of federal,

---

24 See more e.g.: Pierre Bourdieu, "Vive La Crise!: For Heterodoxy in Social Science," *Theory and Society* 17, no. 5 (1988): 773–87; Pierre Bourdieu and Loïc Wacquant, *An Invitation to Reflexive Sociology* (Chicago: University of Chicago Press, 1992); Jen. Webb, Tony Schirato, and Geoff Danaher, *Understanding Bourdieu* (Los Angeles: SAGE Publications, 2002); Alice Sullivan, "Bourdieu and Education: How Useful Is Bourdieu's Theory for Researchers?", *The Netherlands' Journal of Social Sciences* 38, no. 2 (2002): 144–66.

regional, and local patriotic education programs, statistical data from the Organization for Economic Co-operation and Development (OECD), Russian public opinion research centers (Levada Center, WCIOM, the Public Opinion Foundation), the World Values Survey (Wave 6, 2010–2014), and open interviews conducted in 2015–2016. The fieldwork was completed mostly in rural areas of Russian regions (Moscow Oblast, Leningrad Oblast, Pskov Oblast, Saratov Oblast, Novgorod Oblast, Chelyabinsk Oblast, Tver Oblast, Voronezh Oblast), as well as in Saint Petersburg and Moscow. Most of the interviews were conducted face to face, and some via Skype. I found most of the interviewees through the "snowball method" (referral from others), and some I contacted by e-mail. To protect their identities and allow them to speak freely, locations and rough age estimations have been scrambled.

The interviewees, representing different social groups involved in the process of patriotic education, can be divided into two groups. The first group is represented by federal and regional officials (12 interviews) from Moscow, Saint Petersburg, Leningrad Oblast, and Pskov Oblast. These interviews allowed me to understand the features of the normative base of patriotic education, to address as thoroughly as possible my many concerns regarding the legislative documents, and to understand the goals pursued by the Russian state through introducing state programs and other tools of patriotism formation.

The second group includes local officials and guidance counselors (8 interviews), school directors (15 interviews), schoolteachers (25 interviews), and priests in the Russian Orthodox Church (6 interviews). Following the paradigm of habitus as a methodological and conceptual tool, my overall picture of social reproduction of patriotic education in Russia is based on the interviews. This approach has its benefits and limitations. On the one hand, the empirical nature of the major source of information uncovered the inner dynamics of the educational process, with its hidden meanings, covert values, and latent attitudes forming the basis of the revival of patriotic education in Russia; the extensive use of interview fragments throughout the text should help readers form a collective image of my interviewees who, with some exceptions, were remarkably similar in attitudes and background. On the other hand, this approach limits the conclusions of the study to the small number of interviewees. To overcome these restrictions, at least in part, I relied widely on historical literature, educational texts, and supplementary methodological materials mentioned in the interviews as teachers' common sources of information.

1.3 Book structure

This study does not pretend, of course, to uncover all shadows of contemporary patriotic education in Russia, its political echoes, and its ramifications in the international arena. Such an investigation would occupy many volumes. I have attempted to analyze the social features of the model of patriotic education in Russia in order to examine the process of the institution's revealing and the role of social elements in that process. Patriotic education in Russia is a great example of how a political idea can lead to the formation of social structures, and how, in time, those social structures can lead to the restoration of the original political idea. Social structures are often insufficiently investigated within the study of political phenomena, and thus their role is undervalued. This book attempts to rectify this, at least in part, by focusing on the social elements of patriotic education.

Following the introduction, the second part of the book is devoted to the legislative and institutional backgrounds of public policy for patriotic education in the USSR and Russia. Drawing analogies with the Soviet era, some researchers consider the Concept of Patriotic Education, as well as the related governmental programs, as a foundation of the educational process in contemporary Russia. Through the analysis of national, regional, and local legal acts and programs, I argue that the poor quality of these documents disqualifies them from acting as such a foundation. Moreover, I suggest that a careful approach to public programming might be a good alternative to ideology, as the logic of public programs and their evaluation would provide clear objectives, concrete indicators, and measurable correlations of funds allocated for the programs with performed results. However, the quality of state programs for patriotic education is surprisingly poor. They have no real connection to the processes of patriotism formation and are replicated for their own sake and for the support of budget money. With mediocre indicators and performance evaluation, they cannot be considered useful even in maintaining the jingoistic patriotism often attributed to Russian patriotic education. For teachers and school administrators, they are mostly "empty things" stuffed with emotional phrases about the necessity of raising citizens devoted to their Motherland. The real processes, structures, and agents of patriotic education are mostly outside the scope of public programming.

Next, I examine the social roots of patriotic education and their transition from the USSR to contemporary Russia. I develop a general scheme to illustrate the core changes of the model of patriotic education from one period to another. The roots of this model, formed in the 1960s-1970s, were based on communist ideology and the state vision of patriotic education in schools, stressing memorialization of the Revolution and World Wars as an important foundation for social upbringing. This vision was reflected in the concepts of emotion-based learning and the "patriotism of everything," implemented in the practice of education with the help of teachers using pedagogical tools and with the support of youth organizations. The following decades brought changes to the model of patriotic education, but at the same time, the core fabric of this model was surprisingly persistent and self-reproducing. The model was so stable and complete that, after its dismantling in the 1990s, it was able to revive itself upon demand in the early 2000s.

By the 1990s, there was little left from the Soviet structure of patriotic education in schools. There were no state concepts, no plans, and no youth organizations. New challenges in the effectiveness of education and the decline of ideology and propaganda caused the abandonment of emotion-based learning. These made military training, patriotic conversations, and all former state celebrations irrelevant. Patriotic education all but disappeared, however two significant elements of the model survived: the symbolic practice of the Victory Day Celebration, and the teachers' belief in the necessity of education's role in children's upbringing. In the past decade and a half, these vital elements resurrected the whole model of patriotic education, so that in contemporary Russia, the key elements remain, slightly modified from their Soviet form.

The practice of memorialization is perhaps the strongest and most mature element of the patriotic education model. It was supported by the initiative of teachers in the 1990s and is strengthening again today, thanks to the growing attention of the state. School museums, military clubs, search teams, and Memory Guards act as anchor institutions that helped to revive the old model of patriotic education. The teacher-enthusiasts, raised during the Soviet period, reproduce their experiences in contemporary activities.

Even the novel elements of the modern model of patriotic education, described in the last part of the book, do not significantly reorganize or develop the basic structure. The format of patriotic upbringing in kindergartens repeats the rituals of military-patriotic education in the Soviet school. New meanings of citizenship introduced in the 1990s were blocked by a pro-governmental sense of patriotism and spirituality promoted by different educational agents, including the Russian Orthodox Church. However, the novel agents, who began to play a very active role in patriotic education, did not contribute anything radically new, and resorted to long-established patriotic clubs, military games, and lessons of courage.

The development of the patriotic education model shows that it has rooted and expanded in the society, obtaining new adepts in different social groups. And yet, the social reflection in its rational sense does not coalesce well with Russian society, and is instead substituted with nostalgia for the Soviet past, reflected in the teachers' habitus. The future of the patriotic education model is still unclear. Today, the Russian government is making some serious attempts to revitalize the system of patriotism formation. While the current program continues, the revealing elements of the Soviet model of patriotic education, together with new elements, pave the way for their implementation in the society. This process has social roots in the values and attitudes of the teachers, school administration, and society in general.

2. Legislative and Institutional Backgrounds of Public Policy for Patriotic Education

2.1 A Brief History of Public Policy on Patriotic Education in the USSR and Russia

The state policy regarding patriotic education in contemporary Russia began to form in a time of crisis. During the 1990s, Russian society underwent radical transformations in ideological foundations and political and economic systems, which inevitably affected the value orientations of the population, including people's attitudes toward their country and their government. This period of instability saw the first attempts, largely influenced by the historical context and tradition of citizen education in the Soviet Union, to build a system of patriotic education for the New Russia.

The theme of patriotism runs like a thread throughout Soviet history. The Soviet system and the citizen's place in it implicitly involved patriotic orientation, as did the Soviet style of education and training. This conceptual unity did not occur instantly, however. When the Bolsheviks came to power after the October Revolution of 1917, the aim of their political ideology was to build a classless communist society, with the intent of preserving the political regime in order to achieve a world proletarian revolution. Initially, this ideology did not include patriotic education as something vital for the Soviet state and society. However, in 1925, the first People's Commissar of Education Anatoly Lunacharsky wrote about the necessity of encouraging the citizens' "revolutionary patriotism" and their pride in the Fatherland.[25] The transition from proletarian internationalism to Soviet patriotism was denoted in communist ideology no earlier than the mid-1920s.[26]

The idea of patriotic education developed from the ideological halo around the adoption of the Constitution of 1924. The Constitution justified the

---

25 Anatoly Lunacharsky, *Moral' s marksistskoi tochki zreniia* (Sevastopol': Proletarii, 1925).
26 Andrei Abramov, "Patrioticheskaia ideologiia v Rossii: etapy evoliutsii," in *Molodezhnaia politika, vospitatel'naia i patrioticheskaia rabota: Praktika XXI veka*, ed. Mikhail Iudin (Moscow: FGBOU VPO "RGUTiS," 2014), 6–14.

official Soviet interpretation of patriotism as a public consciousness and the sense of belonging to the state as an organizational whole, resulting in the willingness of citizens to defend it and work for its sake. According to David Hoffmann, two key facts linked Soviet ideology and communist education: In 1931, Stalin articulated that the defense of the Fatherland was necessary to protect socialism; and in 1934, nominal head of state and Chairman of the Central Executive Committee of the USSR Mikhail Kalinin said that communist education should "inculcate love for the motherland, for the socialist motherland, and Soviet patriotism. He thus included love for the socialist motherland as an essential part of the communist education."[27]

Patriotism became a key force for unifying the Soviet people. In the 1930s and 1940s, Soviet patriotism "was considered as a conscious, purposeful and effective love for the socialist homeland, based on a deep understanding of the superiority of the Soviet system over all other, non-Soviet systems."[28] The period until the end of the 1950s in the history of the Soviet Union can be characterized as a period of the creation and cultivation of an "image of the enemy" against which the Soviet people must fight.[29] In this regard, the system of patriotic education began to include the development of military skills for protection of the homeland. The military-patriotic element became the quintessence of the Soviet system of patriotic education, intended to promote combat and labor traditions, inculcate respect and love for the armed forces, develop a sense of civic and military duty, promote the mastery of military skills and knowledge, and prepare the younger generation for military service.

After the Second World War, patriotism supported the Soviet political regime and its mission to unite the multinational state. Communist Party ideologists and Soviet bureaucrats carefully formed the system of patriotic education, involving the school, children's and youth organizations, military and sports as-

---

27 David Lloyd Hoffmann, *Stalinist Values: The Cultural Norms of Soviet Modernity, 1917–1941* (Ithaca and London: Cornell University Press, 2003). P. 165.
28 Nikolai Boldyrev, *Vospitanie sovetskogo patriotizma u shkol'nikov* (Moscow: Pravda, 1949).
29 Robert W. Rieber and Robert J. Kelly, "Substance and Shadow: Images of the Enemy," in *The Psychology of War and Peace: The Image of the Enemy*, ed. Robert W. Rieber (New York: Plenum Press, 2001), 3–40.

sociations, and the media. In the basis of this system was the ideological concept of Soviet patriotism, which included unfailing love for socialism, the Soviet government, and the Communist Party, as well as a willingness to defend the country against all threats and enemies. Although the precise meaning of "Soviet patriotism" varied over time, its importance to the concept of the loyal Soviet citizen remained stable.

With the collapse of the Soviet Union in 1991, "Soviet patriotism" formally ceased to exist, and the new Russian government tasked itself with cultivating a *Russian* patriotism in its citizens. Since the late 1990s, patriotic events and education have played an important role in the Russian Federation's state internal policy. At the beginning of the 2000s, several legal acts and governmental documents were adopted, such as the Concept of the Patriotic Education of Russian Citizens (2003), five-year federal programs on patriotic education for citizens (since 2001), and regional programs and laws on patriotic education.

More than ten years had passed since the birth of the New Russia, but the government had not yet considered the question of citizen education, as happened during the early years of the Soviet Union. Experts suggest that in 2001, the second year of Vladimir Putin's presidency, the Russian government enjoyed increased oil and gas revenues and could better focus on public projects, including the sphere of education. Suddenly, a program for patriotic education was required as soon as possible.

Interview fragment
There were historically conditioned circumstances of why it [the first patriotic education program] *was done in a hurry, but they do not justify the fact that there is a formal approach to the programming in patriotic education today. However, then it was all on the personal order and it was urgent. Urgent! There were petrodollars, it was necessary to spend them. Urgently, thoughtlessly, of course... But those who elaborated* [the patriotic education programs], *they did not get much money. They just wrote what they thought. And it was accepted. And what could they think of? All thoughts on education came from someone's childhood. And the Soviet childhood is what they had. With Pioneers and patriots, it was a good childhood, in their memory. It could not be written in another way.*
— A member of a regional Youth Policy Committee (man, 49)

There are several explanations for why the revival of the governmental demand for patriotism and patriotic education happened at the beginning of the 2000s. Françoise Daucé, Marlène Laruelle, Anne Le Huérou, and Kathy Rousselet suggest that the "banner of patriotism" crystallized the "policy of national revival," aiming to mobilize "a detached public around the state and giving renewed prestige to a country whose international status has been questioned."[30] Patriotic education became an umbrella institution to unite the "educational system, the military, and the Russian Orthodox Church, as well as by United Russia and pro-presidential youth movements such as *Nashi* and *Molodaya Gvardiia*."[31] These politics met the society's demand for "normalcy"[32] and nostalgia for the Soviet Union amongst the older generation[33] and Russian youth.[34] It also supported the governmental demand to improve a very particular aspect of civic engagement: the low public support for the armed forces and military duties.[35]

Taking all explanations into account, it is important to note that the legal organization of the resurgent patriotic education was quite different from Soviet times. As in the Soviet tradition, patriotic education in contemporary Russia has been considered principally, or even exclusively, the responsibility of the state. The state decides how its citizens should be educated, as well as the forms the education should take in order to promote loyalty to, and even a kind of zeal for, the state, authority, and the government. However, the new attempts to create the system of patriotic education were not based solely and primarily on

---

30 Françoise Daucé et al., "Introduction: What Does It Mean to Be a Patriot?", *Europe-Asia Studies* 67, no. 1 (2015): 1–7. P. 1.
31 Ibid.
32 Marlène Laruelle, *In the Name of the Nation* (New York: Palgrave Macmillan US, 2009). P. 2.
33 Sergei Oushakine, *The Patriotism of Despair: Nation, War, and Loss in Russia* (New York: Cornell University Press, 2009); Olena Nikolayenko, "Contextual Effects on Historical Memory: Soviet Nostalgia among Post-Soviet Adolescents," *Communist and Post-Communist Studies*, 2008, 243–59.
34 Valeria Kasamara and Anna Sorokina, "Post-Soviet Collective Memory: Russian Youths about Soviet Past," *Communist and Post-Communist Studies* 48, no. 2–3 (2015): 137–45.
35 Valerie Sperling, "Making the Public Patriotic: Militarism and Anti-Militarism in Russia," in *Russian Nationalism and the National Reassertion of Russia*, ed. Marlène Laruelle (Routledge, 2009), 218–71. P. 219.

ideological discourse. The Russian government tried to base patriotic education not on pure ideology, but on programming tools. The Concept of the Patriotic Education of Russian Citizens (2003), which claims to be an ideological background for patriotic education, was based on and supported by government programs, the first of which was adopted two years before the introduction of the Concept. The Concept reflected the totality of officially adopted views on state policy in the field of patriotic education and can be easily classified as ideological. However, it was, almost from the beginning, a "dead" document, referred to by neither federal nor regional programs.[36]

Unlike ideological instruments, governmental programming is an inherently concrete and rational tool of public administration and governance. It involves coordination of the targeted goals, clear steps for their implementation, open data on their financing, and indicators for the program's evaluation. The new program of patriotic education was to be founded *in theory* on a clear, open, and rational formal structure; however, this idea was not put into practice. Now, over a decade and a half since the implementation of the first program, it is obvious that the idea of governmental programming in patriotic education completely failed, producing little more than a formal allocation of budget funds. The reasons for this lay in both the program management practices and the deep structures of the society. This chapter discusses the first reason, and the rest of the book examines the second.

2.2 Governmental Programming for Patriotic Education on the National Level

The official interpretation of patriotic education programming, posted on the website *gospatriotprogramma.ru*, treats patriotic education as a system based

---

[36] The Concept of Patriotic Education defines patriotism as love for the Motherland, devotion to the Fatherland, the desire to serve its interests, and availability to protect it, *up to and including self-sacrifice*. Patriotism is encouraged to improve the morality of the people *and* to facilitate a unified civil society in Russia [italics mine].

on a number of legal acts, specifically the Constitution of the Russian Federation and federal laws related to military service and national security.[37] However, apart from a simple mention of "the system," there are no particulars about how it is organized, and it is unclear how exactly the listed normative acts are related to the patriotic education programs. Nevertheless, four programs of patriotic education in Russia were founded on this vague basis, and this conveyor of targets, indicators, and executors has lasted since 2001.

The first program of patriotic education was undertaken in a hurry, which certainly affected its quality, forethought, structure, and transparency. The goals and tasks of the program were expressed in a very general and abstract way, and there was no indication of how the results could be achieved, managed, and evaluated. The program for 2001–2005 was a hollow document with a real budget. The indicators were formulated in such a way that they could not fail to be performed. However, neither journalists nor economists brought the program's unqualified content to the public's attention. The program for 2001–2005 started a tradition of budgetary disbursement (*osvoenie biudgeta*)[38] in the field of patriotic education that was continued in later programs.

The general layout of the government programs on patriotic education is represented in Table 2.1. The table summarizes the purposes and tasks of each of the four programs, as well as their major executors and budgets. The year-to-year dynamics of these general but important parameters illustrate the formalism in programming and the lack of task succession, despite the stable growth of the budget.

---

37 The Constitution of the Russian Federation, adopted by national referendum on December 12, 1993; Federal Law № 273-FL "On Education in the Russian Federation" dated December 29, 2012; Federal Law № 53-FL "On Military Duty and Military Service" dated March 23, 1998; Federal Law № 5-FL "On Veterans" dated January 12, 1995; Federal Law № 32-FL "On the Days of Military Glory and Anniversaries of Russia" dated March 13, 1995; Federal Law № 80-FL "On the Perpetuation of Victory Gained by the Soviet People in the Great Patriotic War of 1941–1945" dated May 19, 1995; Presidential Decree № 683 "On the Russian Federation National Security Strategy" dated December 31, 2015; Presidential Decree № 1416 "On Improvement of State Policy in the Field of Patriotic Education" dated October 20, 2012.

38 Budgetary disbursement (*osvoenie biudgeta*), a semi-slang phrase in Russian journalism reporting on economics, depicts the practice of a formal allocation of money according to budgetary lines without controlling the quality of the services or goods. This term has historical connotations: In Soviet times, budget expenditure was a kind of economic indicator, assuming that greater spending resulted in greater economic achievement.

Table 2.1 – The major characteristics of the four governmental programs in patriotic education in Russia

Years of Program Realization	Purposes	Tasks	Major Executors	Budget*
2001–2005	Developing the system of patriotic education of the citizens, which, being based on the organization of patriotic feelings and consciousness, can provide solutions for tasks of society consolidation; maintaining social and economic stability; stabilizing of the unity and friendship of the Russian Federation's nations.	– To create the mechanism, which provides establishment and effective functioning of the government's patriotic education system; – to organize the citizens' patriotic feelings and consciousness based on historical values and the role of Russia in the fates of the world; – to raise the personality of the citizen – Homeland's patriot, who is ready to stand up for the state interests of the country; – to organize the complex of regulatory, legal, organizational and methodological support of a functioning patriotic education system.	Ministry of Education Ministry of Culture Ministry of Defense Russian State Military Historical and Cultural Center of the Russian Government (Rosvoencentr)**	177.95 million rubles / about $6.29 million
2006–2010	Perfecting the system of patriotic education, which provides development of Russia as a free, democratic government; developing high patriotic consciousness, loyalty to the Fatherland, willingness to fulfill constitutional duties among the Russian Federation's citizens.	– To proceed with the creation of a patriotic education system; – to proceed with the perfection of regulatory and legal, organizational, and methodological bases of patriotic education; – to attract more scientific institutions, public organizations, working teams, and individuals to take part in patriotic education; – to improve the quality of patriotic education in educational institutions, turn them into centers of patriotic education for younger generations; – to carry out scientifically based organizational and propagandistic activities for the purpose of further development of patriotism as Russia's core moral component.	Ministry of Education and Science Ministry of Culture and Mass Communications Ministry of Defense Rosvoencentr**	497.8 million rubles / about $18.32 million

2011–2015	Further development and perfection of the system of patriotic education of the citizens.	– To enhance the role of state and social structures in organization of high patriotic consciousness of the Russian Federation's citizens; – to perfect the regulatory and legal, methodological, and information support for the functioning of the citizens' patriotic education system; – to organize the society's positive attitude towards military service and positive motivation among young people to perform military service under contract or as a conscript; – to introduce the modern forms, methods, and means of educational work into the activity of patriotic education's organizers and specialists; – to enhance the competence of patriotic education's organizers and specialists; – to develop the material base of patriotic education in educational, working, creative, and social teams.	Ministry of Education and Science Ministry of Culture Ministry of Sport, Tourism and Youth Policy Ministry of Defense Rosvoencentr**	777.2 million rubles / about $19.00 million

| 2016–2020 | Purpose not specified (replaced with the reference to the purpose of the government's policy in the field of patriotic education). | – To develop the scientific and methodical support for the citizens' patriotic education system;
– to perfect and develop the forms and methods of the activity of patriotic education, which has been successfully established, in the light of rapidly changing situations, citizens' age peculiarities, and the need for active inter-ministerial, inter-sectional cooperation and public-governmental partnership;
– to develop the military-patriotic education of the citizens, promotion of service in the Armed Forces of the Russian Federation and law enforcement authorities, to perfect the coaching practice ("shefstvo") of military units over educational organizations and coaching of working teams, business structures, districts, cities, regions, territories, and republics over military units (ships);
– to create the conditions for promoting the volunteer movement, which is an effective instrument of citizens' patriotic education;
– to provide the information support for patriotic education on the federal, regional and municipal levels, to create the conditions for news coverage and means of patriotic orientation for the media. | Ministry of Education and Science

Ministry of Defense
Ministry of Culture
Federal Agency for Youth Affairs** | 1666.56 million rubles / about $26.04 million |

2001–2005

The first government program of patriotic education, "Patriotic Education of Citizens of the Russian Federation for 2001–2005," was adopted on February 16, 2001, in order to develop a "system of patriotic education of Russian citizens, which is capable to ensure problem solving for the consolidation of society, keeping public and economic stability, and the consolidation of the unity and friendship of nations of the Russian Federation."[39] Emphasis was placed on the military component as in the patriotic education system of the Soviet era. The concepts of "strengthening the country's defense capability," "service to the Fatherland," "military duty," "military-patriotic work," and "military service" appear often. While preparation of young people to defend the country became the priority of the program, also important were the citizen's identity formation, the fight against the devaluation of moral values and disrespectful attitudes to the state and social institutions, and promotion of historical heritage and cultural values.[40] There is no system of performance indicators in the program. Desired results, described in general terms, include socioeconomic, moral, and cultural revival, strengthening of the state and its defense capabilities, and achieving social and economic stability.

2006–2010

The second government program, "Patriotic Education of Citizens of the Russian Federation for 2006–2010," continued the earlier program, with the focus shifted towards civil education. "Improving the system of patriotic education, which ensures the development of Russia as a free and democratic state, the formation of high patriotic consciousness, loyalty to the Fatherland, and readiness to fulfill the constitutional obligations by Russian Federation citizens"[41] is indicated as its main purpose. In particular, the program "is based on

---

39 Pravitel'stvo RF, *O Gosudarstvennoi Programme "Patrioticheskoe vospitanie grazhdan RF na 2001–2005 gody, Postanovlenie ot 02/10/2001, № 122,"* available at: http://base.garant.ru/1584972 (as of November 5, 2016).

40 Serguei Golunov, "Patrioticheskoe vospitanie v Rossii: za i protiv," *Voprosy Obrazovaniia* 3 (2012): 258–73.

41 Pravitel'stvo RF, *O Gosudarstvennoi Programme "Patrioticheskoe vospitanie grazhdan RF na 2006–2010 gody, Postanovlenie Pravitel'stva RF ot 07/11/2005, № 422,"* available at: http://base.garant.ru/188373 (as of November 5, 2016).

the principles of the functioning of a democratic state and civil society, and is available for the participation of all state bodies, public organizations (associations), scientific and creative unions and organizations based on their own initiatives."[42]

Unlike the previous program, the program for 2006–2010 offered a list of stated generic performance indicators. These criteria were represented by "moral and spiritual" and quantitative parameters. Moral and spiritual parameters include increasing tolerance, reducing the degree of ideological confrontation in the society, strengthening the unity and friendship of the nations within the Russian Federation, encouraging citizen interest in the development of the national economy, and reducing social tensions. Quantitative parameters include the number of completed research projects on the problems of patriotic education and the extent of their introduction to the theory and practice of patriotic education, the number of trained organizers and experts in the field of patriotic education, the number of military and specialized sports camps, and the number of active patriotic associations, clubs, and centers, including children's and youth groups.

Although the introduction of performance indicators may be regarded as a step forward in the formation of the system of patriotic education in Russia, their ill-conceived and unsystematic character is obvious. Some indicators are repeated several times, and most of them are focused on children, despite stated objectives concerning different social groups. Complicated concepts such as "nationalism," "internationalism," and "identity" are listed without definition. The intended final results of the program, "positive dynamics of growth of patriotism and internationalism in the country, providing favorable conditions for spiritual and cultural growth in society, strengthening the economic stability of the state, and raising the international prestige of Russia,"[43] are so broad and ambiguous as to be a priori impossible. According to the Soviet tradition, the effectiveness of patriotic education is reflected in everything, including economic stability and international prestige, but the tools proposed for achieving these results are either too narrow or too abstract.

---

42   Ibid.
43   Ibid.

2011–2015

The third government program, "Patriotic Education of Citizens of the Russian Federation for 2011–2015," was approved by RF Government Decree on October 5, 2010. The formulation of the program goal attracts attention as a "further development and improvement of the system of patriotic education of citizens."[44] In other words, the hereditary nature of the new program is made clear at the target level, and there were no substantial changes in the formulation of goals.

The program of patriotic education for 2011–2015 established a new list of performance indicators, including the proportion of citizens participating in patriotic education activities relative to the total number of citizens, the percentage of citizens positively evaluating the results of the activities on patriotic education, and the number of trained specialists and organizers of patriotic education. The list of performance criteria proposed by the third program was more specific, yet greatly simplified, compared to the indicators provided in the second program. The exclusion of the quality ("moral and spiritual") component, while increasing the possibility of assessing the effectiveness of the program, calls into question the probability of achieving the final result of the program:

> *the positive dynamics of patriotism growth in the country, increase of social and labor activity of citizens, especially young people, their contribution to the development of the main areas of life and society and state activity, overcoming extremist manifestations of individual groups of citizens and other negative phenomena, the revival of spirituality, socio-economic and political stability, and the strengthening of national security.*[45]

A significant "conservative accent"[46] found expression in the planned outcomes: high security and the maintenance of stability in the social, economic, and ethnic spheres.

---

44 Pravitel'stvo RF, *O Gosudarstvennoi Programme "Patrioticheskoe vospitanie grazhdan RF na 2011–2015 gody, Postanovlenie Pravitel'stva RF ot 10/05/2010, № 795,"* available at: http://base.garant.ru/199483 (as of November 19, 2016).
45 Ibid.
46 Golunov, "Patrioticheskoe vospitanie v Rossii: za i protiv." P. 262.

2016–2020

The latest program for patriotic education in Russia, adopted on December 30, 2015, reflects the new threats facing the country: a heightened geopolitical situation and difficult conditions in economic competition.[47] In these conditions,

> *the aim of the state policy in the sphere of patriotic education is to create conditions for improving the civil responsibility for the fate of the country, to increase the level of consolidation of the society to meet the challenges of national security and sustainable development of the Russian Federation, strengthening the sense of belonging of citizens to the great history and culture of Russia, to ensure continuity of generations of Russians, education of the citizen who loves his country and family, having an active life position.*[48]

Three of the four stated tasks in the program are broadly oriented methodically. The program should contribute firstly to improving the forms and methods of patriotic education, taking into account "the dynamically changing situation, age characteristics of citizens, and the need for active interagency, cross-sectoral cooperation and public-private partnerships"; secondly, to informational support of patriotic education at different levels of government; and thirdly, to the development of the volunteer movement. The fourth and only concrete task, entirely devoted to the military and patriotic aspect, has as its aim "the development of military-patriotic education of citizens, strengthening the prestige of service in the Armed Forces of the Russian Federation and law enforcement agencies, improving the practice of patronage of military units on

---

[47] The text of the program, laid out in early 2015 at the Federal portal of legal acts, contained several different explanations of the external conditions for developing patriotic education. They included "the situation of degradation of basic values," "planting online information, distorting the traditional Russian history and spiritual and moral values through the media, cinema, and literature," and a difficult way of formation of new institutions "through the revolutions and civil war, hard and unpopular reforms." The links at this online document are already defunct. Some citations can be found in Andrey Levkin, "Dokument kak dokument. Patriotizm kak patriotizm," *Polit.ru*, 2015, http://polit.ru/article/2015/04/06/al060415 (as of November 20, 2016).

[48] Pravitel'stvo RF, *O Gosudarstvennoi programme "Patrioticheskoe vospitanie grazhdan RF na 2016–2020 gody, Postanovlenie Pravitel'stva RF ot 10/05/2010, № 1493,"* available at: http://www.garant.ru/products/ipo/prime/doc/71196398 (as of November 19, 2016).

educational organizations and mentoring of labor collectives, businesses, cities, regions, territories and republics of the military units and ships."[49]

The program text contains a description of these tasks, including 48 points of specification. These include improving the legal framework of patriotic education, training professionals and improving their skills, developing social solidarity and a sense of pride in the country, the development of respect for the law and the spirit of the Constitution, improvement of inter-ethnic and inter-confessional relations, intensification of interest in the study of Russian history and state symbols, development of sports and patriotic education, interaction with veteran organizations, and creating conditions for the development of civic activity upon the formation of a patriotic culture in the electronic and printed media, information, and telecommunication networks.

Two obvious markers of the "Soviet spirit" are present in the program. First, the program provides a symbolic link between a healthy lifestyle and militant patriotism. Second, there is a routine link between military and law enforcement organizations and educational institutions.

The first marker is embodied in the resumption of the Soviet complex of physical training called Ready for Labor and Defense (GTO – *Gotov k Trudu i Oborone*). This complex is a revival of that practiced in the Soviet Union, which played a significant role in the system of military-patriotic education of youth from 1931 until 1991. The physical examinations include running, long jump, pulling, tug weights, swimming, shooting from an air rifle or electronic weapons, and other activities. GTO provides established regulatory requirements for representatives of different age groups (age 6 to 70 and older) and for three levels of difficulty. Depending on the results, one can earn a gold, silver, or bronze mark of distinction labeling one "Ready for Labor and Defense."[50] The achievement of the "GTO" distinction can result in practical benefits like better scholarships for students or better salaries for employees of state and public organizations. At the same time, following Soviet best practices, participation in GTO

49　Ibid.
50　This Soviet-Russian tradition of using a spirit of competition ("dukh sorevnovaniia") as a major tool of motivation in youth policies is present in various activities of youth organizations. See: Jussi Lassila, *The Quest for an Ideal Youth in Putin's Russia II: The Search for Distinctive Conformism in the Political Communication of Nashi, 2005–2009* (Stuttgart: ibidem Press, 2014).

testing is becoming an almost required practice for school children and public sector employees, because the patriotic education program requires an increase in the number of people who successfully meet standards of physical fitness and have passed the GTO test. In addition, GTO is a typical example of the politicization and indoctrination of mass sports and healthy lifestyles. If the slogan "Run for your Health" or "Run for your Life" is popular today in many democracies, in the USSR (and now in Russia) this rhetoric was replaced by "Run for your State" or even "Run for your State's Defense."

The second marker is "patronage," a mutual "mentoring" activity of public and military organizations. This is another practice from Soviet times. Formally, patronage assumes some kind of systematic assistance to a "weaker subject," as in the patronage of industry and educational institutions over agriculture, the standouts over the underachieving, experienced workers over young workers, and so on.[51] However, this practice also implies ideological control and political mentoring. The 2016–2020 program for patriotic education reveals this practice, stating that the regulatory and methodological framework of ministries and agencies should pay attention to the re-establishing of military mentoring work. Thus, they should create conditions for strengthening the cooperation of civil, military, and veterans' organizations.

Despite the introduction of these two serious accents, almost nothing changed in the methodological sections of the program. The scheme of the program evaluation, the logic of the formation of the targets of the program, and features of their interpretation are undefined. There are no *specific* guidelines in the program itself for the evaluation of goals and achievements.

Ten key indicators of program implementation are highlighted in the program's application, as shown in Table 2.2. The indicators are based on very unclear and indistinctness rules. Almost all of them are set as the "proportion" of something, although in some cases, such as those regarding patronage and institutional participation, they refer to an increase in the unit of measurement over time, not a proportion, which is a part considered in comparative relation to a whole. Additionally, the use of the word "proportion" without including concrete figures does nothing for clarifying the goals of the program.

---

51 Peter Kenez, *The Birth of the Propaganda State: Soviet Methods of Mass Mobilization, 1917–1929* (Cambridge: Cambridge University Press, 1985). P. 143.

Table 2.2 – Key indicators for patriotic education 2016–2020

Index		Planned values	
		2016	2020
Number of trained organizers and specialists in the field of patriotic education	people	48,000	55,000
The proportion of educational institutions of all types participating in the implementation of the program, from the total number of educational institutions in Russia	%	100	150
The proportion of students who participated in competitive activities aimed at increasing the level of knowledge of Russian history and culture, a city, a region, from the total number of students in the country	%	100	180
The share of Russian citizens who have fulfilled the standards of Russian sports complex GTO, from the total percentage of the population that took part in GTO standards	%	30	70
The proportion of secondary education organizations and professional and educational organizations of higher education that are under the patronage of military units and ships	%	100	150
The share of military units and ships providing patronage to labor groups, businesses, cities, regions, and republics	%	100	150
The share of people who are informed about the program's activities, from the total number of citizens of the Russian Federation	%	100	300
The proportion of regions of the Russian Federation where the regional program was accepted, from the total number of subjects of the Russian Federation	%	90	100
Number of regions of the Russian Federation where the regional center of patriotic education was established	units	80	85
The proportion of voluntary organizations that operate on the basis of federal institutions of higher education, from the total number of federal government educational institutions of higher education	%	25	70

Blurred figures traditionally go hand in hand with the practices of "budget mastering" and "money exploration." The more streamlined the formulation, the easier it is to misrepresent the achievement of an indicator.

Interview fragment

I don't know how these indicators are formed, and I have a feeling that they are formed by hand or head. These are not calculations, because if you take a calculator, you will get not very logical things ... But what? We take a calculator and get these not very logical things, and then look at them and, yeah, we succeeded in these not very logical things for the last year. It's good. And, let's say, in one point we have

lowered. But if we count in a different way, it turns out that it has lowered not so much, and is even preserved almost as it was. Yeah, so, we calculate differently. The fact that there are no definitions and directions is good for us, if you like. It is easy to report. And we do know how to deal with the budget, we don't need the indicators as we have tasks. No, nothing goes in my pocket (laughs). Contests for children, volunteer organizations and all sorts of things. We ourselves know how to redistribute. It is not a fantastic amount of money, actually.
– A member of a regional Youth Policy Committee (man, 48)

The status of the programs

Apart from the unaccountability of the patriotic education programs, there is another problem with their implementation: their official status. Today, the Russian Federation runs 44 government programs. Their financing requires about 70 percent of the federal budget. These government programs are organized into five blocks: "New quality of life" (14 programs), "Innovative development and modernization of the economy" (18 programs), "National security" (2 programs), "Balanced regional development" (6 programs), and "Effective state" (4 programs). These blocks, as well as a list of the programs, are fixed either by the Government of the Russian Federation № 1950-p "On approval of the list of the Russian Federation government programs" (dated November 11, 2010) or in the Decree of the Government of the Russian Federation № 588 "On approving the Procedure for the development, implementation and evaluation of the effectiveness of government programs in the Russian Federation" (dated August 2, 2010). Curiously, none of the patriotic education programs are included in those lists. Indeed, patriotic education has never been included on the official website of government programs (*programs.gov.ru*). Despite this, the patriotic education programs have governmental status. There is no adequate information on which sphere or direction of governmental programming involves patriotism. Representatives of ministries and state departments also have difficulty explaining the status of the program, its historical vicissitudes, and the legal and institutional regulation. The following interviews illustrate this:

Interview fragments

This program was not included in the list of government programs on the website because it doesn't have the status of a Government Program of the Russian Federation governing by Decree 588. Only those which are regulated by it may be posted on the website. However, considering the high social and political significance of this program, an exception has been made for it, and it was approved by the legal act issued by the Government of the Russian Federation. [52] *It has a special status, not in the way that the Program for State Defense has* [the Ensuring the Country's Defense program has a special status of secrecy – A.S.], *but because it is very significant for the society. You should know that the government has a right to issue resolutions of any matter and to give them the format that will be considered advisable depending on purposes and tasks that need to be done.*

– A member of the Ministry of Economic Development (man, 42)

... At the same time, the government program of patriotic education began to be implemented starting with the year 1995, as far as I remember [the first program was implemented in 2001 – A.S.], *and that was long before we adopted the system of strategic planning by realization of the Russian Federation's government programs. And since then it has been systematically prolonged for another five-year period. It has already become a tradition. That is why the decision was made after special coordination consultations with the Ministry of Economic Development of the Russian Federation, and the Ministry is the methodologist in realization of the Russian Federation's government programs. The decision was about declaring this government program once more as an individual standard-setting instrument in a status of government program. At the same time, yes, this document is not on Decree 588's list.*

– A member of the Ministry of Defense (man, 52)

---

52 The newspaper *Novaya Gazeta* in respect to the second patriotic program (2006–2010) says: "The new federal program... was pushed through the government as a result of appeals of the head of one of the Enforcement Agencies to the President of Russia. Back in early July, its approval was under a big question: the government had to approve the list of state Federal Target Programs for the next five years, and the program on patriotism disappeared from that list." It turns out that the Ministry of Finance and Economic Development was against the patriotic program, so it was excluded. However, some Parliament senators, the leader of the Ministry of Defense, and a number of NGOs officially asked President Putin to approve this program as a government program of the Russian Federation and to provide a special budget for it. The President approved the idea and the document was adopted. Source: Alexandra Samarina, "Patrioty dorogo stoiat," *Novaya Gazeta*, July 21, 2005, http://www.ng.ru/politics/2005-07-21/3_patrioty.html (as of November 30, 2016).

It is an interdepartmental and interagency, very complicated program. At first it was completely under the power of the Ministry of Defense, and now it is inter-ministerial. And it has a government status, could there be another way? It has to own an individual website, although we [the Federal Agency for Youth Affairs] *don't support it.*
– A member of the Federal Agency for Youth Affairs (woman, 40)

Thus, the patriotic education programs have their governmental status not as a rule, but by exclusion. They have a "special status" or an "exceptional status," as the respondents from the governmental structures call it. The programs own an individual website, *gospatriotprogramma.ru*, which was set up by the Russian State Military Historical and Cultural Center Under the Government of the Russian Federation (Rosvoencentr) in 2012. Although the current program is implemented by the Federal Agency for Youth Affairs, the information on the website is updated by Rosvoencentr.

The programs on patriotic education are even visually different from other government programs, which are much longer and more distinct. The summaries of programs on patriotic education do not include certain key elements such as target indicators or stages and terms of realization, as well as expected results and cross-regional concretization.

The evaluation of programs in patriotic education

The absence of clear indicators of program effectiveness and common methods of their calculations leads to considerable difficulties in their evaluation. Although the wording of the key statements of each program changes in every reporting year, the content itself does not change significantly. The information about individual regions poses considerable difficulties. In the reporting documents, there is a mismatch in the actual data indicators for one year compared with the following year. For example, in a report for 2012, the indicator of the *number of research works on patriotic education and the level of their implementation into practice by federal executive bodies and organizations* is 6,052 research works and 41% of implementation. However, in a report for 2013, the same indicator for 2012 is shown as 4,738 research works and 51% of implementation. This strange change in the value is nowhere explained and can be considered as either negligence or intentional distortion.

The imbalance between planned targets and actual data from year to year and from program to program suggests that the programs' developers do not review the factual achievements of indicators. For example, from 2011–2014, the factual indicator of the number of research papers on patriotic education exceeded its planned targets by thousands (Figure 2.1). In 2011, the planned indicator called for 12 research papers, but regional authorities somehow collected statistics on 6,052 papers for the reporting year. Despite the discrepancy between these numbers, the planned values were not corrected in the following programs. In 2012, the government expected 16 papers and received 6,301. And so it went for four years. Although those indicators were excluded from the program for 2016–2020, they continue to be reproduced at regional and local levels.

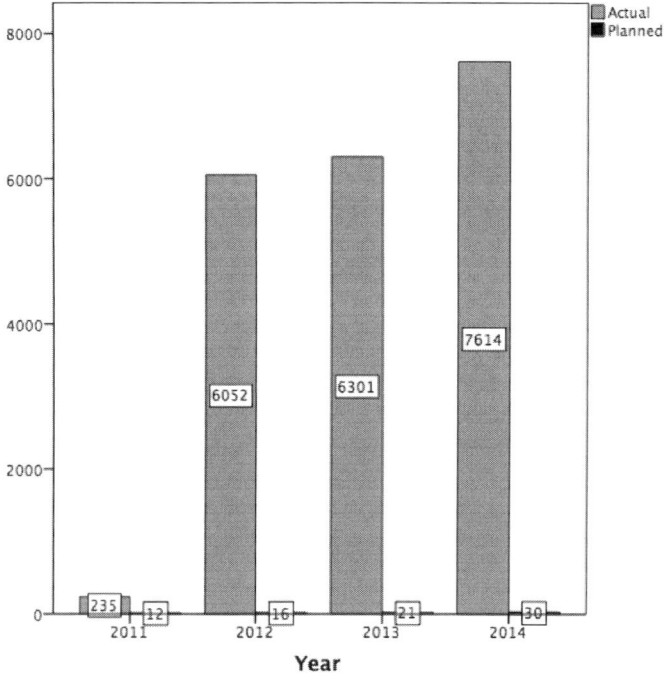

Figure 2.1 – The number of research papers on patriotic education, planned indicators compared to the actual number of papers recorded

Interview fragment
The science and research indicators are a really interesting thing. I count the number of articles in regional universities and the graduation works which go through the Committee. The country is big, and so you get lots of works. I do not even know why they [target indicators] *have not been corrected. To be honest, I did not think about it. In practice, to answer, we ask the... Well, the university faculty, for example, come to our conferences. We ask them: How many, according to your evaluation, how would you say, the things you have researched were somehow implemented into practice? And add the things that the Committee takes to implement from the universities' elaborations... It depends, of course, but I sometimes read and think that something is interesting, but there is nothing to take out of it. It was written for the record.*

— A member of a regional Youth Policy Committee (man, 45)

The average results of a program's performance indicators' achievements in constituent territories of the Russian Federation show that the number of events dedicated to patriotic education, prepared by federal authorities, is the same as or nearly reaches the planned goal almost everywhere (Figure 2.2). The same is true for the number of citizens who take a favorable view of the results of the execution of patriotic education events, the number of citizens who take part in those events, and the number of those studies implemented by federal executive bodies and organizations. These rates are rather even in all of the constituent territories of the Russian Federation and are close to the planned figures. Their charts are practically identical with Figure 2.2.

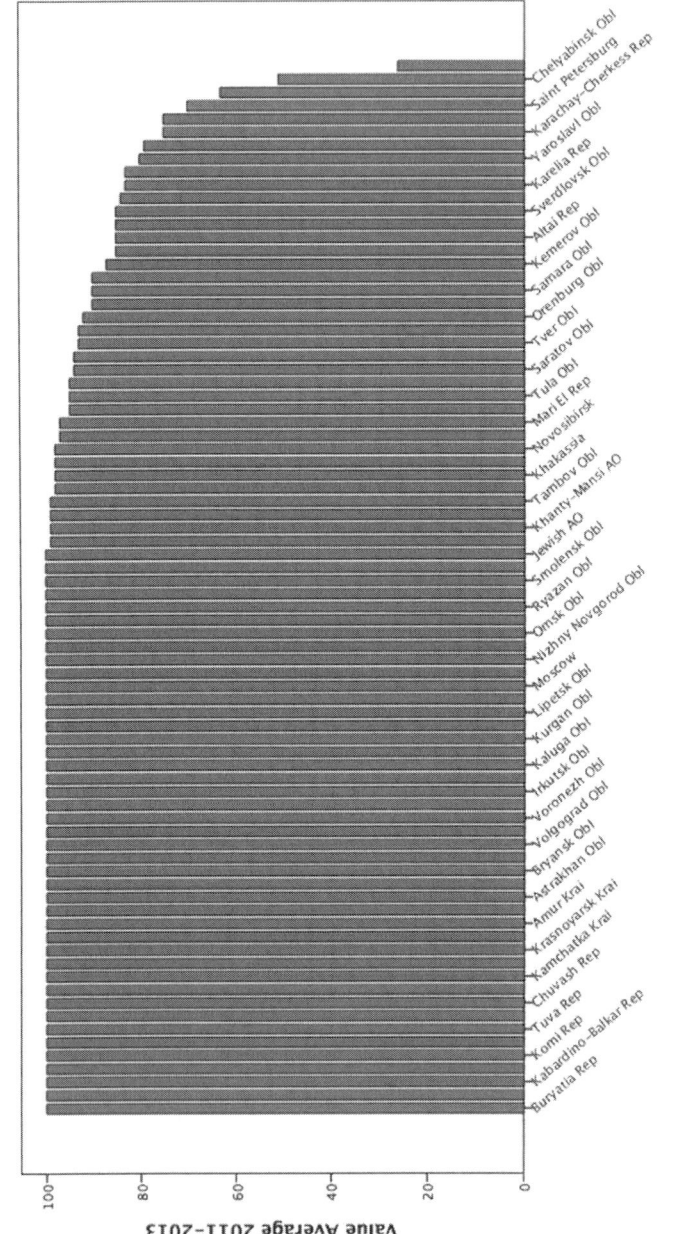

Figure 2.2 – The percentage of events dedicated to patriotic education implemented by federal authorities in different regions of Russia, relative to those planned

The indicators are structured in such a way that they easily allow the demonstration of good results, leading its creators and executors to genuinely believe that the program is effective. However, these indicators show only the federal executive bodies' work efficiency in the area of patriotic education and not the program's social effect. The question of the accuracy of the indicator values remains open because the methods of collecting information are not transparent and are not clarified or explained in official documents.

2.3 Regional and Local Programming for Patriotic Education

Alongside government programs on the national level, there are institutional, regional, and local efforts to promote patriotic education. Regional programs differ depending on their status, financing, and implementation period. They may include special programs, joint programs (patriotic education *plus* sports, inter-ethnic relations, military service training, tourism, etc.), and sub-programs for programs that generally embrace youth policies. Implementation periods for programs vary from two to six years.

Interview fragment
There was a significant growth in the number of laws, programs, and sub-programs over the last month, or even the last couple of months. They are growing up like mushrooms. It is a trend that makes it possible to assume that in a couple of years, Programs for Patriotic Education will be implemented not only at the state level, but at the municipal level as well, and then every single school will adopt it since schools are what all the efforts are about.
– A member of the Federal Agency for Youth Affairs (woman, 40)

As of December 2016, current regional programs for patriotic education were adopted in 56 regions of the Russian Federation.[53] Funding allocation for the regional programs varies from 200,000 rubles ($3,500) per year in the Karachay-Cherkess Republic to 233 million rubles ($3.5 million) per year in the

---

53 About half of the regional programs on patriotic education were adopted as a sub-section of another program, most commonly one on national policy or youth policy. However, even in this case, the patriotic education programs have separate budgets.

Tyumen Region. The examples in Table 2.3 suggest the diversity of the regional programs on patriotic education in Russia.

Table 2.3 – Examples of regional programs on patriotic education

Region	Population, in millions of people	Dates of the current program	Total program budget, in dollars	Number of program indicators
Altai Krai	2.4	2016–2020	445,000	8
Vologda Oblast	1.2	2014–2018	820,000	2
Kaluga Oblast	1.1	2015–2020	341,000	5
Nizhny Novgorod Oblast	3.2	2015–2020	77,000	6
Orenburg Oblast	2.0	2017–2020	1,670	11
Saint Petersburg	5.2	2015–2020	7,996.00	2
Sverdlovsk Oblast	4.3	2014–2020	22,800	14
Tyumen Oblast	3.6	2016–2020	17,940	5
Yamalo-Nenets Autonomous Region	0.5	2015–2018	2,788	10
Yaroslavl Oblast	1.3	2016–2020	1,000	4

The average yearly budget of current regional programs for patriotic education is about $460,000, with the median budget about $120,000 per year. In total, the budget of the current regional programs on patriotic education is about 16.5 million dollars per year, which is almost equal to the five-year budget of the federal program on patriotic education. These numbers, as well as the content of the regional programs and their indicators, are not part of public discussion in Russia. Indeed, they are outside of any statistical analysis and expert evaluation.

The logic of governmental programming suggests that regional and local programs should comply with national programs in accordance with geographic, economic, political, and cultural features of the region. However, when it comes to patriotic education, this logic fails. Regional programs merely repeat abstract wordings and pretentious statements without concretization. Even the distinctive new key words of the current government program (such as *GTO* and *patronage*) have been used in only 8 out of 56 regional programs. Also, the regional programs contain many misprints and discrepancies in description and indicators. All in all, the regional programs are even more unaccountable than the federal program.

Apart from financial ambiguity, regional programs have another interesting feature, mentioned in the interviews with the programs' elaborators and executors: They reflect the major strategy of the Russian political agenda of the last 10 years.

Interview fragment
We should capture some hidden meanings and general tendencies. It is our task to incorporate the political demands, even if they are maybe not said out loud, to the regional programs and policies. Patriotic education is a core issue in those terms. It's a kind of test for us, if we are able to keep the political situation under review and consider it in our actions.
— A member of a regional Youth Policy Committee (woman, 45)

Hidden meanings and unarticulated tendencies in regional programs emerge with the following aspects:

First, there is a tendency to identify patriotic education with military-and-patriotic education, and frequently even with preliminary military training. The list of priority objectives, which is almost the same in all regions, always includes strengthening military and patriotic views of the youth and increasing the quality of preliminary military training for the armed forces.[54] Even the ethnic republics of Russia (Buryatia, Republic of Komi, Tatarstan, Dagestan, etc.), which seemingly should stress the development of tolerance and inter-ethnic cooperation, base their list of patriotic education activities on the military component. Yet the concepts of tolerance, cultural development, citizenship, patriotism, and military service are widely mixed in these programs and frequently replace each other.

For instance, the Program for Strengthening Inter-Ethnic Relations and Patriotic Education (2014–2018) in the Republic of Adygea sets the target of

---

54 This has to do with a tradition from Soviet times, as well as structural changes in the Russian Army (Aleksey Balashov, "Rossiiskaia armiia: Smena modeli," *Mir Rossii* 23, no. 4 (2014): 148–77), that put emphasis on the need to recruit young people.

"patriotic education for citizens of the Republic of Adygea, a consolidated and educated civil society." At the same time, this target is expressed through a range of obscure objectives, such as 1) "patriotic education of the youth, intellectual education for citizens of the Republic of Adygea"; 2) "financial assistance for buying flats for the combat and disabled veterans of Afghanistan"; 3) "providing the youth with incentives for a healthy way of life"; 4) "creation of the environment for the mass media to be involved in the propaganda of patriotism"; and 5) "reducing crime in the Republic of Adygea."

In the Program for Patriotic Education of Citizens and Preliminary Military Training of the Youth for Military Service in the Tyumen Oblast (2016–2020), pacifism is associated with "legal nihilism" and "consumer psychology":

> *The improvement of the system of preliminary military training for the youth will contribute to sustainable replacement of the Russian Armed Forces with healthy, strong, motivated personnel familiar with modern technologies, as well as significantly reduce such phenomena as legal nihilism, political naivety, consumer psychology, and pacifism sentiments among young people.*

To give another example, the sub-program for Patriotic Education of Citizens of the Republic of Mordovia (2016–2018, within the Program for Culture and Tourism Development for 2014–2018) sets as its objective "teaching respect for the Constitution of the Russian Federation." However, this goal is not reflected in any single program event. Moreover, a large part of the program is predominantly dedicated to military education and the memorialization of the Great Patriotic War (World War II) in particular.

In many programs, military and patriotic motives seem far-fetched. For example, the patriotic sub-program for North Ossetia-Alania is said to be targeted at "creation of the environment for successful socialization, effective self-fulfillment of the youth, and use of their potential in the interests of the innovative development of the country *as well as* the improvement of preliminary military training and patriotic education of citizens" [italics mine]. The combination of innovative development and preliminary military training set in the objectives is expected to cause contradiction in the range of targeted efforts. The program's summary outlines specific life values, too, including health, labor, family, tolerance, and human rights. However, throughout the document, it is plain that the focus has shifted from civil and patriotic education to military and patriotic efforts, since all concrete actions in the sub-program require preliminary military training of the youth.

The second aspect involves non-military efforts that support military training for the youth. For example, the major objective of the sub-program for Preliminary Military Training for Children and the Youth in the Chechen Republic (within the Program for Education in the Chechen Republic for 2014–2020) is that of "opposing involvement of the Chechen youth in illegal armed groups, development of preliminary military training of the youth for military service, preparation of the citizens to serve the society and the nation with dignity and selflessness, and fulfilling commitments to defend their country." At the same time, this program embraces not only military efforts (field-days, marches, camps, reestablishment of air and sports clubs in the capital city of Grozny, and network development of pneumatic shooting ranges in the cities and towns of the Republic), but also measures to create and run radio and TV programs on youth problems, to organize youth employment for summer vacations, and to promote motocross racing, carting, car racing, skateboarding, roller-skating, orienteering, and even breakdancing.

Thirdly, the only topic constantly repeating in the federal and regional programs is that of the key part of Russian patriotism, namely the victory in the Great Patriotic War. Almost every regional program enshrines commemoration and celebration of Victory Day as a specific objective, calling for public events that include area study trips and search parties, meetings with veterans, care of the grave of the Unknown Soldier, celebration concerts, and memorial events. This motive is further elaborated upon in local (municipal) programs.[55]

---

55 It is impossible to estimate the exact number of Municipal Programs for Patriotic Education. There are no official statistics – not all municipal administrations have websites, and not all of those that do upload such statistics online. Considering that there are roughly 23,000 municipal administrations in Russia, and that the task to develop such programs on different levels is clearly articulated by the national government, there should be a very large number of such programs underway. Most municipal programs for patriotic education are marked by a lack of financing, while some programs have budgets of up to 1 million rubles (about $16,000) per year. Therefore, efforts are implemented on a voluntary basis (or, perhaps, on a "voluntary-involuntary" basis, as in the proverb from Soviet times) by activists. Understanding of their intentions, motives, and

These programs present specific efforts that, in some respect, correspond with the true range of measures within the Program for Patriotic Education in Russia. These efforts include upkeep of burial places and memorials on municipal grounds dedicated to heroes who perished during the Great Patriotic War; cooperation with veteran's institutions and rendering assistance to veterans; celebration of national holidays such as Fatherland Heroes Day (December 9), International Duties Memorial Day (commemorating the 1989 withdrawal of Soviet troops from Afghanistan, February 15), Defender of the Fatherland Day (February 23), Victory Day (May 9), Russia Day (June 12), Memorial Day of Mourning (June 22), Unity Day (November 4), and Russian Military Glory Day (November 7)[56]; celebration of special holidays related to preliminary training (Conscript's Day, Farewell to the Army Day); propaganda of outstanding and heroic feats of war and labor; museum and library exhibitions related to military glory organized on the occasion of remarkable dates, historic events, and military glory days; area study efforts, including visits to military glory sites; and competitions of military and patriotic paintings, songs, sporting competitions, and photography exhibitions.

Local programs make the same mistakes as those at higher levels. They suffer from incomplete design and possess discrepancies in facts and technical indicators. They neglect the federal documents (in particular the 2016–2020 government program's GTO and patronage features), while at the same time stating ambitious objectives[57] and goals. Those programs frequently contain plagiarism, copying texts from journal articles or Internet entries without including references.

---

   values is a subject for separate research that may shed light on the secrets of ongoing patriotic education in Russia.
56 It is curious that the default list of holidays rarely includes Constitution Day (December 12).
57 For example, the Program for Military and Patriotic Education and Public Spirit of the Youth in the Zarachenskoe Rural Settlement in the Oryol Region for 2014–2016 sets the following objective: "the improvement of the patriotic education system, which is responsible for high targeted social activity among citizens of rural settlements, public spirit and patriotism, pride and devotion to their country, readiness to carry out their civil duty and constitutional commitments, shaping an educated, healthy, and strong young generation that cannot divide their lives from the life of their country."

Despite the ambitious and large-scale objectives, patriotic education at the local level is targeted almost solely at schoolchildren. It is clear that, in the conditions of almost vanishing financial availability for local programs, they can be at least partially implemented only through cooperation with schools. On the other hand, this view clearly contradicts federal concepts that imply that patriotic education is targeted at the whole population of the country.

2.4 Conclusion

The above descriptions show that there are many discrepancies and inaccuracies in the governmental programming for patriotic education at federal, regional, and local levels. One must ask why this practice of "empty documents" is still alive and enjoying the increasing support of budget money. There are two more or less obvious answers to this question. First, the officials involved in the development of programs and routines for all levels of implication are likely incompetent. Second, it is assumed that the governmental programming for patriotic education pursues a completely different goal than what follows from the declarations in the programs. With emotional phrases about the necessity of raising citizens devoted to the Motherland as a smokescreen, the programs themselves form institutional and infrastructural supports to ensure loyalty to the government from certain social groups. Veterans and pensioners, military officers and teachers, and young people's pro-governmental associations, all of whom are the main objects of the programs, are also the traditional base of support for the leading Russian party and the president. In any case, governmental programming in its current state is not the basis for the patriotic education of young citizens of Russia. It falls short of rules of public programming and public evaluation. With poor indicators and performance evaluation, they cannot be considered useful even in maintaining the jingoistic patriotism often attributed to Russian patriotic education.

Interview fragment
The patriotic programs give us the top-dressing [in Russian: *podkormka*, additional nutrition – A.S.], *and we all understand for what purpose. Sure, the teachers, the parents and, heaven forbid, the young children, should not think about purposes other than to raise good citizens for the state. They are not fools, though. So I don't know what exactly they may think, actually. But for us* [the administration], *the political and election motivation of all that patriotic money is obvious. They give us the monies, we spend them to the purpose we need, not only for the patriotism goals. You know, the truth is that you actually do not need money to raise a patriot. However, no monies are ever extra for the municipal school. So this is a deal. A contract. They give us the monies – we pretend to spend them on patriotism – they pretend to believe – we give them the election support. A vicious circle, but it has existed forever.*

— A school director (woman, 50, Leningrad Oblast)

Governmental programming for patriotic education in Russia is proving to be a simple excuse to distribute budget money. The way of formulating and implementing the programs supports Marlène Laruelle's observation that "the patriotism promoted by the Kremlin has turned out to be nothing more than a protean container largely devoid of content."[58]

Theoretically, it is a good idea to provide a link between goals, objectives, actions, and financing in the process of raising new citizens. Also, as other countries' experience shows, it is very effective to set the specific indicators that measure the effectiveness of the program, even for complicated political aspects of the society's life. For example, responsible and thoughtful approaches to public programming became a real basis for nation-building and patriotic education in Singapore,[59] and some programs were successfully implemented in China.[60]

---

58 Laruelle, *In the Name of the Nation*. P, 196.
59 Shuyi Chua et al., "Rethinking Critical Patriotism: A Case of Constructive Patriotism in Social Studies Teachers in Singapore," *Asia Pacific Journal of Education*, 2016; Lily Kong and Brenda S.a. Yeoh, "The Construction of National Identity through the Production of Ritual and Spectacle: An Analysis of National Day Parades in Singapore," *Political Geography* 16, no. 3 (1997): 213–39; Chee Keng John Wang et al., "Patriotism and National Education: Perceptions of Trainee Teachers in Singapore," *Asia Pacific Journal of Education* 26, no. 1 (2006): 51–64.
60 Alisa Jones, "Changing the Past to Build the Future: History Education in Post-Mao China" (University of Leeds, 2007); Daniel Sneider, "Textbooks and Patriotic Education:

However, responsiveness and thoughtfulness do not apply to the governmental programming in the field of patriotic education in Russia. Here, the national program, as well as a huge number of regional and municipal programs, exists in the a priori implementation mode. The programs are built on extremely general terms without any indication of how the results could be evaluated and managed. These programs are a kind of Kant's "thing-in-itself" and do not perform as a basis for anything. The real processes, structures, and agents of patriotic education are outside the scope of public programming.

Wartime Memory Formation in China and Japan," *Asia-Pacific Review* 20, no. 1 (2013): 35–54.

3. The Model of Patriotic Education in Schools: USSR to Russia

In the Soviet Union, and then in Russia, the school system was tasked with political socialization of the youth. School has always been the main institution that provided the translation of settings of civil and social behavior in accordance with the needs of society, and particularly in accordance with the needs of the state. The ideological vector of Soviet schooling was clearly linked to patriotic education. Patriotism served as one of the cornerstones of the communist system, and the state's ideologists and Communist Party leaders generously supported its systematic implementation through education. This support took the forms of financial aid, material benefits to schools, and moral endorsement. In order to receive these benefits, schoolteachers and administrators made their patriotic educational activity visible to the state officials. One way to do this was to write a manual on patriotic education that could serve as an example to other schools and as a signal to the higher authorities. These manuals are usually called *metodichki* and are widely used by teachers in the educational process.

The Contemporary Collection of the Russian National Library contains 1,396 titles of manuals on patriotic education published 1965–2015. The quantitative distribution of the data in Figure 3.1 shows three periods of pedagogical interest in this area. The formation of the pedagogical model of patriotic education took place in the 1960s-1970s, with a gradual decline in the number of manuals written throughout the 1980s, reflecting the changes in this model. After a period of lost interest during the 1990s, the year 2000 ushered in an intense revival of attention to patriotic education.

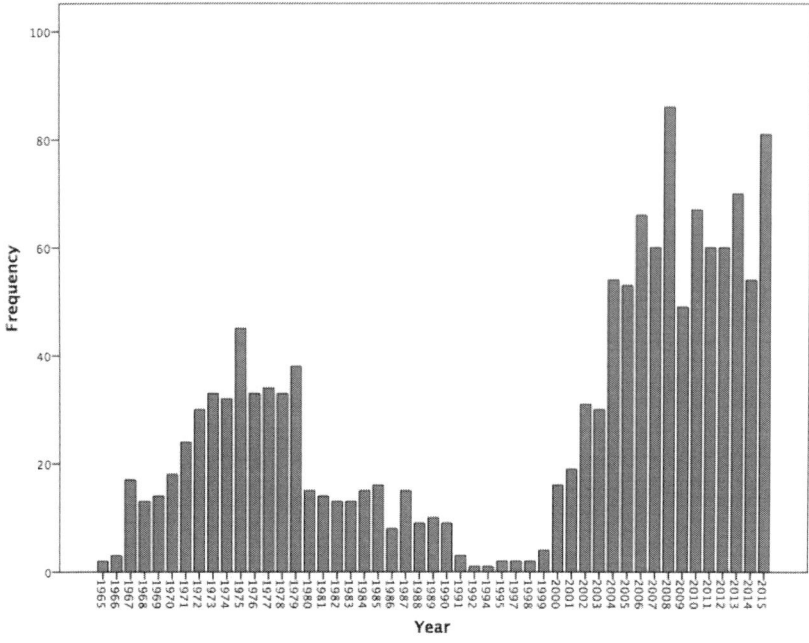

Figure 3.1 – Number of manuals on the subject of patriotic education, 1965–2015 (%, N = 1,396)

The model of patriotic education was formed in the 1960s-1970s as a combination of several basic elements (Figure 3.2.a), but the core fabric of this model began to take shape long before the 1960s, under the influence of the doctrine of socialism. The model of patriotic education was based on the state vision of patriotic education in schools, stressing memorialization of the Revolution and World Wars as an important foundation for social upbringing. This vision was reflected in the concepts of emotion-based learning and the "patriotism of everything," implemented with the help of teachers using pedagogical tools and youth organizations. Each of the following periods brought changes to the model of patriotic education. At the same time, the core fabric of this model was surprisingly persistent and self-reproducing. The system was so stable and complete that, after its dismantling in the 1990s, it was able to revive itself upon demand in the early 2000s (Figure 3.2.b,c).

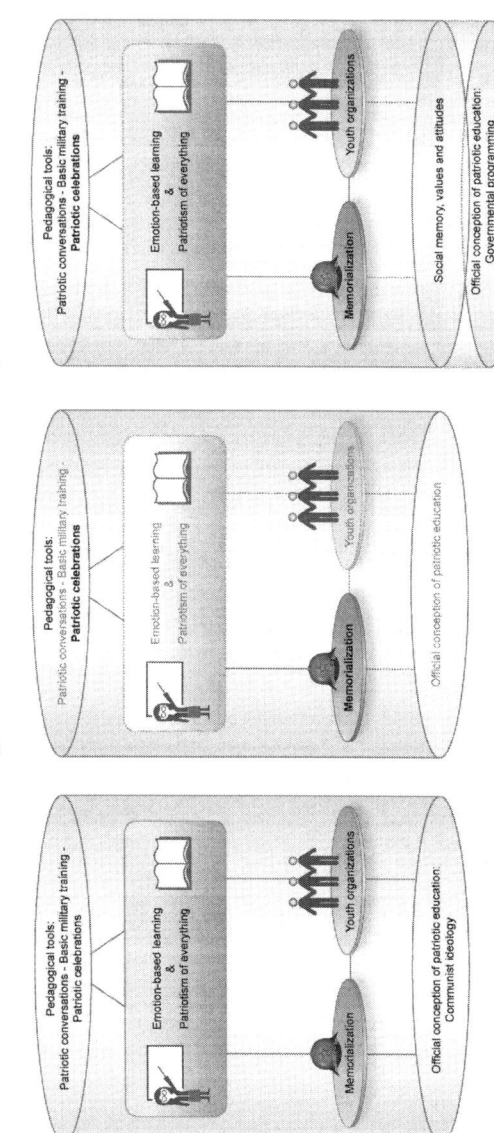

Figure 3.2 – The model of patriotic education and its modification in
a) USSR; b) Russia in the 1990s; c) contemporary Russia

3.1 The Rise and Fall of Soviet Patriotic Education: 1930s–1980s

Soviet patriotism has its roots in the victory of the Stalinist doctrine of building socialism in a single country. With the help of the schools, patriotism spread quickly throughout the population of the Soviet Union. The pragmatic component of patriotism was based on emphasizing the achievements of Soviet power in all spheres of public life, as well as on educating the population in a spirit of devotion to the Motherland. The educational concept of the 1930s reflected the defensive-patriotic tendencies in the ideology of the Soviet state. In every possible way, educational guidance counselors emphasized the link between the worldview of students, school militarization, and patriotism. The following are two examples of methodical instructions for teachers, from 1929 and 1937, which illustrate how easily the educational function becomes subordinated to ideology:

> *Often we can still hear such kinds of reasoning: "Political education is the task of Young Pioneer leaders, in the worst case of a teacher of social science, and there is nothing for chemists or biologists to deal with." This peculiar political neutralism of so-called "neutral" discipline teachers is the residue of bourgeois speculation about the apolitical character of the school. There are great capabilities for political-educational work in the hands of every teacher. ... Our school teaches not Chemistry, Physics or Mathematics in general, but teaches how to use the forces of these sciences to possess the productive forces of the country. (1929)* [61]

> *We should remember that we do not educate pacifists who dream about the peaceful elimination of war – the Soviet student has to understand that war is an inevitable product of class society. Our socialist homeland lives in a capitalistic environment. Fascist governments talk openly about attack on the Soviet Union. That is why it is necessary to teach Soviet students to be ready to repel fascist aggressors, to call the consciousness of necessity to be ready to resist, that is, to strengthen power and technical equipment of the Red Army, which, in case of attack on our homeland, must beat the enemy on their territory. (1937)* [62]

---

[61] Igor Veksler and Rimma Kharitonova, eds., *Vtoraia stupen' sovetskoi trudovoi shkoly. Organizatsiia. Soderzhanie. Metody* (Moscow, 1929).

[62] Natalia Andreevskaia, "Vospitatel'naia rabota na urokakh istorii," *Istoricheskii Zhurnal*, no. 13 (1937): 89–95. P. 91–92.

To bring this patriotic feature of education to life and to realize the official conception of Soviet citizens' upbringing, the school used some organizational tools. In the center of the patriotic education model was emotion-based learning, which became a cornerstone of the process that transformed the priorities of schooling from education to upbringing.

Emotion-Based Learning and the Patriotism of Everything

The main method of patriotic education in Soviet school was emotion-based learning. A teacher should be able to create the "effect of presence" at the level of children's emotions. Thus, students were encouraged to develop a proper assessment of the past, which in turn was considered a starting point to develop a proper assessment of the present. Vladimir Somov cites a methodical document from the 1930s, designed for teachers of History and discovered in a central archive in the Nizhny Novgorod region:

> *Students should see Petersburg workers walking along Petersburg streets and squares to the Winter Palace on January 9[63] and feel their mood and live their lives. They have to experience the joy of workers listening to Lenin at Finland Railway Station. ... There must not be a place for impartial contemplation on History lessons. The destiny of people, which the pupils will learn from History, should deeply impassion the children. They must feel themselves like participants of a fight they study in lessons, they should experience the bitterness of defeat and joy of victory, they should like some and hate others.*[64]

During and after the Great Patriotic War (World War II, 1941–1945), patriotic education was intensified with the recognition of the importance of Russian history and an emphasis on heroic examples. Up to the end of the 1950s,

---

63 The author refers to "Bloody Sunday" or "Red Sunday," which occurred on January 9, 1905 in Saint Petersburg, Russia. Demonstrators marched towards the Winter Palace to present a petition to Tsar Nicholas II and were fired upon by soldiers of the Imperial Guard. In Soviet and Russian historiography, Bloody Sunday is considered to be the start of the Revolution of 1905.

64 Vladimir Somov, "Istoriia kak uchebnyi predmet v sovetskoi sisteme shkol'nogo vospitaniia vo vtoroi polovine 1930-kh godov," *Liudi i teksty. Istoricheskii al'manakh*, no. 6 (2014): 257–70.

a "severe, ineradicable hatred of the enemies of the homeland"[65] appeared in the sections of textbooks devoted to definitions of Soviet patriotism. The true patriot was one "who fearlessly exposed public enemies, philistines, whiners and alarmists..."[66]

Children in primary school received training in patriotic distinctiveness and the formation of love for the place in which the children were born and grew up. Through this feeling, students were meant to develop a love of the vastness of their big country. The greatness of the Soviet Union and advantages of the Socialist system were settled on the basis of carefully selected facts. Thus, students received a wholly positive evaluation of the political regime.

The totality of patriotic education reached its apogee in the 1960s-1970s. Drawing on emotion-based learning, Soviet schools taught what may be described as the "patriotism of everything." Patriotic thinking was no longer a separate task of schooling. The education of patriots began to define the content of practically all school subjects, as well as extracurricular education. Social studies lessons contained the ideology of communism in the context of "theoretical laws," the most important of which were Marxist-Leninist conceptions of war and peace and their economic rationale of the role of defense in the country's development. Geography lessons highlighted the battles that took place in different Soviet territories during the Great Patriotic War. Math classes provided a variety of examples of applied problems related to the "extensive building of communist society."[67] Music lessons were based on classic Soviet compositions, mostly on military themes. Students learned about the historical context of particular songs, almost all of which were linked to the feats of Soviet citizens.

The Organizational Basis of Patriotic Education

While the combination of emotion-based learning and the "patriotism of everything" became a conceptual foundation of the methods of patriotic education, its organizational basis evolved from two elements.

---

65 Nikolai Boldyrev, *Vospitanie sovetskogo patriotizma u shkol'nikov* (Moscow: Pravda, 1949).
66 Ibid.
67 Kairzhan Kozhabaev, "Patrioticheskoe vospitanie uchashchikhsia na urokah matematiki i vo vneklassnoi rabote," *Matemetika v shkole*, no. 1 (1978): 19–22.

Firstly, children's and youth organizations were integrated into school life and broadly supported by the state.[68] Membership in the Little Octobrists or the Pioneer organization, as well as the All-Union Leninist Young Communist League (Komsomol), involved different rules, but all organizations required members to earn merits, the foundation of which were patriotic feelings and actions.[69] This was intended to motivate children and teens to behave properly.

68　The Law "On strengthening the connection between the school and life and the further development of the public education system in the USSR" (1958) adopted by the Supreme Soviet of the Soviet Union; Resolutions of the Central Committee of the CPSU and the USSR Council of Ministers: "On measures of further improvement of the secondary school" (1966), "On the completion of the transition to universal secondary education of young people and future secondary school development" (1972), "Secondary school charter" (1970), "On measures of further improvement of the conditions of rural secondary schools" (1973).

69　When they joined the ranks of the Octobrists, usually between ages 7–9, children were granted a pin badge in a form of a five-pointed star with a portrait of Lenin as a child. Octobrists' activities mostly developed in groups of five. Each group was called a "Star." Children in the Stars were guided by leaders from the Pioneers and the Komsomol. In these groups, children prepared to join the Union Pioneer Organization named after Lenin. Work with the Octobrists was organized mainly in the form of games. The children were expected to learn the basic rules formulated in a simple way:
Young Octobrists are the future Pioneers.
Young Octobrists are hardworking, they like school, they respect elders.
Only those who love to work can be called "Octobrists."
Young Octobrists are truthful and brave, clever and skillful.
Young Octobrists are friendly guys, they read and draw, play and sing.
At age 9–14, students joined the Pioneer organization. At the ceremonial lineup, usually held in a special place like a school museum, children recited the solemn promise of the Pioneer of the Soviet Union. Communists, Komsomols, or older Pioneers handed the newcomers a red Pioneer tie and Pioneer badge.
Pioneering duties included volunteer work as well as games. Children collected scrap metal and waste paper for recycling, helped primary school pupils and cared for the elderly, took part in military-sports games, participated in clubs, and were expected to earn excellent grades at school. Improper behavior was punished by condemnation by the Pioneer Squad Council, which could lead to expulsion from the Pioneer organization.
At age 14, students could become Komsomols. Admission to the Komsomol was conducted individually. To apply, a person needed a recommendation from a member of the Communist Party or from two experienced Komsomols. People could be excluded from the Komsomol for church attendance, carelessness, non-payment of membership dues, or family troubles. Expulsion from the organization threatened a lack of opportunity for future education and career prospects.

More direct rewards existed as well, like inclusion in the Pioneer Book of Honor, receiving the Red Banner or the Order of Lenin, or earning commendations, vouchers to children's camps, or gifts such as books. However, the preferred form of promotion was a collective one. Thus was the *priority of we above I* formed in children's minds.

The second element in the organizational basis of patriotic education was the memorialization of historical events, specifically the Great Patriotic War. Almost every school founded a museum of military glory, and together with the teachers, students organized excavations in the battlefields, during which they searched for relics of war such as guns, uniforms, medals, and other personal items that belonged to soldiers. As the War affected practically every family in the country, these actions were supported by certain emotions associated with personal memories or the recollections of relatives and close friends. School museums played a very special organizing role in this process. As in the case of youth organizations, their activities were directly supported by the state. School museums were founded by the decree of the school director with support from the pedagogical council, Komsomol committee, and Pioneer Squad council. Every such decree had to be approved by the local Board of Education in coordination with the district or city department of culture and district or city committee of the All-Union Leninist Young Communist League (CPSU). In the "Model provision about the museum, working on a voluntary basis" (1978), a school museum was considered a type of public museum.[70] This museum was based on voluntary activity of students, teachers, and parents. The list of a museum's activists often included members of local and state museums, archives, and libraries. A large part of school museums were made up of military-historical museums and Rooms of Military Glory. Many of them were created thanks to the activity of war veterans.

---

70 "A Public Museum is a cultural and educational institution purposefully collecting, storing, exhibiting objects of material and spiritual culture, historical, scientific, artistic or other values. On this basis, the museum leads a broad work in the communist education of the working people." – USSR Ministry of Culture, *Model provision about the museum, working on a voluntary basis*, Postanovlenie ot 04/12/1978, available at: http://www.consultant.ru/cons/cgi/online.cgi?req=doc;base=ESU;n=21597#0 (as of December 5, 2016).

School museums were maintained because of intense interest in the events of the Great Patriotic War. People wanted to preserve the glory of the victory, to remember the tragic past, and to protect future generations from experiencing such a conflict. Museums became the places in which to organize special lessons on the most historically important topics. Members of the Communist Party, participants in the Revolution, veterans of the Civil War and Great Patriotic War, and Heroes of Social Labor often visited school museums to meet children and tell them about their experiences. School celebrations, such as the dedication to Octobrists, Pioneers, and Komsomols, were conducted in the museums, too.

The organizational basis of patriotic education in Soviet schools was strongly supported by a conceptual combination of emotion-based learning and the "patriotism of everything." In everyday school life, this unity of the conceptual and organizing elements was reproduced with three basic pedagogical tools: patriotic conversations, patriotic holidays, and basic military training.

Patriotic conversations

A simple and effective method of conversation, encouraged in all schools in the Soviet Union, covering all age groups and applicable in any context and situation, served to focus young minds on their patriotic duties. Young Pioneer leaders talked with the Octobrists, and chairmen of squads and class teachers talked to the Pioneers. A special role in the preparation and conduction of patriotic conversations was assigned to the senior Pioneer leaders, who reported to the vice director responsible for the extracurricular activity or directly to the school director.

Patriotic conversations, which involved carefully selected factual material, were thematically focused and age-appropriate for the targeted group of children. Conversation topics in primary school were rather general: "Our happy childhood," "Our school museum of military glory," "Who are the Octobrists?" and "Friendship of children of all nations." In high school, conversations became more specific in theme: "The Party is our Helmsman," "Communist ideology is our wings," "Protection of Homeland is our sacred, honorable duty,"

"We accept the torch of revolutionary, labor, and military glory from our fathers and grandfathers."[71]

Some patriotic conversations were conducted by discussing books and movies. Every school library, and sometimes every schoolroom, had a recommended list of books on the topic of "Our Soviet Homeland." The core of this list, formed by the end of the 1940s, included books like "How the Steel Was Tempered" by Nikolai Ostrovsky, "The Son of the Regiment" by Valentin Kataev, and "Timur and His Squad" by Arkady Gaidar.[72] Many of these books were adapted to film.

Soviet cinematography was very productive. On average, Soviet studios released almost 150 films annually, a figure comparable to that of Hollywood, while cinema attendance stood at three times the size of the domestic American audience.[73] Cinematography was considered a transitional tool of patriotic education, applying not only to school, but also to institutions of higher education and the society in general. Organized trips to the cinema, followed by group discussions, were more common than family screenings. The majority of films were about the Revolution and Great Patriotic War.

---

71 Yakov Idel'chik, *Patrioticheskoe vospitanie shkol'nikov (iz opyta)* (Minsk: Narodnaia Asveta, 1968). P. 92–93.

72 "How the Steel Was Tempered" (1932) is an autobiographical novel by Nikolai Ostrovsky. Written in the style of socialist realism, the novel immediately gained great popularity and became the most published work of Soviet literature. From 1932–1986, over 36 million copies of the book were published. The novel depicts the events of the Civil War, periods of recovery in the national economy, and socialist construction.
"The Son of the Regiment" (1944) by Valentin Kataev is about a 12-year-old boy who is discovered by scouts during the Great Patriotic War, fights with them, and carries out combat missions.
"Timur and His Squad" (1940) by Arkady Gaidar is about the adventures of young Timur and his friends. Timur became the prototype for the ideal Pioneer, always ready to help others. In a way, the word "timurovets" became synonymous with the word "Pioneer."
These works, included in either the obligatory or additional reading lists for Soviet schoolchildren, are still encouraged for extracurricular reading in some schools.

73 George Faraday, *Revolt of the Filmmakers: The Struggle for Artistic Autonomy and the Fall of the Soviet Film Industry* (Philadelphia: Pennsylvania State University Press, 2000). P. 9.

Although creative workers in the Soviet Union were under direct supervision by the state, Soviet military movies made for excellent "entertainment cinema," a spectacle with a captivating story, an "ideological show."[74] The Great Patriotic War was depicted multilaterally, covering events on the front lines and at the rear, as well as the partisan movement and intelligence. Millions of people watched films such as "The Battle of Stalingrad" (1949) and "The Dawns Here are Quiet" (1972), and pupils discussed them in literature classes and wrote compositions. The films were also the subject of extracurricular patriotic conversations.

A separate genre of patriotic conversation was *education by example*. Education by example highlighted the roles of specific historical figures and the patriotic nature of their lives. These individuals were Soviet leaders, heroes of the War, and Heroes of Labor, among others. Especially and ubiquitously prevalent was the example of Vladimir Il'ich Ul'ianov, better known as Vladimir Lenin. Education by Lenin's example was dictated by the Academy of Pedagogical Sciences of the USSR. The content of this education centered on Lenin's biography, which portrayed him as a heroic leader of workers. Lenin's life was celebrated in songs, books, films, and other art. Works about Lenin praised him to the skies, lauding his kindness, compassion, sense of justice, and love of nature.

The number of children's books about Lenin increased every year. The first and most popular book dates from 1940,[75] and one of the last, published with an edition of 150,000 copies, is from 1988. The following is a typical passage from such books:

---

74 Ibid. P. 9.
75 "Stories about Lenin" (1940) is a collection of short stories for children by Mikhail Zoshchenko. They describe various positive aspects of young Lenin's life in a way that appeals to children. For example, in "The Pitcher," little Volodya feels guilty because he did not confess after he broke a pitcher; only when he admits his mistake is Volodya able to get a good night's sleep. "The Gray Goat" tells how Volodya convinced his younger brother Mitya that children should be brave. The story "On the Hunt" reveals that Lenin, despite his love of hunting, saved a fox's life by refusing to shoot. Zoshchenko's "Stories about Lenin" were included in the primary school reading curriculum.

> *Little Volodya liked to catch birds. He and his friends set traps for them. I remember he had a linnet in a cage. I don't know if he caught it or whether he bought it or someone gave it to him. I just remember that this linnet lived for a short time, became bored, ruffled up and died. I don't know why it happened, whether Volodya was guilty of forgetting to feed the bird or not. I just remember that someone blamed him and I remember his serious and focused expression while he was looking at the dead linnet, and how he said emphatically: "I will never keep birds in a cage." And he really did not keep them ever after* (Anna Ul'ianova, *Il'ich's Childhood and School Years*).[76]

As children grew up, so did their perceptions of Lenin. In this way, his example was both dynamic and unchanging. By the time children studied Lenin's writings and political life in high school, they were familiar with stories of his childhood, environment, and way of life, and so they explored his ideas with a sense of personal acquaintance. This formed the emotional bias of comprehension of Lenin's gospel and a positive attitude to his life and political actions.

Celebrations

The formation of patriotic values and attitudes was considered most effective through inclusion in activities. Since emotion was an immutable foundation of patriotic education, it is not surprising that the best-perceived activities were public holidays. Schools celebrated the Day of the Soviet Army and Navy (February 23), Labor Day (May 1), the Day of Soviet Victory in the Great Patriotic War (May 9), and the Anniversary of the Great October Socialist Revolution (November 7).

In the mid-1960s, the authorities created a stable model for Victory Day celebrations, a model that is still used today. Every year on May 9, a military parade was held on Red Square in Moscow and broadcast on television and radio. The military parade came to be considered not only as a tribute to veterans, but as a form of state ritual. It was a victory-military form of expression, and it gave the Soviet Union a halo of significance.[77]

---

76 Anna Ul'ianova, *Detskie i shkol'nye gody Il'icha* (Moscow: Malysh, 1988). P. 52.
77 Nina Tumarkin, "Myth and Memory in Soviet Society," *Society* 24, no. 6 (September 1987): 69–72; Christel Lane, "Legitimacy and Power in the Soviet Union Through Socialist Ritual," *British Journal of Political Science* 14, no. 2 (April 27, 1984): 207.

School celebrations were held on the eve of Victory Day. Children learned poems, songs, and dances, and prepared concert performances for parents and veterans. In small towns and villages, the school concerts took place at the House of Culture or the central square. The students' activities also included ceremonies, which took place near mass graves, the grave of the Unknown Soldier, and monuments. The manual on patriotic education from 1949 summarizes the leitmotif of the Soviet school holiday and its basic idea, passed through the decades:

> *The school, family, Komsomol and Pioneer organizations have great capabilities for patriotic education of students in the period of preparation for holidays and especially in the period of their celebrations. Preparation and performance of children's parties, learning poems, preparation of reports, publishing holiday wall newspapers and school magazines, collective listening to the radio, participation in demonstrations and parades, collective visiting of cinema and theaters, meetings between students and notable people – all this can be used successfully to form and secure a sense of Soviet patriotism and Soviet national pride in our students.*[78]

People of all ages responded positively to the celebrations. During the Soviet years, many witnesses to the Revolution and veterans of the Great Patriotic War were still alive, so public celebrations were not just about historical memory, but also about the living memory of generations, as well as oral history. It was with state support that Victory Day became the main patriotic holiday in the country and in the schools.

Basic military training, military games, and gatherings

Basic military training (BMT), or pre-service training, was considered an integral part of the preparation of young people for military service. After 1967, all secondary schools required BMT for boys and girls, starting at age 14. Teachers of BMT were usually ex-officers of the armed forces. Officially, such a teacher was known as a military instructor (*voennyi rukovoditel'*) or, in daily use, a *voenruk*. On average, students had two lessons of BMT each week.

---

78 Boldyrev, *Vospitanie sovetskogo patriotizma u shkol'nikov.* P. 22.

BMT consisted of theoretical and practical training. The theoretical basis was devoted to the study of the composition of the USSR armed forces, systems of military rank and service order, and examination of military regulations and normative acts. Practical training included working with mandatory training materials such as training weapons (Kalashnikov assault rifles, smallbore rifles, air rifles, dummy hand grenades), personal protective equipment (masks, respirators), and means of radiation and chemical protection (dosimeters, gas analyzers). In addition, BMT included marching and training in medical, engineering, topographic, and tactical areas.

Upon completion of the two-year BMT program, *voenruks* organized a retreat gathering for boys in 10th grade, held in a real military unit deployed in the region. There, the students became acquainted with the life of the military forces as well as with the current models of weapons. They also participated in the daily life of the unit, dug trenches for shooting, were engaged in combat training, studied personal protective equipment, and learned to shoot.

BMT was integrated with military-sports games and camps. The first Young Pioneer military-sports game, *Zarnitsa* ("summer lightning"), was conducted in 1967, followed later by a similar game called *Orlyonok* ("eaglet"). These games were included in the plan for the organization of basic military training in secondary schools. *Zarnitsa* and *Orlyonok* represented imitations of military operations, similar to military trainings. Players were divided into two opposing teams, a referee, and neutral observers. The object of the game was to capture the flag of the other team. Each participant wore shoulder straps, and in order to "kill" a player, it was necessary to tear off his straps. Points were awarded for capturing the flag and killing opponents; points were removed for foul play. The winner was decided based on the number of points scored or upon capturing the enemy's flag.

Besides mandatory BMT, the All-Union Voluntary Society for Cooperation with the Army, Air Force, and Navy (DOSAAF) offered opportunities for training in military-technical sports like parachuting, crawler vehicles and track driving, gliding, aircraft sports, shooting, and orienteering. According to various sources, DOSAAF had from 65 to 98 million members.[79] It performed two important functions. First, it provided Soviet people with an opportunity for recreation that would not otherwise be available. Second, it ensured military training for the youth and prepared them for the Army. In branches all over the country, DOSAAF offered defense instruction and training in military skills and sports. It provided "war games and contests for young and old, stressing especially such manly sports as motorcycle riding, fencing, marksmanship, grenade throwing, and obstacle racing. It organized mass parachute jumps and long marches, frequently led or supervised by army officers. It invited boys to learn to operate radio equipment, to pilot planes, to scuba-dive, and trained a million or so technical specialists each year."[80]

Sustainability of the model of patriotic education

The aforementioned institutions and methods of patriotic education were sustainable and universal. Youth organizations, memorialization practices, and different pedagogical tools were flexible, changeable, adaptive, and ideologically grounded. Despite their simplicity, or perhaps because of it, these methods upheld a model of patriotic education (Figure 3.2.a), a structure based on the state vision of patriotic education in schools, which appeared in the concept of emotion-based learning and the "patriotism of everything." The close interconnectedness and mutual support of multiple elements provided for the self-reproduction and self-preservation of this structure.

The adaptive qualities of the model became apparent in the late 1970s when party ideologists announced a reduction of militarism in education and upbringing. The word "patriotic" in education received a new prefix: "international." The school system, as a state-dependent institution, reacted with absolute willingness to accept changes in political attitudes. Lessons began to emphasize the friendship of peoples, fidelity to the community of socialist countries, and love for a multinational homeland. At a glance, education and upbringing became *internationally patriotic* both in form and content.

---

79 Michael Lucky, "Soviet Officer: A Credible Adversary" (Maxwell Air Force Base, Alabama, 1986).
80 Robert G Wesson, "The Military in Soviet Society," *The Russian Review* 30, no. 2 (1971): 139–45.

However, the old ideological sense of patriotism did not disappear. Methodologists, teachers, leaders of youth organizations, and school directors reformatted it into "heroic-patriotic education" and "ideological-patriotic education," which continued to exist together with the new internationally patriotic mode. Heroic-patriotic education presumed the education of youth in the combat and labor traditions of the Soviet people. The ideological-patriotic education supposed promotion of Marxist-Leninist ideas and stressed their extensive successes in all spheres of public life.[81] Thus, patriotic education still included the development of a sense of civic and military duty, respect and love for the armed forces, the propaganda of combat and labor traditions, and the development of courage, acquisition of military knowledge, physical conditioning, and endurance of the school children.

3.2 The Decline of Patriotic Education: 1980s–1990s

In the mid-1980s, state and societal focus on patriotic education was fading due to the changes in national and international political situations and educational reform. The reform was aimed at a radical renewal of the Soviet school, especially its curricula. Courses such as Computer Science, Ethics, and Psychology of Family Life were introduced.[82] Also, the reform included better training and pay for teachers and other educational workers. Better conditions of life for everybody involved in school life became a state priority. In the 1980s, many graduates of pedagogical universities not only received job positions in brand new schools, but even received apartments, mostly in rural areas and small cities. The total number of the country's teachers increased from 2.6 million in 1981 to 3 million in 1986.

For the young teachers, it was not obvious that ideology should be valued above learning. Old values and attitudes were incompatible with the new developments in education. However, complete removal from patriotic education

---

81 Arsenii Milovidov, *Kommunisticheskaiia nravstvennost' i voenno-patrioticheskoe vospitanie* (Moscow: Znanie, 1979).
82 Beatrice Szekely, "The New Soviet Educational Reform," *Comparative Education Review* 30, no. 3 (1986): 321–43.

was impossible, as it was still considered the major force for creation of citizens loyal to communist ideology and the Soviet state. Thus, young teachers continued certain pedagogical traditions to maintain a façade of patriotic education and to avoid penalties from the supervisory authorities.

> *Interview fragment*
> *I graduated from pedagogical university in 1983 and then came to a totally wonderful new school. It was located in a new building, just built. Its collective was new, too; almost everyone was young. And the children were "new," too, because beforehand, only a primary school was in that village, and to get a secondary education, children had to move to the city. We were young, and although we followed some slogans, yet, we really liked everything new that happened. The air already smelled of spring, although we were still fearful that the spring would not come. There were a lot of slogans, again, but they were different. They were about humanization and humanitarization of education. We believed that we would teach in a new way. We began to learn to question the pressure under which we grew up... I cannot say that we stopped believing in the Soviet ideals, we didn't. But we learned how to build Potemkin villages, how to play a show to perform what we were not interested in. It gave us free time for all new things that we considered useful to ourselves and our students. All the rest, everything we did not believe in, was a show. Just making performances, no serious and terrible ideology with which we were fed up. We got real pleasure from doing this. It was our "carnival night."*[83]
> – Primary school teacher and deputy of extracurricular activity (woman, 55, Saratov Oblast)

In order to maintain the façade of patriotic education, the school staff returned to old methods: patriotic conversations, the merits of historical figures (including Lenin), school museums, patriotic holidays, and basic military training. Nevertheless, as the years passed and the events of World War II became distant memories, the lessons of basic military training shed their ideological burden. The practice of throwing grenades or shooting a rifle gradually lost its

---

83 In *Carnival Night* (1956), the classic musical comedy by Eldar Ryazanov, the House of Culture prepares for its New Year's Eve extravaganza, but the interim director schedules serious educational presentations and lectures instead. The spritely young House of Culture workers band together to thwart the director's plans, and in the end, they celebrate New Year's Eve with fun and entertainment.

pragmatic objective and became an interesting pastime or an entertainment for schoolchildren.

Interview fragment

I became a teacher in 1985. Before that, I studied at Ped [Pedagogical Institute], was in the army, and before that studied at school. And in 1985, I suddenly saw the difference. The difference of expectations. When we were in school, everything around BMP [Basic Military Preparation] was very serious. I won't lie and tell you that all of us would perform those 100 meters of skiing to protect the Soviet borders (laughs)... but it was impossible to cheat, it was easy to get exiled from everywhere... And we were always told that physical training is a key thing to raise a fighter. War, the potential war, was everywhere. Seriously. And by the mid-1980s everything has passed away, very quickly. You know, it was 1985, there was a thaw in the political situation and so on... But how fast it was accepted by the people, by the schools! As if they were waiting for it, as if everything that was serious before never existed! My school was new and the teachers were young. The pathetic was expelled, you know. We still had the BMP. They crawled with grenades, shot from a rifle... but it was fun! Fun, but not a mission for the children.

– Basic Military Education teacher (man, 58, Pskov Oblast)

By the 1990s, there was little left from the Soviet structure of school patriotic education (Figure 3.2.b). There were no state concepts, no plans or other facilities that the school could consider as the basis of its educational activities. The goal to construct a new Russian state eclipsed practices of memorialization and remembrance. The Octobrists, Pioneers, and Komsomol were dissolved in 1991. New challenges in the effectiveness of education and the decline of ideology and propaganda caused the abandonment of emotion-based learning. These made military training, patriotic conversations, and all former state celebrations irrelevant. The model of patriotic education was forgotten, no longer necessary to the authorities.

However, two elements of the model survived to become the foundation for the future revival of patriotic education. One of these elements is the celebration of Victory Day, officially revived in 1995 as the major state holiday. This symbol of the past contrasted with new holidays such as June 12, the Day of Declaration of State Sovereignty of the Russian Federation (the Day of Russia since 2002), the meaning of which, according to opinion polls taken at the time, was not clear to most citizens.[84] Unlike this new and, in a sense, contrived celebration, Victory Day was clearly understood to be veneration of the past, as well as a real connection to Russian family histories. Victory Day also supported feelings of group solidarity and national dignity, very important in years of crisis.

The Victory Day Celebration was introduced at schools in a historical format, as it was in Soviet times. The symbol of the Soviet Union was widely used during the celebration, as it was the banner under which people fought in the Great Patriotic War. Meetings with veterans, maintaining the grave of the Unknown Soldier, and organizing search expeditions returned to the life of the school.

The second element of the old system of patriotic education had never disappeared: the teachers. Those who taught in the 1990s grew up within the Soviet structure of patriotic education, and many of them taught within in its framework in the 1980s. They could not suddenly change their pedagogical settings and teaching tools, which were time-tested and understood to be proven, nor could they abruptly alter the idea that students needed upbringing and training as well as education. Indeed, a firm belief in their pedagogical mission to raise good citizens sustained many teachers during the years of economic crisis. Therefore, teachers transmitted core values from their formative experiences in the Soviet Union to a new generation of students in the New Russia.

Interview fragment
It was hard to relearn the history. Every time I went to the classroom, I considered in detail what and how I would teach the students something that I taught automatically for years. I was preparing at night, although there were no sources for self-education. What sources did we have? The TV and a couple of newspapers, which came to school with a huge delay, because no one could take them from the post office for weeks because it was closed, having no money. The magazines on history were good, by the way. They even began to publish a new one, "Rodina,"[85] *and it was even*

---

84 Anna Sanina, "Citizenship and Civic Values in Modern Russia," in *Citizenship, Inclusion or Exclusion? A Contemporary Survey*, ed. S. J. Maldoran (Oxford: Inter-Disciplinary Press, 2011), 51–57.

85 *Rodina* ("Motherland") is a popular illustrated science and history journal headquartered in Moscow, established in 1989 by the government of the Russian Federation and the

called "Novaya Rodina" [New Motherland] for some time, I suppose. But it was expensive to subscribe to it. We lived in hungry years, our salary was detained, it just was not paid for six months, easily. And of course, the magazines were out of the question. We came to our students with a heavy heart and sometimes with a hungry stomach. And especially with the older children, I often sighed about the Soviet years. I did. I told them something, but stopped short. I didn't want such a past for them, but at that time, I didn't see the future. I wasn't sorry for myself, I was almost a pensioner, but I was sorry for the youth.

– History teacher and deputy of extracurricular activity (woman, 65, Leningrad Oblast)

These two surviving elements of the Soviet structure of patriotic education – teachers with Soviet experience, and Victory Day as the most important patriotic holiday – were enough to revive all the other elements of the old structure within a few years.

3.3 The Basics of Succession

Most of the teachers who taught in the 1980s also taught in the 1990s, and a significant number of them continue to teach today. It is almost impossible to estimate the number of teachers whose professional values and attitudes were formed under the Soviet ideology. Open-access statistics, both Russian and international, give only average data of teachers' ages. According to the most recent international survey, TALIS (2012), which included Russia, the average age of Russian teachers is 52 years.[86] The Higher School of Economics' 2016 survey shows that on average, 77 percent of teachers are at their employable age (55 years for women and 60 years for men).[87] This percentage is lower in

---

Administration of the President of the Russian Federation. In 2007, it was awarded the state honorary badge "For active work on patriotic upbringing of the citizens of the Russian Federation."

86 "Teachers: OECD Data," 2013, https://data.oecd.org/eduresource/teachers.htm (as of December 20, 2016).

87 Leonid Gokhberg, Irina Zabaturina, and Natalia Kovaleva, eds., *Indicatory obrazovaniia: 2016 : Statisticheskii sbornik* (Moscow: NRU HSE, 2016), https://www.hse.ru/data/2016/03/21/1128209800/Индикаторы образования 2016.pdf (as of December 20, 2016).

such key disciplines as Russian Language and Literature (71.7%), Mathematics (67.5%), Physics (67.7%), and Chemistry (66.8%). For History teachers, this indicator is higher: 78.6 percent are at their working age. However, this data could be explained by the fact that History was combined with such disciplines as Economics, Social Studies, and Law. These subjects were not taught separately in the Soviet school, so the teachers of these subjects would be younger than those in the "classical" disciplines.

There is no actual research describing teachers' age distributions in Russia's regions or in the different types of settlements (rural, city, megalopolis). However, the current discourse on social media and my interviews with teachers suggest a sad reality: Young teachers do not stay at schools, especially in rural areas, because of low salaries and societal devaluation of teachers' hard work. If it is true that the average age of Russian teachers in any school is about 52 years, the picture is clear: Teachers who were 52 years old in 2012 received the classic Soviet patriotic education both in school and at the Pedagogical Institute. The "average" teachers from the official statistics are likely those who started their careers in the early 1980s, the ones who implemented patriotic education in order to maintain the façade of patriotism at school.

Interview fragment
There are no young people at the school. We have a particular staff team, and so it has remained for 20 years... oh, no, for more... for 30 years... No, since 1980, when our school was opened. They, I mean us, we still stay in the core. Almost 40 years, isn't it? Oh... (laughs) No, it's a tragedy, of course. We will leave soon. We are barely hanging on here. Every year we think, we hope... each of us, that a new girl will come, and I will retire in peace. I will pass everything to her. But she does not come, that girl. No girls, no boys, nobody wants to. There was one last year, she gave two lessons and said that it was enough for her... it's a hard job. So we still stay.
  – History teacher and deputy of extracurricular activity (woman, 60, Pskov Oblast)

"We," who determine the agenda of the educational process, seem to be between the ages of 40–45 in Moscow and Saint Petersburg, and 60 and older in Russia's regions, especially in the village schools. These people came through the Soviet school system as pupils, learned the methodological basis of teaching tools at University, and taught in Soviet schools. They survived the hardest economic and political crisis, and yet they did not change professions, as did many of their colleagues. They remained teachers, and they sincerely believe that it is their duty to raise the new generation. It is unsurprising that the old principles and approaches guide them as they work with contemporary children.

Interview fragment
> *It seems like we do not care who has the power. We are professional and thus candid, according to any kind of education, and patriotic education as well. Even in the 1990s, when they said that we do not even have to raise the children. Even now, when they say that we have to raise them in freedom. We raise them in the way we used to. This is our mission, we have been taught this way. Under Gorbachev, and under Yeltsin, and under Putin. If we look back on who is in power, we will destroy everything. Thus, we learned to take everything into account, everything they tell us. But we use our heads and souls and do what we are supposed to.*
> – Math teacher and deputy of extracurricular activity (woman, 60, Leningrad Oblast)

The "we" represents itself in the organizational structure of the school, which has hardly changed since the Soviet period. The school director plays a determining role in a school's life. Contemporary schools may have collegiate or public management bodies, like the School Staff Council, Teachers Council, Parents Council, or Learners Council. Their functions vary, but they generally comply with the strategy chosen by the school director. The school director maintains unity and is personally responsible for everything that goes on within learning and extracurricular activities. The school director is also responsible for the school's relations with local and regional authorities, from whom comes financial support. Generally in Russia, the rule of *financial support in exchange for loyalty* continues. For obvious reasons, school directors are reluctant to speak on this topic in interviews, but some manage to provide indirect testimony:

Interview fragment
> *As a director, I am responsible not only for the educational process, but also for the people, for staff to have their salary and for children to have their teachers. And for the material issues as well. Who would give money for the floor paint? We have had the windows replaced. New doors. That is the thing. We do not force anyone to*

choose [at the elections – A.S.]. But we create the area for cooperation with those who help us. We can invite someone to talk at the Teachers Council. Yes, usually they want to talk before the elections. They talk in different ways. But this process of building the relationship, it is a very long and delicate process. We have to pay something in return for their loyalty, including the material loyalty to us. And they need loyalty as well from us, and if we give them loyalty, we will not lose anything, I assume. Because otherwise we will lose. We will not have the school otherwise. At least there will be not such a nice and warm school building.

– A school director (woman, 63, Leningrad Oblast)

Some foreign and Russian oppositional media consider school directors and teachers part of the current regime. Along with the government workers, military authorities, military school cadets, police officers, and other state-financed organizations' occupations, teachers form the category of so-called "organized electors." They are expected to vote for the ruling party. Moreover, in the last two Duma election cycles in Russia, the teachers were blamed for ballot-rigging and other falsifications.[88] The issue of loyalty is urgent, and the school director has all the tools to address it.

The school director has deputies, including the vice director responsible for extracurricular activity.[89] This position, as well as the position of a teacher-organizer, is directly linked to the organization of extracurricular activities like clubs, recreational activities, and sporting events, as well as for patriotic education of the children. Interestingly, as a rule, especially in schools with staff of varying ages, those positions are occupied by people who were Pioneer leaders or Komsomol leaders in their youth.

---

88 One of the most recent and widely discussed facts of fraud in the Duma elections took place in Rostov-on-Don in 2016. Surveillance cameras recorded teachers lining up to make a "wall" to hide their ballot-stuffing colleague from view. The video posted on YouTube: goo.gl/TaSDJ7 (as of November 5, 2016).

89 Different schools may have a different name and different official position for the person responsible for education. He or she may report directly to the Director or a member of the unit responsible for the extracurricular activity. Such people are in every school. Moreover, some schools have a position called "deputy director of patriotic education" or "deputy director for military-patriotic education." There are even exceptional cases of schools having a Pioneer leader position, such as, for example, in the Nygdinskaya school in the Alarsky District of the Irkutsk Region (job description at http://nig-din.alaredu.ru site; direct link goo.gl/hef2eB (as of November 5, 2016)).

Interview fragment

In the 1990s, no one remembered that we have not only to educate, but also to raise the children, that this is the main important function of the school. They have abandoned it, have disowned it as a Soviet remnant. Without thinking, without calculating the consequences. And that impinged upon children very badly. We got a soulless generation, which only cherishes material things. Thank God they started to bring everything back at the end of the 1990s. They realized that upbringing is necessary. And its format is the same as it was, because the nature of upbringing has not changed. And yes, our former Pioneer leader does this, but what is the problem with that? She is experienced, she has experience. She understands how to do it. Come and try to organize 200 pupils and 25 teachers. She knows how, she can. Well, I do not have to choose someone else, someone who understands nothing in this, but has never been a Pioneer leader... It would be ridiculous.
– A school director (woman, 60, Pskov Oblast)

The deputies of extracurricular activity have several functions. They organize ongoing and long-term planning of activities with students, coordinate activities, control the work of student clubs and other after-school activities, develop the methodology of extracurricular events, and collaborate with local and regional authorities, mostly with education departments. The last element of their activity is probably the most interesting. According to interviews with school directors, the cooperation between schools and district (local) and regional education departments is unsystematic and peremptory. Officials frequently send schools obsolete plans or guidelines. They oblige teachers and school administrations to generate reports, but almost never send feedback or proposals on improvements. This forces those responsible for extracurricular activities at the schools either to rush events or to falsify reports.[90]

---

90 This situation is not related to laziness or the unwillingness of teachers to delve into the essence of educational processes. The obvious reason for such formalism is lack of time. According to recent studies, only 48.6% of contemporary Russian teachers work within the approved standards of 18 contact hours per week, and 46.4% have twice the workload. On average, a teacher has from four to six classes every day, six days a week. Also, 64.1% of teachers fulfill the responsibilities of a homeroom teacher. In addition, teachers are responsible for organizational and methodical work, like filing reports and preparation of plans. According to the 2013 OECD survey, only 9.5% of teachers have time for additional educational work and extracurricular activity. Source: "Teachers: OECD Data" (as of November 5, 2016).

Interview fragment

Suppose I receive a document from the local Education Department. That we have to, let us say, organize and hold an all-school poetry contest until March 25, and that the contest should be dedicated to the memory of something, and we also have to choose the winner and to send the winner's poem to take part in a regional contest. And the letter comes on March 22... Oh, yes, that was exactly the same date and the contest was dedicated to May 9, Victory Day. I remember now. But let's suppose (laughs). Well, I check the dates of the messages. The letter was sent from the Ministry [of Education and Science] *on January 15, from the regional Education Department on February 20, and from the District it was sent to us on March 22! Electronically! Well, what were they doing with those letters that it took so long? I don't know. All right, here comes the letter. What can we do? Well, I go to the teachers and tell them, "Well, colleagues, here is what they ask. Do you have something already composed?" I have to, because, you know, it is impossible to make children write a poem in one night! But it's ok, we always write poems about May 9. We found something acceptable, we wrote that we had held the contest, and we sent what we found <...> I do not see a problem with that, or something dishonest. Because we do not write poems instead of the children. We did not hold the contest, but the poems are real, it was a child who composed it. Well, of course we helped them, but it does not matter.*

— Primary school teacher and deputy of extracurricular activity (woman, 50, Chelyabinsk Oblast)

Recall the average age of contemporary teachers and the origins of their teaching activities. For most of them, those origins are in the 1980s, a time of big changes in the educational system and rethinking patriotism's place in school and society, of reconsidering patriotic education, of the gamification of basic military training, and of changing attitudes to patriotism from that based on faith in a bright future to the pragmatic and rational. The teachers' experience of patriotic education in the 1980s included the elements of imitation, falsification, and window dressing, entirely different from the flourishing years of patriotic education in the 1950s-1970s. The 1980s provided teachers with an experience of patriotic education "lite," of using educational instruments mostly as mimicry, without true faith in the cultivation of patriotism.

3.4 Conclusion

In the last decade and a half, the Victory Day Celebration and teachers' attitudes have resurrected the system of patriotic education. They are clearly the basis of the model's isomorphism and are key to explaining how the embodied attitudes and values of the educational agents have led to the homologous structures. Today, the objective structure of patriotic education is like that of the Soviet period both in content and in method (Figure 3.2.c).

The critical difference, however, is that the government conception and programs are only formally declared as a basis for patriotic education. On the level of a particular school, they mean nothing and do not guide teachers or school administrations. No one at school tries to understand the goals or intentions of these documents; often, no one reads them.[91] Vice directors responsible for extracurricular activity are mostly guided by a so-called training manual (*metodichka*) of patriotic education. These manuals, which became a substitute for the conceptual basis of patriotic education, are generally written by teachers, for teachers. Sometimes the authors are local or regional educational guidance counselors, but they are not public officials or authorities. As a rule, these training manuals contain three sections: the goal of patriotic education and its meaning; a description of the main forms of work on patriotic education, which are altogether military-patriotic (memory duty, book of memory, military-sport clubs, school museums of glory, etc.); and finally, plans and methodological recommendations for military-patriotic work in educational institutions, such as lesson plans, lesson summaries, and celebration scripts. Very rarely does a manual include a brief summary of the current government program of patriotic education. Although there exists an official version of how patriotic education should be developed, there is no connection between it and the direct activity of the school.

---

91 None of the interviewed teachers and principals had read the current government program of patriotic education. Respondents reported lack of time. Some respondents were genuinely surprised by the question and said they did not consider the program worth reading.

Whereas the Soviet state subsidized its interest in the development of patriotic education by supporting school practices of memorialization and activities of youth organizations, as well as providing a framework of ideological values that kept the system united and workable, in contemporary Russia, the government promotes patriotic education by, for instance, requesting that schools hold particular events. In the majority of cases, no financial support is offered for the events. The main thing the government needs is a report that will be included in the summary of the indicators' achievement. The current process of patriotic education is unstructured, underfunded, and ineffective, even though effectiveness is one of the key requirements of public programming.

However, there are tendencies toward future changes. Today, the Russian government is making some serious attempts to revitalize the system of patriotic education. While the current program continues to live its own life, the revealing elements of the Soviet model of patriotic education, together with new elements, pave the way to the implementation of the official ideology. This process has clear social roots in the values and attitudes of the teachers, school administration, and society in general.

4. Historic Elements and Structures in Contemporary Patriotic Education

At a glance, patriotic education, as an element of the Russian educational system, has sprung up as if from nowhere. This revival is generally associated with various political events, such as the growing impact of the government on society after the start of Vladimir Putin's third term in 2012, the reaction of the Russian government to the liberal protest activity in the country in 2011–2012, and the aggravation of international tensions caused by the annexation of Crimea and the Syrian conflict.

However, for teachers and school administrators directly involved in the process, the revival of patriotic education is logical and progressive. It is interpreted in terms of a "return" (*vozvraschenie*) to traditions, to roots. The theme of recovering traditional values appears in nearly every interview with teachers and school directors.

> *Interview fragment*
> *Today I can say that patriotic education is reviving. It is pervasive, anyway, in every school, every class. It provides us with those essential communication frameworks, which turn the usual educational process into upbringing. We have a really strong tradition to take it as a way to come back to our roots of upbringing. I think that this is the strongest track in our school's life. Though we keep up with the times as well, we change something or reject something. These are the right tendencies, which allow to combine traditions and innovations.*
> — History teacher and deputy of extracurricular activity (woman, 45, Moscow Oblast)

Indeed, the contemporary version of patriotic education has changed. New objects, new meanings, and new agents appear that did not exist or were not so pronounced in the Soviet period. Despite these important differences, the basic model has remained almost untouched and peacefully coexists with new elements and additions.

4.1 The Substitution of the Conceptual Basis

In the Soviet model of patriotic education, a strong organizational basis consisted of two elements, namely memorialization and youth organizations, which were part of the state's concept of patriotic education. Although that concept was not noted in any separate document, it flowed from communist ideology. In the New Russia, the government decided to recommence patriotic education using methods of governmental programming, which, as an instrument of public administration and governance, is preferable to ideology. This method of programming requires continuous evaluation and assessment of goals, means, and results; however, as practiced, this method is proving inefficient. It also appears ineffective, for the current official concept and program of patriotic education are not relevant documents to patriotic activity in schools. This is admitted at the regional level of government.

Interview fragment
Strictly speaking, nobody has read the Law on Education[92] for a long time, let alone the patriotic education programs. When we work with schools, when we need to persuade them to do something or to implement something new, we write standard phrases. "Pursuant to the Federal Law on Education" is among them. But I am more than confident that if we had some fun and inserted some fake information about this law, no one would notice, because nobody reads the law. But when you ask about the legal basis and in what way it is associated with schools, I have a definite answer: no way. In no way is it associated with schools. <...> It is rare when a school has such a teacher who is competent enough in the legal field, at least in the field of educational activities.
– A member of a regional Committee on Education (man, 55, Leningrad Oblast)

Interviews with teachers and school directors confirm that there is currently no connection between the conceptual foundations or governmental units of patriotic education and the activities of schools and preschools. Instead, teachers follow a long-established habit and use special professional manuals (*metodichki*). For these teachers, *metodichki* substitute for the governmental conceptual basis of the educational and pedagogical processes.

---

[92] Federal Law № 273-FL "On Education in the Russian Federation," dated December 29, 2012, is the major legal document in the field of education in Russia.

Part of the educational work prescribed in contemporary manuals involves patriotic education.

Metodichki across the country are similarly written and include structured lesson plans, scripts of celebrations, recommendations for school libraries, and so on. Rarely do manuals act as a mediator of governmental programming in the field of patriotic education, merely retelling the main points of the program. In most contemporary manuals and textbooks devoted to patriotic education, references to questionable sources are common, as are Soviet-era understandings of patriotism. For example, the 2016 book "The formation of patriotism in preschoolers by the example of the image of the Armed Forces" includes the following:

> *Patriotism is a very complicated, multifaceted human feeling, which is incredibly rich in its content. By definition of the National Sociological Encyclopedia, patriotism is a moral and political principle, a social sense, the content of which is love of country, pride in its past and present, a willingness to subordinate one's interests to the interests of the country, the desire to protect the interests of the country and its people.*[93] *The Great Soviet Encyclopedia defined patriotism as love of country, devotion to it and desire for one's actions to serve its interests. Summarizing, we can say that patriotism is the love of one's native land, pride in its people, respect for the defenders of the Fatherland, respect for the national anthem, flag, coat of arms of the homeland; it is a deep, internally stable connection of the individual with his or her people, with their Motherland. And it is not just the information that children must receive, but also the truths that must affect their feelings.*[94]

The Great Soviet Encyclopedia (*Bol'shaia Sovetskaia Entsiklopediia*), the largest Russian-language encyclopedia published in the Soviet Union from

---

[93] This book uses definitions without references. A Google search suggests that by "National Sociological Encyclopedia," the author is referring to the website http://voluntary.ru, which provides neither the names of the authors of the entries nor the names of project managers. Moreover, it is stated that the encyclopedia "cannot guarantee the accuracy, adequacy or completeness of the information." Such a dismissive attitude to sources and the rules of citation is characteristic of contemporary school manuals for patriotic education.

[94] Natal'ia Vorob'ëva and Ol'ga Sapozhnikova, *Formirovanie patriotizma u doshkol'nikov na primere predstavlenii o vooruzhënnykh silakh* (Moscow: Itellekt-Center, 2016). P. 8.

1926 to 1990, claimed to be the major Marxist-Leninist general-purpose encyclopedia. It contained universal and "proper" definitions for almost everything. In the aforementioned discussion of patriotism, it is unlikely that the authors are underlining a commitment to the Soviet system. Rather, they believe that the Encyclopedia is a credible and proper source for the definition of a key term. Noteworthy is the emphasis on feelings, a classic Soviet educational element (*"it is not just the information that children must receive, but also the truths that must affect their feelings"*).

Emotional background became the basis for transforming the school's priorities from education to upbringing in the 1930s. At that time, it served as a reason for the formation of the "patriotism of everything." Contemporary Russian manuals about patriotic education suggest that this tendency is returning. For example, the following are definitions of the tasks of patriotic education from manuals written in 1949 and 2009, with key terms highlighted:

> Soviet patriotism is a great moral power. It determines the behavior of the Soviet people, it is the source of **courage**, source of soulful nobility. ... The whole way, the whole structure of Soviet life, the heroic past and especially a great present of our country causes the development in the younger generation the feelings of ardent love for the Homeland. <...> The patriotism of the Soviet school should not be something abstract, contemplative. Love of the country must awaken in them a desire to do specific tasks in their work to serve the people and the Soviet state. Patriotic **duty** of students and their **obligation** before the Homeland are defined first and foremost by **the high quality of their studies**. (1949)[95]

> For a student to be a patriot means first of all to be a worthy citizen of his country. **To study well**, to be ready to perform their constitutional **duties** and **responsibilities** in the Russian Armed Forces. It is necessary to inspire students with examples of national history, to remind them of the loyalty of the Motherland to **military duty** in tsarist Russia, in the years of Soviet power. The defining characteristics of those times were the **dedication, courage** and **bravery** of our countrymen. We should deliver the education according to these examples. (2009)[96]

---

95 Boldyrev, *Vospitanie sovetskogo patriotizma u shkol'nikov*. P. 4, 11.
96 Vasilii Mikriukov, *Voenno-patrioticheskoe vospitanie v shkole: 1–11 klassy* (Moscow: VAKO, 2009). P. 16.

Putting aside the Soviet pathos in the first definition and considering only the meaning of the tasks set before the teacher and students, the meaning of these two passages is the same. Children must learn to be worthy and courageous citizens of their country. Understanding study as service to the country rather than as a source of knowledge is what determined the Soviet pattern of educational process. Today, educational guidance counselors replicate this idea, and many teachers then transmit it in their daily educational practice. They also apply the idea of emotion-based learning to extracurricular activities, revealing the old forms of memorialization and youth organizations.

4.2 Memorialization

In the contemporary Russian school, the element of memorialization has been extensively developed. Memorialization practices were active in the "decade without patriotism," as one teacher called the 1990s in an interview, and they are even more active today. Of course, most are devoted to the Great Patriotic War (1941–1945), but they also include the wars in Afghanistan (1979–1989) and Chechnya (1994–1996; 1999–2009).

Memorialization supposes historical and heroic views of patriotic education. School museums are the main agents of development and implementation of plans for patriotic education, volunteer activities, and search parties. In small towns and villages, they often become the centers of social life. Often the only educational center in the community, school museums determine an ideal image of the person who should be brought up both by parents and school.

Interview fragment

Our school isn't big, we have less than 400 students. And we live in the same village and know all the parents, and school is in the center [of village life], *and the museum is in the center of our school. And we try to educate children to be true human beings. And we all are on the same wavelength, because parents of even those children who are in elementary school now, they are still Soviet-era people, they have Soviet attitudes. We have no choice but to remember the Soviet era. With our level of life, with our wages and other things, we can only be nostalgic for the Soviet era. And in the center of this, there is a museum that organizes all the work. The museum attracts*

school administration, village administration. You asked in what degree they determine our plans and tell us what to do… Well, here we are to define their plans and tell them what to do and how! It is they who include our activities in the village and even into the district plans of different kinds of activities, like celebrations, parades, and so on.

– History teacher and head of the school museum (woman, 65, Novgorod Oblast)

School museums often work hand in hand with patriotic clubs in schools. Marlène Laruelle classified the latter as clubs of "extracurricular activities, largely oriented toward promoting values and Soviet patriotism."[97] School museums are often organized and supported by History teachers, while the activities of clubs are supported by Physical Education and Life Safety teachers. As a rule, the museums have two main themes: the memory of the Great Patriotic War, and the broader memorialization of the history of the land. These two themes are always considered as two separate topics. The Great Patriotic War as a subject of museum activities often requires more time, more exhibits, and more attention than the age-old history of the land. In some schools, the Great Patriotic War exhibition is elaborated in a single symbolic unit with the Afghan and Chechen wars. This is especially true for schools with graduates killed in those wars.

Interview fragment

We try to develop not only as a museum of combat glory, but also as a local history museum. Pupils are divided into two subgroups, one of them is responsible mostly for the nature of the native land, streets' toponymy, history… You know, like peacetime history. Another one deals only with the Great Patriotic War, families of the deceased, their histories. We also remember and communicate with the parents of our graduates lost in Chechnya.

– Geography teacher and head of the school museum (woman, 60, Tver Oblast)

Materially, the school museum is typically a separate classroom. There are posters with photos and fragments of text hanging along its perimeter, which tell about the school's history, locality, and region. Under the posters,

---

[97] Marlène Laruelle, "Patriotic Youth Clubs in Russia. Professional Niches, Cultural Capital and Narratives of Social Engagement," *Europe-Asia Studies* 67, no. 1 (2015): 8–27. P. 11.

there may be items found in search parties or given to the museum as gifts. Because the museum hosts lessons, discussions, and some meetings as well as serving as a place for memorialization, there are desks at the center. Organizationally, school museums are often tabulated as extracurricular activities, or clubs. They are not institutionally museums, as they were in the Soviet era. Following the formal rules of school extracurricular activities, the museums have a plan, a timetable, and a list of the major activities approved by the school director.

> **Box 4.1 – Introductory note to the working plan of the "School Museum" club (for the 2015–2016 academic year, 2 academic hours per week)** [abridged]
>
> - The museum motto: "Honor the past, live the present, seek the future!"
> - We enter the future looking back at the past. – Paul Valéry.
>
> The relevance of the program is determined by the current socio-economic and educational reform of the school, its significance to the revival and development of spiritual and moral values, the need of formation of high moral and ethical principles of students, and preparing young people for active participation in the development of civil society and the Russian statehood. The role and importance of the school museum increases in relation to the need to implement national and regional programs of patriotic education of youth.
>
> **Goal**: To provide conditions for the formation of motivation of the individual to learn the history of the native land, and the development of creative and intellectual abilities in various types of museum activities. The school museum, as a part of open educational space, is designed to be a connecting thread between school and other cultural institutions and public organizations.
>
> **Objectives:**
>
> 1. An efficient use of preserved and exhibited original historical documents for education of pupils in the spirit of patriotism, civic consciousness, high morals.
> 2. Research of past school traditions.
> 3. Organization of research work in order to replenish the museum fund.
> 4. To consolidate and continue the development of motivation of children to participate in museum activities.
> 5. Fostering a culture of communication with older people, strengthening ties between the educational institution, cultural institutions, and public organizations for the solution of problems of education of children and youth's sense of citizenship and patriotism.
> 6. Filling the leisure time of children with research-collective work, studying and describing the museum items, creating exhibitions, conducting tours, conferences.

7. Carrying out, at the museum's lessons of courage, meetings with veterans of war and labor.

8. In the process of research activities, pupils should master the various techniques and skills of local history and museum activities.

Forms of work in the school museum:
- research;
- lessons in the museum;
- meetings, conferences, courage lessons, quizzes, lecturing work;
- excursions;
- independent study.

One of the conditions for the successful organization and activity of the school museum is a continuity of its assets. It is supported by including students of different age groups among its members.

The main activities of the school museum:
1. The search activity.
2. The research activities of students.
3. The excursion and educational activities.
4. The design activity.
5. Patronage work (meetings with veterans, conducting tours).
6. Public relations (creating the museum's website).[98]

Source: courtesy of Anna Mikheeva, Head of the Museum and a teacher of History at Pliusskaia Secondary School, Pskov Region

In the past decades of autonomous existence, the school has carried out three major activities – volunteering, Memory Guards, and search teams.

The volunteering activities aim at the preservation of historical memory. They include the upkeep and improvement of memorable places and military burial sites, as well as social support for veterans. Today, this trend is national in scope. According to its official website, the all-Russian public movement "Volunteers of Victory," founded in 2015, currently involves 157,000 people. The main objectives of the movement are saving the historical memory of the Great Patriotic War and involving the young generations in great historical events. It is also aimed at the civic, patriotic, spiritual, and moral education of Russian citizens; preserving and defending the identity, culture, and traditions of the

---

98   The museum's website is http://shkolaklub.narod.ru (as of December 20, 2016).

Russian Federation; and collaboration with public organizations of civic-patriotic education.

Memory Guards (*Vakhty Pamiati*) are events dedicated to the memorialization of battles and the dead. One of the most popular all-Russian Memory Guards is the Candle of Memory (*Svecha Pamiati*), which takes place on June 22 in remembrance of Nazi Germany's 1941 invasion of the Soviet Union (Figure 4.1).

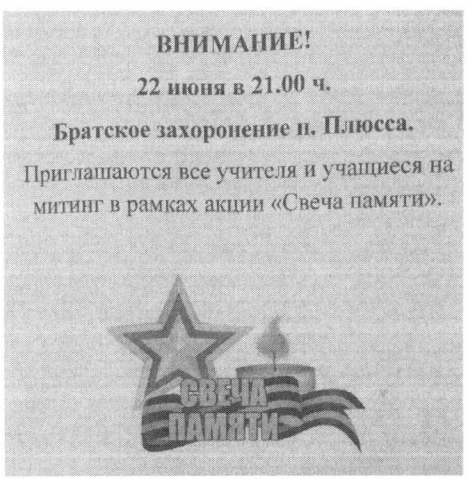

Figure 4.1 – School announcement (Pskovskii Region):
"Attention! The 22nd of June at 9:00 pm. The mass grave of the village of Pliussa. All teachers and students are invited to the rally 'The Candle of Memory.'"

The search team activity includes search expeditions to battlegrounds of the Great Patriotic War, studying topography, working with archival documents, maintaining soldiers' graves and monuments, and reconstructions of military battles. Search teams often identify themselves with the school museums, but not because they want to encourage the schoolchildren to participate in the search work or reconstructions. They have different reasons related to their uncertain legal statuses and constant difficulties in obtaining permission to handle weapons. Also, they are "regularly accused of feeding the black market in historical weapons."[99] Having these difficulties, they associate themselves with school museums in order to exist, but there is otherwise little connection between search teams and school museums. As a rule, the successful and active search teams consider the museum's activities as unserious and childish.

For a quarter of a century after the collapse of the Soviet Union, the museums' activity rested on the shoulders of activists. Personal interest, even that of a single person, is key to the museums' survival.

Interview fragment
The logic is that if somebody is interested in something, he or she will do it. I've been doing it for 40 years. And everyone's accustomed to my doing it, and I've gotten used to how to attract others. School administration, district and regional [administration], veterans, military instructors, students' parents. Everybody is involved. <...> In our region, patriotic education is the most important one. We tried to teach Economics, for example... well, there is nothing – everything is destroyed, no business, nothing. You can't educate children on the emptiness. But these things [patriotic education] we have. We have good results. This year, seven people have entered either in the military or police. Bound for their destinies... I think the province is more patriotic. There are no such requests as in the city where all people do is think how to get more money or how to spend free time. Here children read and think.
– History teacher and head of a school museum (woman, 67, Pskov Oblast)

Nevertheless, teachers' personal interest cannot provide the sole basis for a museum's material growth. This is why most heads of museums, teams, and clubs were so enthusiastic about the recent governmental ideas for the creation of the all-Russian organization aimed at upbringing.

4.3 Youth Organization(s)

Attempts to restore a patriotic youth movement on a national scale began in the early 2000s. The nostalgic orienting point for this was the Soviet children's organization, the Pioneers. In 2004, pro-government party United Russia (*Edinaya Rossiya*) initiated the creation of a "pupils' party," the children's movement

---
99 Laruelle, "Patriotic Youth Clubs in Russia. Professional Niches, Cultural Capital and Narratives of Social Engagement," 2015. P. 14.

called "Bear Cubs of Russia" (*Medvezhata Rossii*). Its symbol combined elements of the New Russia (the bear and the tricolor Russian flag) with that of the Soviet era (the red necktie of the Pioneers). Activities of the "Bear Cubs" included *timurovskaya*[100] assistance to elders and the disabled, community service such as tree planting and litter cleanup, and patriotic concerts. Journalists and the public accused the children's group of being political and blamed them for a return to Soviet ideals, as well as for setting old-school goals and using old-school means. The initiative was soon forgotten.

Nevertheless, the idea of reviving the Pioneers remained, and was instead reproduced at the level of pro-government intelligentsia. In 2012, film director Stanislav Govorukhin, who served as the head of Putin's electoral headquarters, called for the restoration of the Pioneer organization at a meeting with Moscow teachers: "Pioneers must return, and the word 'pioneer' is beautiful. If I heard that the Pioneer organization had been created, I would be happy."[101] Such statements were supported by both teachers and school directors, especially those of regional schools.

Interview fragment
The intelligentsia is known to be different. Not that I'm against the liberals, but I agree that they have already distributed something very extreme, which is alien to our traditions, our values, our priorities in raising children. I have a warm attitude toward those who stand for the return to the best that we had, and the Pioneer organization is one of those bests. It is clear that there should not be domination by ideology, but the organization must exist.
— A school director (man, 60, Saratov Oblast)

By the 1990s, some schools implemented initiatives of children's associations. Reproducing habits formed in Soviet times, the teachers considered

---

100 As mentioned in Chapter 3, Timur (from Arkady Gaidar's book "Timur and His Squad") was one of the most popular heroes for Soviet children. The "Bear Cubs of Russia" organization's reference to Timur was neither accidental nor used to stress a return to the Soviet era. Rather, "timurovskaya" is a commonly understood expression, having an action-related as well as moral meaning.

101 "Stanislav Govorukhin predlozhil vossozdat' pionerskuiu organizatsiiu," *Novaya Gazeta*, February 16, 2012, https://www.novayagazeta.ru/news/2012/02/16/53966-stanislav-govoruhin-predlozhil-vossozdat-pionerskuyu-organizatsiyu (as of December 20, 2016).

themselves responsible not only for education but also, and mainly, for their students' upbringing. In the early 2000s, several regions of the Russian Federation saw the resumption of the Councils of Counselors (*Sovety vozhatykh*) and children's movements declared to be the heirs of the Pioneers.

To give an example, Verkhnesspasskaia School in the Tambov region is home to a children's organization called *Ritm* ("Rhythm"), founded in 1999. Since 2011, the organization has been named for the "internationalist warrior Gennadii Boltnev, deceased in Afghanistan." The history of the movement shown on the website relates its modern organization with the time of the Pioneers. Its main directives are "civil-patriotic, spiritual-moral, creative, sport-health, labor." Rules of the organization replicate those of the Soviet Octobrists: "We are merry guys"; "We are strong, brave, handy, and skillful"; "We study well and love to work"; "We respect the elders and take care of the juniors."[102]

Such organizations are widespread in Russian schools, especially in rural areas. Their existence is largely socially determined by the status of school as the last surviving cultural sanctuary. This status, especially relevant during the crisis of the 1990s, persists. The initiative for establishing these organizations, as for school museums, often came from teachers who had worked at the school since Soviet times. They were the leaders and inspirers of these organizations. One teacher related the story of the creation of such an organization:

Interview fragment

Our village began to be destroyed in the 1990s. All the youth were leaving, there was nowhere to work. Many of those who remained were drinking. Children came to school lost. Terrible to say, sometimes they, too, drank. Hooliganism was increasing terribly. They prowled in the evenings and nights, and I was afraid to be spotted when walking home from school late. One day, I went to the director and said that it was necessary to restore the educational work, at least at the school level. It was 1998, probably, or even 1997. I said that we should not abandon the children – we are the school! The director supported me. She said that she had thought about it, too. She asked me if I was ready to take part in that, because she could not pay me anything, not even release me from curricular hours. I said yes. I was 55 years old then.

— History teacher (woman, 75, Tver Oblast)

---

102 "Detskaia organizatsiia Ritm imeni voina-internatsionalista Gennadiia Sergeevicha Boltneva," n.d., verhspas.68edu.ru/vospitanie/ritm.htm (as of December 20, 2016).

In the 1990s, many youth organizations had a local and rather closed character. They rarely interacted with other similar organizations from neighboring schools. However, this closeness was associated not only with institutional constraints but with the lack of money for transport and material costs associated with collaboration. So, symbolically, they were entirely localized in the environment of a particular school, most of all in the school museum, and associated with practices of memorialization. However, for most schools, their activities had great educational value. For years, the vast majority of school organizations were not supported by the state financially, organizationally, or politically. Local, regional, and federal authorities were not interested. The first three federal programs of patriotic education sidestepped many such organizations. School organizations, like school museums, were supported by the enthusiasm of the teachers. Recently, however, the situation has changed.

The Russian Movement of Schoolchildren

The Russian government became intensively interested in organizational work in schools in 2015. The first nation-wide, large-scale project of a new children's organization was the all-Russian, public-state, children-youth organization "Russian Movement of Schoolchildren" *(Rossiiskoe Dvizhenie Shkol'nikov)*, RMS. Its founder is the Federal Agency for Youth Affairs (Rosmolodezh). According to its charter, the movement is non-political and is intended for all children over eight years of age.

Formally, the RMS is a voluntary, autonomic public association established to promote "state policy in the field of education of the younger generation" and "identity formation based on the characteristic of the Russian society's system of values."[103] The last phrase is a direct reference to another document from 2015, the Presidential Decree "About a strategy of national security of the Russian Federation." This document manifested the "traditional Russian spiritual and moral values," which include "the priority of the spiritual over the material, the protection of human life, rights and freedoms of the individual, family,

---

103 Charter of all-Russian, public-state, children-youth organization "Russian Movement of Schoolchildren." Adopted by a consistent congress of the Russian Movement of Schoolchildren. Protocol №1 from the 28th of March, 2016. https://рдш.р ф/docs?page=2 (as of December 20, 2016).

creative work, service to the Fatherland, the norms of morality, humanity, mercy, justice, mutual aid, collectivism, historical unity of the peoples of Russia, and the continuity of the history of the Motherland."[104] Despite the universality of these values, they were marked by this document as traditionally (and even exceptionally) Russian. The expression "traditional Russian spiritual and moral values" (or simply "traditional values") has become a pro-government dog whistle used in speeches and written propaganda. The semantics of this expression involve the juxtaposition of "incorrect" Western values and "proper" Russian values.

Mostly due to this emphasis on tradition, the approval and operation of the RMS was surrounded by the nostalgia of Soviet symbolism. President Vladimir Putin signed the decree on the establishment of RMS on October 29, 2015, the anniversary of the founding of the All-Union Leninist Young Communist League (Komsomol). The first Congress of the RMS took place in 2016 on May 19, the date on which Soviet children celebrated Pioneer Day.

These nods to nostalgia were intended to help engage all schools in the new movement. However, that symbolism was not articulated directly. The government did not want to demonstrate the intention of total involvement of all the schools in that process.

Interview fragment
We acted very carefully. Not only because the Duma elections were coming and the uncontrolled talks about "Back to the USSR" were undesirable for us. We just didn't want our idea to be immediately destroyed at its root. It took us too much time to prepare a database to work with schools to involve all of them in the movement. These are social technologies, they are used by governments all over the world, it is not our invention. When everybody joins, it is easier for you to join, too. These are technologies of collectivism.
– A member of the Federal Agency for Youth Affairs (man, 40)

---

104 President RF, *"O strategii natsional'noi bezopasnosti Rossiiskoi Federatsii, Ukaz ot 31/12/2015, № 683,"* available at: http://www.consultant.ru/document/cons_doc_LAW_191669/ (as of November 20, 2016).

Immediately after the signing of the decree, the Public Opinion Foundation carried out a survey[105] that reported that only 17 percent of people had "heard something" about the establishment of the RMS, and only 6 percent knew about the decree. The vast majority of Russians heard nothing about the RMS. In general, however, people supported the idea of an organization modeled after the Pioneers. More than half of respondents said that the Pioneers was a good organization and that future organizations should use the experiences of the past. Younger people between ages 18–30 were opposed to such a plan – from their point of view, an organization must meet the requirements of modernity and should not look like a Soviet one.

For some time, the patriotic orientation of RMS was unclear. In the text of the RMS Charter, the word "patriotic" appears only once, in the context of collaboration with public associations "having a patriotic, cultural, sporting, and also charity direction."[106] Nevertheless, at the first congress of the RMS, a military-patriotic track was highlighted separately, along with personal development, civic activism, and media (Table 4.1).

RMS activists wrote program manuals, one of which is dedicated to the general principles of working with students, with the others devoted to each of the RMS tracks. The texts of the manuals are published on the RMS's official website and can be used by anyone; however, the target audience for the manuals is not schoolteachers and directors, but district and regional committees

---

105 The Russian nationwide survey was carried out from October 31 to November 1, 2015. One thousand respondents over 18 years of age were interviewed in 104 Russian cities. The questions concerned the relevance and benefits of the new RMS organization, as well as its differences and similarities with the Pioneer movement. According to the survey, support for the RMS is greater among older people, respondents with average incomes, and residents of small towns; those who oppose the RMS are mostly young people (18–30 years old) with high incomes who reside in the Central Federal district (including Moscow); 45% of the respondents believe that children they know will want to join such an organization, and 19% do not think that children will want to join. This percentage is higher among young people (25%), young people with higher educations (33%), and people with good financial situations (28%). "O Rossiiskom dvizhenii shkol'nikov," *Fond Obshchestvennoe Mnenie*, November 16, 2015, http://fom.ru/Obraz-zhizni/12394 (as of December 20, 2016).

106 Charter of all-Russian, public-state, children-youth organization "Russian Movement of Schoolchildren."

and education departments. These groups are expected to play a major role in recruiting the maximum number of students to the movement.

Table 4.1 – The Russian Movement of Schoolchildren activity tracks

Track	Objectives
Personal development	– development of creativity; – promotion of a healthy lifestyle among students; – promotion of professions.
Civil activism	– To save and develop friendly relationships between nations in Russia and to unite in a single Federal state, to promote national cultures and languages; – to contribute to the formation of active life positions of students and create conditions for development of children's initiatives; – to form in pupils a conscious valuing of the history of their country, city, area, people; – to develop in children a sense of patriotism, national pride for their country; – to stimulate social activity of students aimed at providing help to needy categories of people; – to help organizations of culture in arranging and carrying out public events; – to provide help and assistance in carrying out ecological events; – to intensify the desire of students to organize activities in the framework of search teams.
Military-patriotic	– Together with responsible teachers, to form a school system of normative and legal support for activities in the field of military-patriotic education; – to organize the work of military-patriotic clubs on the basis of educational organizations and to involve children; – to organize specialized events aimed at increasing children's interest in service in military units, including military training, military sports games, competitions, and promotions; – to organize educational programs, interactive games, seminars, master classes, open lectures, meetings with interesting people, heroes of our country, and veterans; – to provide coordination of the school's military-patriotic activities with public associations and public organizations in the framework of social partnership.
Informative-media direction[107]	– To create an Information and Media Center (IMC) to realize the system of informational interaction between participants of the RMS; – to create and test indicators and criteria for evaluating activities of the information and media direction of the RMS; – to create a system of interaction with information and media partners.

The basic training manual "Methodical directives for a senior counselor of the educational organization" announces two "natural" needs of children:

---

[107] The written objectives do not clearly describe the specifics of students' activity in the framework of this track. Most likely, it supposes the creation of school newspapers, preparation materials for local newspapers and magazines, and school activity in social networks.

"the intention to unify" and collectivism. In addition, as follows from the title, this manual recovers the figure of the counselor (*vozhatyi*) as a key figure in children's education:

> *The key figure of RMS's activity in educational organizations, who keeps principles and norms fixed in the Charter of RMS, is a counselor. Counselors are leaders trusted by children who can make goals, plan, and stimulate activity within the tracks; also, they are tutors who professionally motivate children and teenagers to constructive and creative activities, and senior friends who can motivate children to realize themselves in offered tracks of the youth organization.*[108]

Methodical recommendations regulate and frame daily counseling activity. This activity includes communicating with three main groups: students, a teachers' committee (tutors, teachers, school administration), and parents. The main objective of the senior counselor is the formation of a "primary branch" of the RMS in school on the basis of "mass and voluntary participation."

Interview fragment

The accent on communication between the authorities and schools has suddenly, very quickly shifted from education to upbringing. Like everybody in our district, we entered the RMS. For us, this was unexpected and brought a lot of extra work. But the kids liked the action. There was a solemn line, they were awarded with badges and ties. Of course, we have ambiguous attitudes toward this. It turned out that we kind of had to organize everybody. I consulted with colleagues and we decided that we should not refuse, due to political reasons, so to speak. When I say political, it is not in terms of the situation in the country, but in terms of the strategic development plan of our school. In short, we were afraid that schools who had already entered the RMS will have benefits compared to those that have not. So we decided that it was better to be there than not to be.

— A school director (woman, 55, Leningrad Oblast)

In 2016, regional committees were developing plans to work with schools in the capacity of upbringing. Now, schools are, almost by force, introducing a position for a senior counselor. Teachers receive many more tasks than before.

---

108 Elena Levanova et al., *Metodicheskie rekomendatsii dlia starshego vozhatogo* (Moscow: MPGU, 2015) https://рдш.рф/docs?page=1 (as of December 20, 2016).

Many of the tasks are related to military-patriotic education as a separate track of the RMS.

Yunarmiya: The Young Army

Military-patriotic direction is carried out by the Russian military-patriotic youth movement *Yunarmiya* ("Young Army") in coordination with the relevant clubs of young frontier guards, young rescuers, young traffic inspectors and police's assistants, and movements of the Russian Cossacks. *Yunarmiya* was formally founded the same day as the RMS (May 19, 2016) as a subordinate RMS structure. Today, however, the scale of this organization already claims to have the status of an independent movement.[109]

The declared goal of *Yunarmiya* is not only military-patriotic education, but development of the youth's interest in geography, the history of Russia, and its nations. Nevertheless, the infrastructure of the movement is tied to the locations of military units, military educational institutions, the All-Union Voluntary Society for Cooperation with the Army, Air Force, and Navy (DOSAAF), and the central sports club of the army. The role of a special all-national place for training is given to Patriot Park, the military-patriotic park of recreation and culture near Moscow.[110] The most common type of head of the regional *Yunarmiya*

---

[109] Confusion of subordination and division of functions of the RMS and *Yunarmiya* existed from the outset. In an interview with school directors and teachers, people are surprised to learn that *Yunarmiya* is formally a part of the Russian Movement of Schoolchildren. They sincerely believe that they are two different organizations. The Open Russia project materials give reason to believe that the same opinion is typical for many regional authorities. Roman Popkov, "Yunarmiya Generala Shoigu," *Openrussia.org*, August 12, 2016, https://openrussia.org/media/140099/ (as of December 20, 2016).

[110] Patriot Park (http://patriotp.ru), called a "military Disneyland" by some, is a large-scale entertainment and exhibition area dedicated to the Russian Armed Forces. On over 5,000 hectares of land sit an aviation museum, the museum of armored vehicles, the artillery museum, exhibition weapons, and military equipment. The Park has different clusters dedicated to various kinds of the armed forces: Ground Forces, Air Forces, Navy, Aerospace Defense, Strategic Rocket Forces, Airborne Troops. There is also a historical-memorial complex called "Guerilla Village" (*Partizanskaya Derevnia*), which includes staff dugouts, stables, shelters, medical service, storage of weapons and ammunition, a workshop for making explosives, kitchen, bakery, bath, and objects that recreate the everyday life of the Russian partisan detachment during World War II. All major activities of the Ministry of Defense take place there, such as exhibitions, competitions, and reconstructions of battles. Many activities are aimed at young people and

organization is a former enforcer (*silovik*), or a person close to the security forces who is a part of the regional ruling elite or demonstratively loyal to them.[111]

The main forms of *Yunarmiya* activities are military-sportive games, military-patriotic clubs, and special formations of *Yunarmiya* participants. The best *Yunarmiya* groups are encouraged to participate in military parades, to attend large-scale activities of the Ministry of Defense such as International Army games, the International Military-Technical forum, the Days of Innovations at the Ministry of Defense, festivals, and sports competitions, and to get involved in numerous public projects.

Thus, despite the declared peaceful goal of the *Yunarmiya*, its content is completely militarized. The movement was founded on the personal initiative of Minister of Defense Sergei Shoigu and was designed with obvious zeal and pleasure. The movement quickly acquired the necessary symbolic attributes and emotional halo, which bring together elements of novelty, coolness, and Soviet nostalgia.

Yunarmiya members wear a special uniform.[112] The *Yunarmiya* emblem is a star on a red eagle background, with the red color reminiscent of Soviet youth movements (Figure 4.2). The motto "If not you, then who?" is a reconfiguration of the Komsomol motto, "Who if not we?" This motto was later borrowed by Russian Special Forces, and appears in slightly modified form as the motto of the Russian Airborne Troops: "Nobody but us!"

---

children. A separate sector of the park is devoted to the *Yunarmiya*. Patriot Park is the largest tourist destination in the Moscow region, with branches set to open in all regions of Russia.

111 Popkov, "Youngarmiia Generala Shoigu."
112 The website юнармейцы.рф sells the *Yunarmiya* uniform, which includes a jacket, polo, cap, belt, bag, boots, hip bag, and socks, for 19,410 rubles ($300). In comparison, the minimum wage level in Russia is 7,500 rubles ($125) per month, and the average monthly teacher's salary is 32,000 rubles ($530). Children who join the *Yunarmiya* receive free uniforms. Based on the official figures on the number of members indicated on the website юн-армия.рф (42,019 as of January 21, 2017), the total cost of the uniforms to the Russian budget is approximately 815 million rubles ($13.5 million).

Figure 4.2 – Soviet and Russian youth organization badges
From left to right: Octobrist badge, Pioneer badge, *Yunarmiya* badge.

The modern *Yunarmiya* is based on the youth voluntary public organization "Movement of Young Patriots," which in turn was formed by the merger of military-sports games (*Zarnitsa* and "Eaglet"), school military-patriotic clubs, and school museums of military glory. These are local organizations that, like the aforementioned children's club "Rhythm," survived the collapse of the Soviet system of patriotic education.

These formerly neglected school museums, clubs, groups, and organizations are now offered not only government support and social networking, but further benefits as well. Organizers of military-historical clubs, search teams, and school museums are the most rewarded targets of *Yunarmiya* recruiting. Once forgotten, they have suddenly received long-awaited attention from the state, a special status, and recognition of the missionary character of pedagogical activity.

> ***Interview fragment***
> *I finally don't have to worry for the future of my club, of our school museum, of our children and graduates. More than 30 generations of students have gone through our school museum of military glory. Shoigu is a good man, I feel like he himself supports us. He understands us and speaks to us in the same language. He sends his people, I have someone with me now. Recently we were visited by retired veterans, they showed weapons to our children and talked to them about real things. Children have been discussing this for a month! They saw nothing but rusty helmets, and there was a real gun!*
> – History teacher and head of a school patriotic club (woman, 70, Pskov Oblast)

Every school that joins the *Yunarmiya* is expected to open a Room of the Youngarmer (Figure 4.3) as a place for study and recreation. The room must be equipped with samples of small arms, a special mannequin for practicing medical care skills, multimedia learning equipment, and a stand with the models of small arms in service to the Russian Army. The Room of the Youngarmer also stores the flag, the book of the squad, and the literature on military-patriotic education. The layout is presented on the official website, www.young armiya.ru.

Figure 4.3 – Youngarmer's Room
On the left: the layout of the Room of the Youngarmer. The attributes of the room include a mannequin of a soldier holding a cat, the coat of arms of the *Yunarmiya*, a map of Russia, President Putin's portrait, the *Yunarmiya* flag, and the inscription "The eagle power has millions of eaglets, and we are the pride of the country."[113] On the right: a real Room of the Youngarmer at the time of opening. Children are dressed in *Yunarmiya* uniform. On the walls are posters with military themes, a map of Russia, the Russian coat of arms and emblem of the Ministry of Defense, and portraits of Vladimir Putin and Defense Minister Sergei Shoigu.[114]

One detail in the room layout draws particular attention: the figure of a man in green combat fatigues without insignia, with a gun, holding a cat. This is an allusion to the Russian military and the annexation of Crimea. In early March, 2014, strategic areas in Crimea were occupied by heavily armed men in camouflage uniforms without insignia. They did not engage in conversation

---

113 "Voenno-patrioticheskoe dvizhenie Youngarmiia," 2016, http://www.youngarmiya.ru/2016/07/vse-otvety-o-yongarmiy.html (as of December 20, 2016).
114 Photo from the official website of the public *Yunarmiya* VKontakte page. Direct link to photo: goo.gl/DCC7RB (as of December 20, 2016).

with representatives of mass media, but they behaved "very politely."[115] The phrase "polite people," accidentally launched by blogger Boris Rozhin, became an Internet meme. One of the most famous images of "polite people," a photo of a masked man in green combat fatigues holding an orange cat, spread as a visual symbol of the euphemism for the modern Russian military "showing its presence" abroad. The image of the soldier with a cat appeared on shirts, bumper stickers, collectible figurines, and children's toys (Figure 4.4).

Figure 4.4 – Symbolic exploration of the "Polite People" image of the Russian Army
From left to right: picture of a soldier taken during the annexation of Crimea[116]; model kit, "Modern Russian Infantry 'Polite People'"[117]; bumper sticker reading "Polite People."[118]

The obvious political and military context of the rapid development of the *Yunarmiya* is evident not only in small symbolic details, however. Sergei Shoigu, who never drew the connection between the *Yunarmiya* and the RMS, stressed the special status of the *Yunarmiya* movement and its members:

---

115 "Vezhlivye liudi kak novyi obraz Rossiiskoi Armii," *RIA Novosti*, May 16, 2014, https://ria.ru/defense_safety/20140516/1007988002.html (as of December 20, 2016).
116 "Vezhlivye liudi i kot," *Novii Krym*, December 3, 2014, http://www.newscrimea.ru/vezhlivye-lyudi-i-kot/ (as of December 20, 2016).
117 "Internet-shop Karopka," 2016, http://karopka.ru/community/user/10232/?p=2&MODEL=429214 (as of December 20, 2016).
118 "Internet-shop Rusticker," 2016, http://rusticker.ru/naklejka-na-avto/polite_people/product/3609 (as of December 20, 2016).

Patriotic Education

In a very short time, the Yunarmiya will become the most mobile, huge and efficient children-teenagers' military-patriotic organization of our country.
- Shoigu's speech at the ceremony of registration of the *Yunarmiya* as an all-Russian youth movement on July 29, 2016[119]

We will do everything to ensure that you are the strongest, smartest, most beautiful and most important, worthy citizens of our country <...> you will have opportunities to participate in all our events. You will have the opportunity to fly airplanes and jump with a parachute, to dive under the water and hike on our warships and submarines. You will have the opportunity to shoot anything that shoots, except the rockets. You will have the opportunity to drive all that we have.
- Shoigu's speech at the first all-Russian forum of the *Yunarmiya* on May 28, 2016[120]

School directors and teachers prefer not to discuss the militarized nature of the movement, but they note the clear organizational advantages they receive from participation in it. The national organization provides familiar and necessary methodological guidelines of what to do and how.

Interview fragment
...it turns out, well, that all is contained in the system. It is not anymore like – there is a tutor, there is a patriotic education and a lot of unfamiliar things... they promised the room [the Room of the Youngarmer], but there's no room yet. But it is not the room, but that now I have an idea what to do with my kids and don't go myself but do it in the spirit of the system. I really missed the systematic planning, and a sense that what you're doing, someone else needs this, including the state.
 – Primary school teacher and deputy of extracurricular activity (woman, 54, Leningrad Oblast)

In the three days after the signing of the decree that established *Yunarmiya*, 104 pupils joined the movement. In two months, 76 regional *Yunarmiya* headquarters were created all over the country. Today, the *Yunarmiya* covers all citizens of the Russian Federation.[121]

---

119 "V Rossii sozdano voenno-patrioticheskoe dvizhenie Youngarmiia," *Interfax*, August 3, 2016, http://www.interfax.ru/russia/521787 (as of December 20, 2016).
120 "Shoigu: Osnovnaia zadacha Yunarmii - vospitat' patriotov RF, a ne voennykh," May 28, 2016, http://special.tass.ru/armiya-i-opk/3321648 (as of December 20, 2016).
121 The official website юн-армия.рф shows that by the end of 2016, there were 26,742 Youngarmers, that is, 0.1 percent of all Russian pupils.

> **Box 4.2 – Oath of the Youngarmer**
> *Joining the ranks of the Yunarmiya in the presence of my comrades, I solemnly swear: To be always loyal to my Fatherland and the Yunarmiya brotherhood, to comply with the Charter of the Yunarmiya, to be an honest Youngarmer. To follow the traditions of valor, courage, and comradely mutual assistance. To be always the defender of the weak, to overcome all obstacles in the struggle for truth and justice. To strive for victories in academics and sports, a healthy way of life, to prepare myself to serve and create for the good of the Fatherland. To honor the memory of the heroes who fought for freedom and independence of our country, to be a patriot and a worthy citizen of Russia. With honor and pride, to bear the title of the Youngarmer. I swear!* [122]

With the rise of the RMS and the *Yunarmiya*, the political meaningfulness of patriotic education reached a higher level. Today, Russia has all the prerequisites for a general indoctrination and strengthening of control over the institutions of patriotic education. However, whether or not these conditions would be implemented depends on many factors, not least of which is the international situation. It is possible that the *Yunarmiya* system and the student movement will routinely reproduce practices of memorialization, volunteering, and local history, while the federal and regional budgets for patriotic education continue to exist with questionable effectiveness.

The implementation of the RMS and *Yunarmiya* happened very quickly. With zeal or hesitation, schools accept these institutions as an organic part of a lost system, made possible because the social structure and cultural basis of the Soviet school is still present in the Russian school. After all, emotion-based learning and the "patriotism of everything" existed long before the RMS and *Yunarmiya*.

4.4 Patriotic Content of School Subjects

The patriotic content of school subjects grounded in emotion-based learning is another Soviet schooling custom used in contemporary education. Today, it is

---

[122] "Yunarmiya, Military-Patriotic Movement. Official Webpage," 2016, http://юн-армия.рф/about/.

mostly associated with local history and knowledge of the native land. As Tatyana Tsyrlina-Spady and Alan Stoskopf show, the History curriculum in many ways follows Soviet tradition, orienting "towards fulfilling its major social goal of developing pride in Russia's past and present and shaping school students into loyal Russian citizens, especially by utilizing the Russian notion of the hero to achieve this type of loyalty to the state."[123] History becomes the most patriotism-oriented subject, with a primary purpose of legitimizing the patriotic agendas of the state and the pursuit of a common ideology.[124] However, there are tendencies toward spreading the emotional aspect of learning, as well as patriotism itself, to almost every school subject. Notable are similarities to the Soviet practice of emphasizing the exceptionality and superiority of what is Russian over what exists in other countries.

Interview fragments
In every subject, there is a theme which can be related to the history of one's native land, something to tell children about patriotism. In every subject, in History, and in Literature, and in Biology, and in Geography. And... so now, in connection with crisis it became more difficult, but previously, different teachers used to necessarily go in for expeditions on native land, to collect materials. Geographers, biologists, historians, librarians. Everyone in their own interests, and then we prepared a conference. Once a year, it was very useful experience, because we could use all those materials in the lessons, preparing exercises.
   – Geography teacher and head of the school museum (woman, 60, Tver Oblast)

In literature classes, we generally have a task to educate patriots. But not just patriots, but thinking patriots, reflexive patriots. We try to show what distinguishes our culture from the West, what is our peculiarity. The kids, for instance, watch "War and Peace" after reading the book, and we watch not just our film by Bondarchuk [the 1965 film directed by Sergei Bondarchuk], *but a new serial, which is British* [2016, directed by Tom Harper]. *And together with the kids, of course, we come to the conclusion that*

---

123 Tatyana Tsyrlina-Spady and Alan Stoskopf, "Russian History Textbooks in the Putin Era: Heroic Leaders Demand Loyal Citizens," in *Globalisation and Historiography of National Leaders: Symbolic Representations in School Textbooks*, ed. Joseph Zajda, Tatyana Tsyrlina-Spady, and Michael Lovorn (Dordrecht: Springer, 2017), 15–33. P. 15.
124 Tatyana Tsyrlina-Spady and Michael Lovorn, "A Curriculum of Ideology: Use and Abuse of Modern History Education in Russia and the United States," *International Dialogues on Education: Past and Present* 2, no. 2 (2015).

> they can't fully understand and correctly reflect our Russian soul. I believe that this emphasis on the specialness of culture is patriotic education.
> — Literature teacher (woman, 50, Moscow Oblast)

Teachers can share methods for developing patriotic and military-patriotic studies in various courses by writing articles for online newspapers and social networks. In these articles, they share their experiences and present suggestions for delivering patriotic information when teaching a particular subject. For example, an article titled "Military-patriotic education of pupils in Math lessons" offers a methodology for contextual tasks for students in 5th grade. The author recommends, during the study of segments, angles, and scale,

> to note that a good knowledge of these and other issues, and the ability to apply them in practice, are necessary to conduct the paramilitary game Zarnitsa; they are essential for serving in the ranks of the Russian Army, as the skills of orienteering and determining the distance to objects "by eye" are required not only of the commander, but every ordinary soldier.[125]

The author, a mathematics teacher in a rural school in the Chuvash Republic, mentions emotion-based learning as a rationale for inserting patriotic content into math lessons:

> The patriotic duty of students during the training period in the school is to get "good" and "excellent" marks, to harden physically, to cultivate the moral and volitional qualities of a citizen of Russia. <...> Every teacher knows that learning should be emotional and initiate positive emotions. <...> We the Math teachers can do a big favor to future soldiers, telling them about the application of mathematics in military service.[126]

In an article titled "Patriotic education and upbringing in physics lessons," a teacher in a rural school in the republic of Saha (Yakutiya) suggests that an emphasis on the patriotic feelings of Russian scientists can increase students' motivation to study:

---

[125] Elena Nikiforova, "Voenno-patrioticheskoe vospitanie uchashchikhsia na urokakh matematiki," *Pervoye Sentiabria*, 2005, http://festival.1september.ru/articles/212619 (as of December 20, 2016).

[126] Ibid.

> Studying light pressure with pupils, it is useful to report that Piotr Lebedev perfomed a truly scientific exploit <...> For the patriotic education of students, such a significant fact from the biography of Piotr Lebedev is important. In 1911, a scientist who worked for 20 years at the university left in protest against the reactionary actions of the Ministry of Education. Piotr Lebedev was left without an apartment, his favorite job, and the means of living. At this time, he received an invitation to the Nobel Institute in Stockholm, where they promised him good working conditions, freedom of action, and a lot of money. But the scientist refused the offer and remained in his Motherland. As a true patriot, he could not leave his Fatherland.
> Studying nuclear reactions and their energy output, it makes sense to turn for educational purposes to the biography of Igor' Kurchatov <...> Shortly before his death (in 1960), he said: "I am happy that I was born in Russia and dedicated my life to the nuclear science of a great country. I deeply believe and know that our people, our government, our society will use the achievements of this science only for good."[127]

In 2014, one of the most popular Russian math textbooks for primary schools did not pass the state examination because the content of the book was not deemed conducive to the development of patriotism:

> [T]he textbook's context does not help with patriotism formation. Heroes of the writings of Janny Radary, Sharl Perro, the brothers Grimm, Alan Milan, Astrid Lindgren, Erich Raspe, dwarfs, elves, fakirs with snakes, and the three little pigs are hardly called to form a sense of patriotism for one's own country and nation.[128]

The expert who carried out the evaluation specified in her claims that, of the 119 cultural and mythological characters in the textbook, only nine are related to Russian culture or folk tales; letters of the old Slavonic alphabet are carelessly depicted "in blue ink and scrawl" while Roman numerals are written clearly; and the fairy who comes to the aid of children in tasks does not exist in Russian culture.

---

127 Raima Konobulova, "Patrioticheskoe obuchenie i vospitanie na urokakh fiziki," *World of Teacher*, October 31, 2015, http://worldofteacher.com/9218-patrioticheskoe-obuchenie-i-vospitanie-na-urokah-fiziki.html (as of December 20, 2016).

128 Andrei Kozenko, "Patrioticheskoe vychitanie," April 8, 2014, https://www.znak.com/2014-04-08/pochemu_odin_iz_samyh_populyarnyh_uchebnikov_po_matematike_ne_proshel_gosudarstvennuyu_ekspertizu (as of December 20, 2016).

In a more recent example of the tendency toward emotion-based learning in mathematics, 4th grade students in the 2016 Novosibirsk Math Olympiad were asked this question regarding currency: "The dollar is twice the price of the ruble, and the euro is three times more expensive than the dollar. Which is better: 17 rubles or 3 euros?" Mathematically, the correct answer is "3 euros," equal to 18 rubles. However, when the children gave this answer, it was counted as incorrect. The recommended answer was "17 rubles."[129] Upset parents received this explanation from the teachers: "We live in Russia, and Russian rubles are our money."[130]

The "patriotism of everything" allows unlimited focus on the emotional aspect of education, mainly on the emotions of supremacy. In the end, this inevitably leads to a reduction in critical thinking. Such a patriotic, emotional focus is voluntary on the part of teachers, according to their inner convictions. As the political situation in the country turns toward formation of ideology based on Russian superiority, these trends have the potential for rapid growth and development in the direction of nationalism.

4.5 Pedagogical Tools

The Soviet conventions of patriotic conversations, patriotic holidays, and basic military training as tools of patriotic education were preserved in almost every Russian school during the 1990s and 2000s. Although there were attempts to modernize these tools, as is apparent from the frequent use of the word "innovative" in patriotic education manuals, the attempts nevertheless included dressing up the old military patriotism. Indeed, "innovations" sometimes involve nothing more than MS PowerPoint presentations.

---

129 "Mamu shkol'nitsy vozmutili absurdnye otvety na zadachki pro rubli i flomastery," *NGS. Novosti*, October 11, 2016, http://news.ngs.ru/more/50094613 (as of December 20, 2016).

130 "Na Shkol'noi Olimpiade Vernyi Otvet Okazalsia Matemticheski Nepravil'nym. Zato Patriotichnym," *Meduza*, October 11, 2016, https://meduza.io/shapito/2016/10/11/na-shkolnoy-olimpiade-vernyy-otvet-okazalsya-matematicheski-nepravilnym-zato-patriotichnym (as of December 20, 2016).

Patriotic Conversations

Teachers report in interviews that state institutions infrequently prescribe the topics of classroom discussions. Unlike the situation with Soviet patriotic conversations, when a pool of questions for discussion was formed by the agenda of the Communist Party, there are no obligatory topics to discuss with the students. Patriotic conversations by teachers' initiative are also not widespread. During routine meetings with students, teachers prefer to discuss problems with the children's behavior, communication with classmates and adults, and healthy lifestyles.

However, when instructions exist, they take the form of federal "mandatory recommendations." One such mandatory recommendation is the all-Russian lesson. The all-Russian lesson is taught in all Russian schools on the same day and on approximately the same subject recommended by the Ministry of Education and Science. Recently, the subject was the annexation of Crimea.[131]

According to the official recommendations of the Ministry of Education, the purpose of a united lesson is the development of a sense of patriotism and pride for one's country, forming the Russian civil and civilizational-cultural identity of pupils on the basis of historical events associated with the reunification of Crimea and Russia. A single lesson consists of compulsory and variable parts. The compulsory part includes the story of the referendum in Crimea and Sevastopol. The guidelines for the lesson explain:

> *At this stage of the lesson, it's preferable to invite some important guest (representative of the legislative or executive power) who could explain how the referendum was organized, what difficulties were met, and how they were solved. Fragments of documentaries on the referendum and on the day when Crimea was joined to Russia can*

---

[131] In March 2015, the Ministry of Education and Science recommended the all-Russian lesson framework to celebrate the anniversary of Crimea and Sevastopol joining the Russian Federation. Ministry of Education and Science of the RF, "All-Russian lesson— We are together!'" March 3, 2015, http://минобрнауки.рф/новости/5229 (as of December 20, 2016).

be shown. Allow time for the children's stories about how their families were touched by these events. It is important for this stage of the lesson to be vivid and emotional.[132]

The variable part of the lesson involves a discussion with students titled "What is Crimea for Russia?" The recommended format is the "Line of History," listing the main events that characterize the historical relations of Russia and Crimea, ending with the following words:

> *In the evening* [of March 18, 2014], *a festive concert was held on Red Square in Moscow. Speaking from the scene, President of the Russian Federation Vladimir Vladimirovich Putin said:*
> **Perhaps nobody was sleeping in Sevastopol this night. The night sky was lit by flashes of fireworks. The eyes of the people shone with tears. This is the day they have been awaiting for 23 years.**
> **Crimea was waiting for a miracle, its people believed that it will happen, they have done a lot to make this miracle come true, and we helped them in this, because "We are together!" Because Crimea is Russia!** [133]
> [in bold in the original]

Teachers prefer to execute such orders almost literally, slightly altering the material based on the age of the students. This is connected to pedagogical culture and a perception of state authorities as pedagogical authorities.

> **Box 4.3 – Class discussion: "Crimea is ours!"**[134] [abridged]
> Purpose: to acquaint pupils with the celebration of the annexation of Crimea to Russia; to educate love and respect for people, the history of the country; to cultivate the sacred feelings of love for the Motherland.
>
> Teacher:
> "… Our lesson's topic is dedicated to Crimea for a reason. What do you think it might be connected to? Why do people say that Crimea is ours again?

---

132 Ministerstvo Obrazovaniia i Nauki RF, "Primernii scenarii uroka dlia uchashhihsia osnovnoi shkoly, Posviashhennogo Godovshhine Priniatiia Kryma i Sevastopolia v Sostav Rossiiskoi Federatsii," 2015, goo.gl/Uw1C3F (as of December 5, 2016).
133 Ibid.
134 Liudmila Kondakova, "Klassnii chas na temu 'Krym - Nash!'", *Mul'tiurok*, March 20, 2016, https://multiurok.ru/milakonda/files/klassnyi-chas-na-tiemu-krym-nash.html (as of December 5, 2016).

(Children give answers)
"The history of the Crimea is long and interesting. During the reign of Empress Ekaterina II [Catherine the Great], the Crimea became a part of the Russian Empire. However, as the years passed and as a result of political maneuvers, the Crimea was a territory of the neighboring state of Ukraine. In the course of recent events that took place in this state (the political-military coup), the people living on the peninsula of Crimea and the city of Sevastopol expressed their desire to be part of Russia, asking for protection from the aggressive new government of Ukraine. So, on March 18, 2014, by popular vote on a referendum, an interstate agreement was signed on the adoption of the independent Republic of Crimea by the Russian Federation and foundation of the new subjects of the Federation-Republic of Crimea and the federal city of Sevastopol. In this regard, I ask everyone to stand."
Hymn of the Russian Federation.
Teacher:
"Let's talk about the Republic of Crimea, about its famous cities, the life of the people, climatic conditions, flora and fauna. <...> Today is the celebration of the reunification of Russia and Crimea. Let's invent a symbol for this holiday."

Figure 4.5 – A child's drawing based on the lesson "Crimea is ours!"
The inscription inside the heart says, "Crimea is Russia.[135]" Outside the heart is written, "We are one."

Continuing another Soviet tradition, the state authorities made some attempts to implement *education by example* as a particular genre of patriotic

---

135 Ibid

conversation. Of course, the focus of such conversations was President Vladimir Putin. In their analysis of contemporary Russian textbooks, Tatyana Tsyrlina-Spady and Alan Stoskopf discuss how Putin is depicted as a "hero-unifier who can protect the State from its enemies, such as terrorists and separatists, in order to safeguard enduring Russian principles and values"[136] who "strengthens traditional Russian values of Orthodoxy, protects the national unity, encourages patriotism, promotes culture and science, and enables the Russian people to move forward into a greater Russian glory."[137]

The obligatory textbooks are supported by special books about Putin's personality and humanity. These books are recommended for use in schools, but teachers and school administration often understand this recommendation to be mandatory. For example, the 2004 book "Vladimir Putin. Parents. Friends. Teachers"[138] was directed to be purchased by Russian schools in 2012.[139] Fewer copies of this book were published than the famous book about Vladimir Lenin, Anna Ul'ianova's "Il'ich's Childhood and School Years," but it was perhaps the first example of a governmental order to schools in post-Soviet Russia. Written by President Putin's childhood teacher Vera Gurevich, the book received praise from Anatoly Kartashov, President of the Regional Association of Veterans of Military Counterintelligence, who wrote the introduction. According to Kartashov, the book is "a wonderful example for patriotic education of the young generation":

> This true book largely answers the question that people continue to ask around the world: "Who is Mr. Putin?"—showing our president as an honest, intelligent, highly educated person, and we, the representatives of law enforcement agencies, will continue to provide worldwide support in his quest to build a new and strong Russia.[140]

---

136 Tsyrlina-Spady and Stoskopf, "Russian History Textbooks in the Putin Era: Heroic Leaders Demand Loyal Citizens." P. 22.
137 Ibid. P. 24.
138 Vera Gurevich, *Vladimir Putin. Roditeli. Druz'ia. Uchitelia*, 2nd ed. (St. Petersburg: Izdatel'stvo Iuridicheskogo Instituta, 2004).
139 Alexander Chernykh, "Prem'er kak primer," *Kommersant*, February 8, 2012, http://www.kommersant.ru/doc-rm/1868451 (as of December 5, 2016).
140 Gurevich, *Vladimir Putin. Roditeli. Druz'ia. Uchitelia*. P. 3.

In the spirit of the tales of Lenin's youth in "Il'ich's Childhood and School Years," the book recounts Putin's childhood, his school successes and problems, and relates personal memories of young Volodya, who "knew how to get along with all the guys, and didn't ever fight or bully, and did not offend the weak," and "had many companions, two friends, but perhaps no enemies."[141] The book consists of moral and instructive stories that generally act to mythologize the image of the Leader:

> *Many years ago, we were on holiday in the South, and Volodya went with us, as Vladimir Semenovich* [Putin's father] *asked. Where we rented a room, the hostess had a cat that "walked by herself" <...> Early in the morning, the cat gave birth to kittens in the yard, and the hostess put them in a garbage bucket, covered it, and left. Volodya jumped out of bed and let the poor creatures out. Two were dead, but he saved three. <...> It seemed that he forgot about the incident and wasn't mean to her* [the hostess]. *However, this was not the case, although he still greeted her, spoke politely, brought food from the store at her request if he went to buy it for us. One day he bought us sausage that was fragrant, juicy, delicious <...> The hostess came into the kitchen, inhaled the aroma of the product without speaking to anyone, and said with a Ukrainian accent: "I so much want a sausage." Volodya answered, "Go and buy one at the shop, they brought a lot there." Hearing this answer, I was stunned. The hostess left. I asked Volodya: "It seems that you begrudge her the sausage?" The answer was: "I don't hold grudges, but I don't treat evil people." He said it suddenly and bluntly. I had no more questions.* (Vera Gurevich, *Vladimir Putin. Parents. Friends. Teachers*).[142]

Vladimir Putin is himself the co-author of a textbook. In 1999, a book called "Let's Learn Judo with Vladimir Putin" was published and has since been republished several times. In 2008, a training video based on the book was filmed in which President Putin himself demonstrates fighting techniques. In 2016, Russian schools, mostly primary schools, received 7 million copies of the textbook set "The Art of Judo – From Games to Skill," authored by Putin and Arkady Rotenberg, Vice-President of the Judo Federation of Russia.[143] The

---

141 Ibid. P. 43.
142 Ibid.
143 Evgenii Kaliukov, "V rossiiskie shkoly postupit 7 mln uchebnikov Putina i Rotenberga po dziudo," *RBK*, June 30, 2016, http://www.rbc.ru/society/30/06/2016/57752e6d9a794 72c97f32963 (as of December 5, 2016).

president's image is used in the argument for a healthy lifestyle, as well as the role of sports in national security.

> ***Interview fragment***
> *In our school, there is no opportunity to teach judo. We do classic sport training. However, in the Life Safety Lessons, which I also teach, we watch a film about Vladimir Vladimirovich [Putin] every year. Students are keen on this, and I connect their interest exactly with the figure of the president. They don't just watch, but they go to a library to borrow the book. This year, two students joined the district section of judo, but to take part in the lessons, they have to make a long trip, an hour and a half, so they can't go all the time. So, the video tutorials, plus the President as a teacher, are invaluable.*
> — Physical education and Life Safety teacher (man, 55, Voronezh Oblast)

Life Safety Lessons, Military Gatherings, and Games

Since the beginning of the 1990s, lessons in military preparation have been preserved as a part of Life Safety Lessons. Traditionally, the teachers are men, former soldiers, which is significant because 85 percent of teachers in Russian schools are women. Life Safety Lessons are popular with many children, and not surprisingly, the methodological basis and traditions of teaching are similar to those from the Soviet era. The situation changed, however, once the activation of the *Yunarmiya* promised students the latest military equipment.

A 2011 textbook titled "Basic Military Preparation" contains the same sections as Soviet textbooks on the subject: fire training (Kalashnikov, rules of fire, hand grenades, protective equipment); drill; engineered barriers (antipersonnel and antitank); military topography; tactical training; military field training; radiological, chemical, and bacteriological defense; military medical training; and physical training, including hand-to-hand combat. This textbook is positioned as a collection of materials that can be used in extracurricular activities and Life Safety Lessons in schools and colleges. The author claims that "the tutorial helps to solve problems of military-patriotic education of young people, teaching a healthy and safe lifestyle, and raising a patriot of the Fatherland."[144] That the content of the textbook has not changed much from Soviet times is clear from the illustrations (Figure 4.6). The book does not contain any up-to-date information about weapons, contemporary strategies of military operations, or the newest threats (e.g. terrorist attacks) and personal protective equipment.

Military sports and military training in the 10th grade are a traditional component of Life Safety Lessons. The restored *Zarnitsa* game almost entirely repeats the scenario from Soviet times. Its main phases include an obstacle course, first aid and carrying the victim, assembling a Kalashnikov submachine-gun, setting up tents, packing a backpack, making a fire and boiling water, orientation with a compass, performance of military songs, and drawing the group symbol.

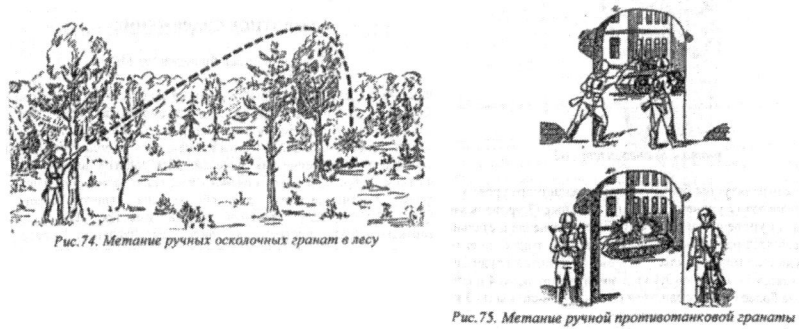

Figure 4.6 – Illustrations from "Basic Military Preparation" (2011)
On the left: "Throwing concussion hand grenades in the forest";
on the right: "Throwing an anti-tank hand grenade."

School military training usually takes place in winter or summer, and only boys can participate. For up to five days, they are immersed in the everyday work of military conscripts. Military training school, carried out jointly with the local military, teaches subjects such as military life; the organization of the

---

144 Boris Simonenko, *Nachal'naia voennaia podgotovka* (Briansk: Poligram-Plus, 2011). P. 4.

guard and internal services; elements of combat such as shooting, tactical, physical, and medical training; the issues of radiation; and chemical and biological protection of troops.[145]

> **Box 4.4 – "Our military trainings," an essay by a student from a rural school**
> At the end of June, we set off for military training. We were preparing for that event all year in Life Safety Lessons. We understood that it was a serious event and wanted to honorably represent our school.
> In the morning, the girls saw us near the school. They wished us luck and some of them wished they could go with us. We also wished they could!
> In the military unit on the parade ground, we were met by the administration. The commander talked about the general rules of conduct, and then the soldiers showed us a presentation on hand-to-hand combat. On the first day, we were shown the barracks, spoke about the timetable, had a tour of the museum of the military unit, and were shown the weapons of war.
> After sleep, our army life began. We stood at the command "Rise!" (and once even at the command of "Alarm!"), ate in the soldiers' canteen, did exercises, sang patriotic songs, watched films on military subjects and, of course, we studied. We were taught to provide first aid for various injuries. We ran races and did long jumps and pull-ups. We were given bulletproof vests, helmets, and machine guns. Wearing all those, we learned the ways of soldier movement in battle. We studied the assembly and disassembly of guns and learned to shoot from the prone and standing positions.
> We also had to watch a TV program, "Time" [Vremya], because we needed to know about the main events happening in our country during the day. We liked the canteen very much! We ate almost everything, both soup and the second course, and of course fruit salad!
> The interior of the classrooms was very interesting and in the patriotic mood. Some classes had posters with the state symbols, anthem, and portraits of the President, Prime Minister, and Minister of Defense. The corridors of the barracks where we lived were also covered with posters: the great Russian generals, with their famous quotes—Suvorov, Kutuzov, Zhukov; religious literature shelves; and boards proclaiming the conditions and benefits of military service.
> After dinner, we usually had a lecture on the political situation in the world, about the modern meaning of the Russian Armed Forces, about the Great Patriotic War and its veterans, about the benefits of serving in the army, and about the dangers of alcohol

---

145 Ministerstvo Oborony RF & Ministerstvo Obrazovaniia i Nauki RF, *Prikaz ob utverzhdenii instruktsii ob organizatsii obucheniia grazhdan Rossiiskoi Federatsii nachal'nym znaniiam v oblasti oborony i ih podgotovki po osnovam voennoi sluzhby v obrazovatel'nykh uchrezhdeniiakh srednego (polnogo) obshhego obrazovaniia, obrazovatel'nykh uchrezhdeniiakh nachal'nogo professional'nogo i srednego professional'nogo obrazovanija i uchebnykh punktakh*, February 24, 2010, http://base.garant.ru/198025/#ixzz4SP3TqROw (as of December 5, 2016).

and drug addiction. Teachers and the military told us about their personal experiences and said they had never regretted their choices, they were happy to defend the Fatherland. Every day in the evening, there was also a ceremony for the best participants of the day. Their names were noted in the "combat sheet." Sometimes to note the best guys, the teacher brought them down and declared gratitude to the guys, who loudly answered before the formation, "I serve the Russian Federation!"
Everything was organized at the highest level, we felt like a real military! We were even visited by the girls on the final day for a "date." We showed them all we managed to learn, and then had lunch together in the canteen. I loved our military training and I would love to do it again.

Patriotic Celebrations

Celebrations are an essential part of patriotic education. As an element of the model of patriotic education (see Figure 3.2), they have been preserved since Soviet times and were even observed during the decade when patriotism was not inculcated in the citizenry. This is especially relevant to the Victory Day celebrations on May 9. Both teachers and local authorities consider Victory Day to be the cornerstone of the formation of patriotism in modern Russia. The other two major celebrations are Russia Day (June 12) and Unity Day (November 4).[146]

Interview fragments

We have always tried to keep the celebration of May 9 in the schools, even when it was not celebrated officially. Even when there was no parade, we had our own little parades in our towns and villages. Wherever possible, we supported the teachers who wanted to root the memory of the War. School museums and patriotic clubs have played a great, enduring role. We [the Department of Education] always tried to make this holiday something united for our district. We wrote reports to the newspaper, we announced competitions for children, we gave the money for carnations [a traditional gift to war veterans]. We actually took part in this holiday, making speeches, and I think it was also important for children and especially for teachers.
— Guidance counselor of the district Department of Education (woman, 48, Pskov Oblast)

Russia Day is a day of freedom. Victory Day is the day of our power, of our memory, a reminder that we are strong. National Unity Day is a day of unity together... all nations,

---

146 Sometimes Defenders of the Fatherland Day (February 23) is included in the list, although many schools consider it more like "boys' and men's day," matched with International Women's Day on March 8. Perhaps this celebration is the only one in which a military theme is not connected to patriotic education.

all united. This triad correctly shows what is happening in contemporary Russia, it creates in children the right vision, the image of the country. If you overload the holidays, it will be a mess. There's still the New Year and the 8th of March. And the graduation party, Day of the Farewell Bell... Although Day of the Farewell Bell has also become very patriotic lately. We try to show that by graduating kids into the world, we have given patriots to our country.

— Biology teacher and deputy of extracurricular activity (woman, 46, Leningrad Oblast)

Russia Day has been celebrated on June 12 every year since 1992. On this day in 1990, the Declaration of Sovereignty of the Russian Soviet Federative Socialist Republic, which was to become the new democratic legal state, was adopted. The Declaration asserted the priority of the Constitution and laws of the Russian Federation on the legislative acts of the USSR; equal legal opportunities for the newly formed political parties, public organizations, and associations, formal and informal; the principle of separation of powers; and the need for a substantial expansion of the rights of the subjects of the Russian Federation.

Despite the significant legal background of this holiday, Russia Day is usually celebrated with expressions of love and affection for the country. The celebrations are widely associated with traditional Russian images, such as birch trees, woven bast shoes (*lapti*), handicrafts like Gzhel porcelain and Khokhloma painted wooden bowls, and folk singing and dances. However, the particular moment of June 12, 1990, has little symbolic meaning for the way this day is celebrated.

Interview fragment
Russia Day is a day of a new Russia and of the old Russia, not of the USSR. It is a day of justice. It is not just about a day, June 12, 1990, but about historical justice. Our roots are in the Russian traditions, and that is what we are celebrating on Russia Day.

— Geography teacher and head of the school museum (woman, 60, Tver Oblast)

Unity Day has been celebrated on November 4 since 2005, in connection with the government's plan to end celebrations on November 7, a date connected with the anniversary of the October Revolution of 1917. The idea for a celebration on November 4 was expressed by the Russian Interreligious Council, for on November 4, 1612, soldiers freed Moscow from Polish invaders. It is believed that in this battle, the people demonstrated heroism and solidarity, regardless of their origin, religion, and position in society.

The scripts of this holiday vary, but they all include the idea of unity of the "brotherly peoples" of the former Soviet Union. Soviet symbols remind participants of their shared Soviet heritage; for instance, child performers might wear Soviet school uniforms (Figure 4.7).

Figure 4.7 – Performance at a Unity Day celebration
Students from the Ulyanovsk region perform the hymn of the Russian Movement of Schoolchildren in Soviet school uniform. The inscription in the background says, "The Russian Movement of Schoolchildren."[147]

Both Russia Day and Unity Day use contemporary Russian state symbols in performances. Skits, poems, and speeches include the colors of the modern Russian flag, the text of the Russian national hymn, and symbols of the Russian coat of arms. The most popular patriotic holiday in schools, however, is Victory Day, a celebration full of Soviet symbolism and history.

---

147 A screenshot from the public video from November 4, 2016. URL: goo.gl/QYFo4u (as of December 20, 2016).

The victory of the Red Army and Soviet people over Nazi Germany in the Great Patriotic War of 1941–1945 is celebrated on May 9. As in Soviet times, school holidays include poems about the war, an imitation of the parade on Red Square, and reenactments of solders' lives. Often, part of the celebration involves a procession to lay flowers on the tomb of the Unknown Soldier.

The holiday maintains the Soviet traditions of celebration and acquires new rituals. One of the grandest such rituals is "The Immortal Regiment," started in 2012 by activists in Tomsk to commemorate their grandparents. "The Immortal Regiment" is a procession of people with portraits of their loved ones killed in the Great Patriotic War. From year to year, this ritual involves an increasing number of localities. In 2015, the event attracted about 12 million people, and in Moscow, the procession was headed by President Putin. Although this event is surrounded by controversy over whether it may have been ordered by local authorities,[148] teachers and principals note the enthusiasm of the students and their interest in this action.

Interview fragment
[T]here was an interview that said something like 75 percent of modern people had family members who fought in the Great Patriotic War. However, significantly fewer people, around 20 percent, remember details about who fought and where.[149] And so, that is why we and our children like such an action. In a playful way, they learn about their family, learn the details of the history, and the history then becomes personal history. I believe that it can be very helpful in life.
– A school director (man, 45, Moscow Oblast)

---

148 Varlamov, "Organizatorov 'Bessmertnogo Polka' ulichili v nabore massovki," Livejournal.com, May 7, 2016, http://varlamov.ru/1705935.html (as of December 5, 2016).

149 This refers to the interview of the Public Opinion Foundation, in which a telephone survey of 1,000 citizens aged 18 years and older with a random sample of mobile and landline telephones was held on April l9, 2015. According to the survey, 79% of Russians said they had relatives who took part in the war. However, only 29% of respondents could recall the locations or the operations involving members of their families. Statistical error does not exceed 3.8%. The Public Opinion Foundation, "Velikaia Otechestvennaia voina v semeinoi istorii," 2015, http://fom.ru/Proshloe/12142 (as of December 5, 2016).

Victory Day, as a holiday that unites Russians, has maintained popularity for over 70 years. However, in comparison with Soviet times, the holiday remains perhaps the only symbolic field for the construction of the Russian nation that is widely used in school patriotic education. The heroic, militarized, victorious celebration combines well with the other elements of patriotic education from the Soviet era, like school museums, search groups, and basic military trainings. The observation of Victory Day in the contemporary school is a celebration of the deeds of heroes. Interestingly, the aim of preventing future wars, inherent in the nature of the Soviet version of the celebration, is frequently omitted. The importance of the victory becomes so critical for the formation of national values and the image of the nation in contemporary Russia that the tragedy of war fades into the background. This need for victory takes surprising forms in society in general,[150] and this common attitude is reflected in schools. "Victory" becomes a single grand narrative assembling patriotic and nationalistic trends, shifting understandings of peace toward the experience of the Cold War era rather than toward the concepts of democratic citizenship of the 1990s.[151]

Victory Day celebrations allow participants to experience the victory of 1945 anew every year. This victory, although long past, becomes a metanarrative of a "final victory." Its meaning in discussions about the need for peace is declining, while the sense of the country's gratitude to the dead is highlighted, and this accent is supported at higher levels by the media discourse of the military power of the Russian government.

---

150 Many Russian people use symbols of the Great Patriotic War and its celebration in a frivolous manner. For instance, the black-and-orange-striped Ribbon of Saint George, used since 2005 at Victory Day ceremonies out of respect for the veterans, is widely used to decorate dishes, thrift shops, and even strip clubs. At Victory Day parades, babies are dressed in military uniform. Rear windows of cars are decorated with the inscription: "1941–1945: We can repeat that." For more examples, see: Anna Sanina, "Competing for a citizen: 'Visible' and 'invisible' forms of state identity in Russia," *Journal of Eurasian Studies* 3, no. 2 (2012): 126–46; Anna Sanina, "'Whom Are You Kidding?' Visual Political Irony in Contemporary Russia," *Forum: Qualitative Social Research* (forthcoming, 2017).

151 Tatyana Tsyrlina-Spady and Michael Lovorn, "Patriotism, History Teaching, and History Textbooks in Russia: What Was Old Is New Again," in *Globalisation, Ideology and Politics of Education Reforms* (Cham: Springer International Publishing, 2015), 41–57.

Interview fragments

In the classroom, when we learn about the Great Patriotic War, I always bring the lesson to talk not just about heroes, but about children-heroes. Our current pupils should be aware that their peers or even younger children were able to do great deeds, to lay down their lives for their country. Of course, war is a disaster, it is death, hunger and hardships. But they need to feel the sense of victory and the role of little heroes in this victory. This is the only lesson where I do not allow discussions. We have a classroom full of pacifists, ready to speculate on the importance of life and the world... who can argue that this is important? But they can't know the whole story, the whole atmosphere of the war, and I want them to imagine it. And I tell them how I remember myself being pupil, and what our teachers who actually participated in that war, what they told us, and I require them not to discuss, but to listen very carefully.

— Teacher of History and Social Science (woman, 61, Saint Petersburg)

This is my personal favorite celebration, and I do my best to pass my feelings to my students so they will like Victory Day, too. They are so small, though, they are so open to that victory feeling, that it is easy to fulfill their needs. We discuss the Victory Day history all the time, and I proudly tell them that WE WON. And this is such an undeniable fact, that we won, that they come to believe that we can win in everything, and this is so inspiring for them.

— Primary school teacher and deputy of extracurricular activity (woman, 54, Leningrad Oblast)

4.6 Conclusion

The key elements of patriotic education, developed in the Soviet school, are preserved in a slightly modified form in contemporary Russia. The essential difference is the current lack of a conceptual basis. State programming for patriotic education has been conducted at the federal and regional levels since the early 2000s, but schools never conceived of it as a real framework for their activities. New youth organizations such as the Russian Movement of Schoolchildren and the *Yunarmiya* do not focus on the state programs of patriotic education, either. Their objectives and funding are provided mainly by the Ministry of Defense and the Federal Agency for Youth Affairs. Schools make up for the lack of a working conceptual and legal basis for patriotic education with manuals, which borrow much from the Soviet experience of patriotism and emphasize the military-patriotic view of the process.

The practice of memorialization is perhaps the strongest and most mature element of the general model of patriotic education. It was supported by the initiative of teachers in the 1990s, before the new Russian state paid any attention to it. School museums, military clubs, search teams, and Memory Guards act as anchor institutions that help to maintain the old model of patriotic education. The figure of a teacher-enthusiast managing these associations is central. These teachers, raised during the Soviet period of patriotic education, reproduce their experiences in modern activities. At the same time, the sublimation of patriotic education in the 1980s allowed them the essential experience of formal response to the requests of authorities and creating their own patriotic lessons. This makes teachers important agents of patriotic education in contemporary schools, for, state recommendations aside, it is the teachers who ultimately decide what to teach the children.

The logical concern is: What may happen when these teachers retire? Will their methods of patriotic education continue with a new generation of teachers? This has no clear answer. Much depends on state policy in the sphere of patriotic education and especially on methods for developing its ideological basis. At the same time, studies of teachers' social and cultural identities suggest the sustainability of their habits[152] and assume that changing the model of patriotic education will require a slow process of internal changes in such a conservative organization as the school. Current trends suggest that the practice of memorialization will continue to play a significant role in patriotic education.

The Soviet model of patriotic education, fundamentally preserved through the adoption and maintenance of old elements, is flexible and enduring enough to have acquired new elements and new meanings in the years since 1991. These new elements and meanings are examined in the next chapter.

---

[152] Valeria Ivaniushina and Daniil Alexandrov, "Is there a differentiation of teachers in the Russian school system?", *Sotsiologicheskie Issledovaniya*, no. 9 (2016): 59–65.

5. Novel Elements of Patriotic Education in Contemporary Russia

The general outline and basic elements of patriotic education have been mostly preserved since Soviet times; however, the last 15 years have seen this basic model enriched with new targets, new meanings, and new agents involved in the formation of patriotism.

5.1 New Targets

In a departure from the tradition of the Soviet period, contemporary patriotic education aims to reach preschoolers as well as schoolchildren. An analysis of the catalogue of the Russian National Library (nlr.ru) demonstrates that from 1970–1989, only four patriotic education manuals, less than 1 percent of the total, were aimed at children of preschool age. From 2000–2016, however, there were 77 manuals aimed at preschoolers, or approximately 10 percent of the total. These manuals for kindergarten teachers include summaries of daily lessons, scripts for the weeks of patriotic education, and patriotic holidays and excursions appropriate for children ages 3–7.

Manuals for preschool teachers are meaningfully divided into two groups. About half of the manuals, despite the patriotic titles, do not reflect patriotic education in the traditional Soviet sense. Sometimes they include scenarios for Victory Day celebrations, but mostly they consider general questions about discovering the surrounding world and learning concepts of family, home, and native land. They suggest activities directed toward ideas of friendship, solidarity, and nature conservation. Such manuals typically focus on the importance of educating children about Russian and Soviet tradition, folktales, games, and celebrations. These educational tasks are implemented through conversations ("Family and home," "Nature of Russia," "Russian nesting dolls"), short excursions ("forest corner," "pharmacy," "Orthodox Church"), holidays ("Maslenitsa," "Easter," "New Year"), and games.

The other group of manuals, on the contrary, focus on military-patriotic education (Figure 5.1). These manuals include games to acquaint children with the structure of the armed forces of Russia, military history of the country, and the Great Patriotic War and Victory Day. In so doing, military topics are proposed for study not only in the format of exceptional events, like celebrations or thematic weeks, but as an everyday object of children's attention.

Figure 5.1 – Covers of the manuals for patriotic education for preschool teachers
From left to right: "You took an oath – not a step backwards: Designing the thematic weeks in the work on patriotic education with children ages 5–7," and "Educational Sandbox: The formation of patriotism in preschoolers on the example of their ideas about the armed forces" for children ages 3 and up.

To give an example of everyday activities, the manual titled "Educational Sandbox"[153] proposes to simulate the battles of the "glory of Russian weapons in different eras." It suggests using a sandbox filled with toy humans, animals, and fairy tale characters, as well as models of military equipment, walls, and

---

153 Natal'ia Vorob'ëva and Ol'ga Sapozhnikova, *Pedagogicheskaya pesochnitsa: Formirovanie patriotizma u doshkol'nikov na primere predstavlenii o vooruzhënnyh silakh* (Moscow: Itellekt-Center, 2016).

fortifications. All of these figures are, for some reason, called "symbols of socialization" by the authors.[154] According to them, "thanks to the principally liberation character of the Russian weapon campaigns," these games form in the preschoolers "a deep respect for the army as the protector, as well as an attitude toward military service as an honorable duty."[155] Additionally, "children should not only be equipped with certain knowledge about the military forces and the heroism of the people in different eras, but above all, this knowledge should be presented in emotion-based form."[156] (Box 5.1)

Box 5.1 – Fragments of the class "There is such a profession – to defend the Motherland!" for children ages 4–6[157] [abridged]

Structural component	Words and actions of the adult	Actions of the children
Entry ritual	Greeting of the children, call to go to the sandbox. On one of the side corners, a toy Russian soldier from any era appears. Throughout the class, this figure asks all questions, accepts and evaluates responses, gives tasks, and governs the behavior of children.	
Main part	Soldier: "Our home is good and beautiful! What do we have? Are there any mountains? Are there any rivers? What grows in gardens, in the fields? Look what a beautiful and rich country we made!!! People live everywhere. And there is such a profession – to defend the Motherland!	Children build mountains and draw rivers in the sand, adding figures of trees.
	Who protects the Homeland?	Children answer.
	It is the soldiers, sailors, and officers.	
	To protect our homeland against threats that can come from the sea, we have a Navy. Now go to the tables, choose one figure each, and create a fleet on the sea.	Children choose ships, boats, and submarines, and complete the task.
	But the threat may be not only from the sea but from the air! And here the air force keeps watch! These are planes, and helicopters, and even space ships! And brave and intelligent pilots control this equipment! Make them airfields! If you want to hide them, clear the forest, flatten the sand and place the planes and helicopters!	Children build airfields with aircraft.
	We also have miners who lay mines to hinder the movement of enemy troops. Put mines in the sand here."	Children bury toy mines in the sand.

---

154 Ibid. P. 20, 22.
155 Ibid. P. 15.
156 Ibid. P. 26.
157 Ibid. P. 28–30.

Celebration scripts for preschoolers replicate scenarios of school celebrations (Box 5.2). They include concerts of military songs, stories about the war, meetings with veterans, and war-themed craft projects. During preparation for the Victory Day celebration, the vocabulary of preschoolers is enriched with words such as "war," "enemy," "veteran," "to win," "to lose," "memorial," and "Ribbon of Saint George." Obviously, young children cannot understand the social and political nature of such complex concepts.

> **Box 5.2 – The script of a Victory Day celebration for the younger group (3–4 years old) in a kindergarten[158]** [abridged]
> Problem: Lack of knowledge about Victory Day, ignorance about veterans of the Great Patriotic War.
> Participants: Children of the younger group, teachers, parents.
> Objective: Formation of moral values.
> Tasks:
> 1. To give the children initial information about the Great Patriotic War. To give knowledge about the defenders of the Fatherland, the functions of the army.
> 2. To activate auditory and visual analyzers, to develop children's speech, imagination, and thinking. To develop the ability to communicate with one another, encouraging children to work together.
> 3. To develop in the children pride and respect for the veterans of the Great Patriotic War, to develop a sense of pride for their Homeland and the ability to listen to adults.
> 4. To activate the vocabulary: Motherland, hero, veteran, victory, soldier, army, defender, memorial.
> Teacher: "May 9 is the most important holiday celebrated in our country. What is this holiday? What is this victory? Over whom? Victory Day is the greatest and the most serious holiday for Russia and for many other countries. <...> It was a terrible and long war. One early June morning, fascist Germany attacked our peaceful country. All the people rose up to defend the homeland: our army, and women, and the elderly, and even children." (During the conversation, the teacher gives explanations and responses to the children, summarizes their questions, shows visual material, etc. The conversation should be emotional, lively, and should increase the activity of children. During the conversation, the teacher provides the new information to clarify or deepen children's knowledge about objects and phenomena.) <...> "Our valiant soldiers drove out the Nazis and came to Berlin. It happened on May 9, 1945. And since then, every

---

[158] Elena Bikbulatova, "Proekt v detskom sadu 'Den' Pobedy'. Mladshaia gruppa," *Kladovaia razvlechenii*, 2016, http://kladraz.ru/blogs/elena-konstantinovna-bikbulatova/proekt-den-pobedy.html (as of January 5, 2017).

citizen of our country and people in other countries celebrate this holiday. Now listen to the poem:

The Day of Victory came,
The best holiday on Earth.
We have a lot of fun today,
Both the adults and kids!

For no one has forgotten the valiant heroes and their exploits. There are many monuments in memory of the heroes of the war built across the country, as well as the mass graves in which those who were killed in the battles were buried." (shows illustrations) <…>

The children read poems:

We were not born yet
When in the military tempest of fire,
Deciding the future centuries' fate,
You fought the battle, the Holy battle.

The mature nature of this celebration suggests that its main task is not informative or educational. The emphasis is on the development of emotional background and shared values. The goal of such rituals, celebrations, and group activities is to make young children love the state, its symbols, and its past while the children are too young to contradict or protest. As children age, they will understand the military history of Russia as a history of victory, and this will be the foundation of emotion-based learning.

Interview fragment

We have kindergartens that are very successful in terms of patriotic education. Of course, we do not perceive seriously that children aged 4–5 would remember the fights and battles, but they will definitely feel what it is like to be proud of their country – we consider it very important to show them this, even at an early age. Of course, we need the support of the family, but if kindergartens properly organize their work, then children start to think and realize that there is a country and that it must be protected.

– Guidance counselor of the district Department of Education (woman, 48, Pskov Oblast)

The expansion of the Soviet model of patriotic education to include younger pupils is another indication of its embeddedness in the social structures of the Russian society. Education and its upbringing function are funded by the state and designed to respond to the government request for loyalty and political support of the existing system. In the Soviet era, this request was explained in the need to maintain an ideological foundation, but in the Russian education system, this need does not formally exist. Nevertheless, the model of patriotic education is socially reproduced within the school system and at the preschool level, as well. The kindergarten teachers and guidance counselors of preschool education recognize the model as something from their own childhoods. As a result, contemporary children enter this system very early and remain inside it until they graduate from school.

The expanded model of patriotic education involves some new meanings and connotations that do not change much of its content, but bring it in line with the spirit of the post-Soviet time.

5.2 New Connotations

The collapse of the Soviet Union and the task of building a new Russian state have affected social rhetoric and attached some additional semantic features to the model of patriotic upbringing. These features are associated with an intricate mixture of patriotic and military-patriotic education with two other meanings. The first meaning considers civil aspects of patriotic education. The second meaning could be described as spiritual, moral, ethical, and religious. Although these are not dominant contexts and are largely variations on military-patriotic education, their use is very common not only in educational processes, political discourse, and public documents, but also in scientific works of Russian researchers.

Civic-Patriotic Education

In the early 2000s, when the first program of patriotic education was adopted, the political discourse in Russia still had a residual dominance of the civil and democratic rhetoric of authorities. Problems of building a civil society, overcoming cultural trauma,[159] and the formation of national Russian identity were at the center of statements made by government officials and political

---

[159] Jeffrey C. Alexander et al., *Cultural Trauma and Collective Identity* (California: University of California Press, 2004).

leaders. For example, in 2003, President Putin spoke of the national idea of Russia in terms of economic revival: "The main thing is to ensure the growth of the economy. This literally determines the country's future: the competitiveness of a country in all spheres, in all areas."[160] In contrast, in 2016, answering the same question about the national idea, Putin said: "We have no, and cannot have any other, unifying idea except for patriotism."[161]

In the situation of the 2000s, the request for patriotic education was carried out in terms of civic-patriotic education (*grazhdansko-patrioticheskoe vospitanie*). This term was partly applied to the civic studies that by that time already existed in schools. After the collapse of the Soviet Union, Russian education actively promoted the ideas of civic education aimed at formation of legal consciousness and democratic attitudes and values. Civil society activists focused on several problems of civic education in Russia, pointing out that textbooks are outdated, do not provide up-to-date ideas about the legal system, and do not form specific behavior skills; the educational environment lacks the available formats for presentation of legal issues (simplified training modules, TV shows, cartoons); and the current practice of civic education cannot lead to the formation of a legal culture of personality.[162] Many of the educational institutions promoting these ideas were concentrated in Moscow and Saint Petersburg, although the regions also had centers or programs of civic education. Teachers were involved in learning this subject through participating in courses and conferences that were often organized with the support of human rights activists and educational and humanitarian projects sponsored by European or American funds.[163] Russian public movements aimed at modernizing the educational system in the New Russia also played their role. Despite all this, there

---

160 Vladimir Putin, "Beseda s finalistami konkursa 'Moi dom, moi gorod, moia strana,'" *Kremlin.ru*, June 5, 2003, http://www.kremlin.ru/events/president/transcripts/22021 (as of January 10, 2017).
161 Vladimir Putin, "Vstrecha s aktivom Kluba liderov," *Kremlin.ru*, February 3, 2016, http://kremlin.ru/events/president/news/51263 (as of January 10, 2017).
162 Nataliia Eliazberg, ed., *Grazhdanskoe obrazovaniie - pedagogicheskii, sotsial'nii i kul'turnyi fenomen* (St. Petersburg: Soiuz, 2006). P. 13.
163 For example, the Soros Foundation conducted teacher conferences and grant competitions on civic education for teachers. Today, the majority of such foundations and organizations fall under the Russian Federal Law "On noncommercial organizations," № 121-FZ adopted on July 20, 2012. This law bans activities of organizations that receive

are few experts or adepts in civil law and civil democratic practice compared with the total number of teachers socialized under the Soviet model of education and upbringing. For the majority of teachers and school directors, the task of civic education was new, so they understood and implemented it through the tools that were accessible and comprehensible to them, and the greatest of those tools was patriotic education.

Interview fragments
We began to understand this civil [education] like this: it's like former patriotic [education], only moral and democratic. We were faced with civic education in the 1990s, then it was like a fashion. The historians, I remember, were gathered at some Soros courses, and they brought out the books and used them in the classroom. That time I was just a teacher, not a director, and I remember that we discussed that for the teachers of Literature it would nice to have such courses, too. Historians promised to tell us this and that, but somehow it did not happen all it once. We read new books then, of course, but we didn't attend any courses. And why it was a problem is that the courses usually give some techniques or methods, and we used to teach the children with the methods. So we came to the conclusion that it's a better to use the old methods than no methods at all, and thus in general, we adhered to the direction of patriotism, although we certainly touched rights and freedoms in the discussion.
– A school director (woman, 55, Leningrad Oblast)

Civic studies [grazhdanovedenie], this school subject was introduced to our school curriculum in the mid- or late 1990s, when it was difficult for us to teach even history and social studies, and civic studies was especially difficult to teach. Because we didn't know how to interpret. The history we had [in the textbooks] ended with the collapse of the Soviet Union, and the "New Russia" topic had, I wished, one paragraph. In the crisis years, children were very surprising regarding the passages written in the textbook about civic responsibility, about the state of law. They just laughed,

---

funding from foreign governments. With the adoption of this law, activities regarding civic education became difficult. There are only a few organizations and foundations in contemporary Russia that are actively involved in educational activities in the field of rights and freedoms (Moscow Helsinki Group and Sakharov Center) or anti-corruption education (Transparency International). In this situation, the choice of perspective and teaching methods of school subjects related to the state and societal relations rests to a large extent with the schoolteachers. In their turn, due to cultural priorities and a lack of time, teachers often prefer to rely on the point of view of the guidance counselors from regional education departments, as well as on published manuals on patriotic education.

and rational arguments didn't work for them, because the children saw what a mess was happening. What could we tell them? That tomorrow they will have a bright future... a bright future is also something from ideology, right? The ideology was sort of forbidden. So we had to appeal to the emotions and feelings of patriotism, and to show that our great country is great, that we ascended after the Great Patriotic War, and thus to inspire the faith that we'll rise up again soon. I used these techniques always, and when I taught civic studies, too. The faith worked, and the faith is patriotism.

— Teacher of History and Social Science (man, 57, Tver Oblast)

The discussion about what civic education is, and how it differs from patriotic education, was developed in the Russian scientific environment. Its peak came during the mid-1990s to mid-2000s, mostly in the reputable journals of the Russian Academy of Sciences ("Sociological Studies" and "Political Studies") and in other publications discussing citizenship, civic engagement, civic identity, civil religion, and civil education.[164] These discussions were often initiated with the support of national science foundations and nonprofit organizations. The researchers demonstrated the necessity of formation of civic education in Russian schools and universities. They considered the rationality of studying problems of civil, national, and ethnic identity in a multinational country; assessed the risks of patriotically oriented civic education; and stressed the responsibility of academics, journalists, and public figures for the distribution of civic knowledge and practices of legal education. However, the number of participants in this debate was very limited. It rarely had an impact on management

---

164 Isak Froumin, "Grazhdanskoe obrazovanie: spornye momenty i vozmozhnye tendentsii," *Direktor shkoly* 5 (1997): 57–66; Andrei Ioffe, "Sovremennye vyzovy i riski razvitiia grazhdanskogo obrazovaniia v sovremennoi Rossii," *Prepodavanie istorii i obschestvoznaniia v shkole* 9 (2006): 19–24; Ol'ga Lebedeva, "Patrioticheskoe vospitanie: vernopoddannicheskoe ili grazhdanskoe?", *Pedagogika* 9 (2003): 77–82; Alexander Gofman, "Sotsiologiia i grazhdanskaia religiia v Rossii," in *Sotsiologiia i sovremennaia Rossiia* (Moscow: SU HSE, 2003), 84–107; Vladimir Magun and Leokadia Drobizheva, eds., *Grazhdanskie, etnicheskie i religioznye identichnosti v sovremennoi Rossii* (Moscow: Institute of Sociology of the Russian Academy of Sciences (ISRAS), 2006); Alexander Sungurov, "Grazhdanskoe obrazovanie: v poiskakh optimal'noi modeli regional'nogo razvitiia," in *Sotsial'noe partnerstvo i razvitie institutov grazhdanskogo obschestva v regionakh i munitsipalitetakh: praktika mezhsektornogo vzaimodeistviia* (Moscow: Agentstvo Social'noi Informatsii, 2008), 275–84.

decisions[165] and almost never affected the attitudes of the real agents of patriotic education: school directors and teachers.

The echo of civic education remained alive in some governmental decrees in the early 2000s. For example, the Concept of Modernization of Russian Education, adopted in 2001, considered upbringing as the primary priority in education, but implied civic upbringing and did not directly mention patriotism:

> *The most important tasks of upbringing are the formation of students' civil responsibility and legal consciousness, spirituality and culture, initiative, independence, tolerance, successful socialization in society, and active adaptation in the labor market.*[166]

By that time, however, the civic component in the governmental documents was matched by the patriotic one. In state standards for school education approved in 2004, the civil and patriotic invariably coexist in the definition of tasks of learning basic school subjects.[167] The Russian language should foster "citizenship and patriotism," and Literature should form "civic consciousness, patriotism," and "civic and patriotic pathos." History should bring up "patriotism, respect for history and traditions of our Homeland, to the rights and freedoms of the individual, democratic principles of public life." Even foreign language courses were intended to raise patriots. State officials acquainted with the background of elaboration of such documents say that they met a clear demand from teachers and directors to reveal patriotic discourse on the level

---

165 In 2004, the "Civil G8" organization provided a draft of a new government program, "Civic education of the population of the Russian Federation for 2005–2008." In this program, civic education was defined as activities for education, training, and awareness aimed at the formation of knowledge, skills, values, and competencies necessary for humans as citizens of Russia. However, this project was recognized as duplicating the existing program on patriotic education and was not adopted.

166 Ministerstvo Obrazovaniia RF, *O Kontseptsii modernizatsii rossiiskogo obrazovaniia na period do 2010*, 02/11/2002. http://base.garant.ru/1588306/#block_1000#ixzz4Td8stAS3 (as of January 10, 2017).

167 Ministerstvo Obrazovaniia RF, *Ob utverzhdenii federal'nogo komponenta gosudarstvennykh obrazovatel'nykh standartov nachal'nogo obschego, osnovnogo obschego i srednego (polnogo) obschego obrazovaniia*, 03/05/2004, http://base.garant.ru/6150599/#ixzz4TdAFhG3P (as of January 10, 2017).

of school governance, and thought that this demand matched the political situation in general.

> **Interview fragment**
> *There were discussions at various levels, and we understood that teachers do not understand us. They were accustomed to talk in terms of patriotism, and for the first time in many years, our president began to talk about patriotism, that we need to reveal it, that we need to be proud of our country, and so on. And here were the teachers, watching TV, and asking us why we have forgotten patriotism – Look, even the president says we should bring it up, finally. And then we introduced "hyphen patriotism"* [civic-patriotic]*, simply because it was easier and more intuitive for teachers.*
> – Member of a regional Youth Policy Committee (man, 48)

Patriotic meanings of civic education were specified in the governmental documents and then in manuals. They formed a strong connection between the concepts of patriotism and citizenship on the level of school education, and this connection persists today. Teachers and principals use "civic" and "patriotic" as synonymous or complementary terms.

> **Interview fragments**
> *I see the task of school as the formation of respect for traditions in children, the introduction to our Russian spiritual values and to the folk culture. We must prepare children for life, that is, they should be mature, active individuals, capable of solving the tasks posed by the state. That is, we need to educate citizens who love their country, patriots capable of performing their civic duties. Thus, of course, we keep the issues of civic education, the formation of patriotism, in the primary place.*
> – A school director (man, 57, Pskov Oblast)

> *The formation of civic identity is the task that is very important for us now. Not only because it is defined somewhere from above* [by the government]*, no. We accepted the task even before the programs, manuals, and so on. We believe that our graduates should, first, love their country, and second, understand that they belong to our state, that is, they live here, they study here, and will work for its good. This is civic identity, this is the awareness of belonging to the community of citizens, which is based in particular on patriotism, on love of the country.*
> – A school director (woman, 45, Leningrad Oblast)

For school directors and teachers, the priority of patriotic education over civic education was preferable because, in contrast to civic education, patriotic education was clearer in its nature and its tools of implementation. In interviews, the semantics of civic and patriotic constantly intersect, while the rational and cognitive elements that underlie civic education are replaced by the emotional basis of patriotic education, and often by blind patriotism.[168] This emotional basis is complemented by another meaning, developed parallel to civil rhetoric, which is spiritual, moral, ethical, and religious patriotic education.

Moral-Patriotic Education

The spiritual, moral, or ethical meaning of patriotic education is today even stronger than the civic meaning. This is well illustrated by the Google Books Ngram Viewer distribution (Figure 5.2) in which the hyphenated word combinations "spiritual-patriotic" (*dukhovno-patrioticheskoe*), "moral-patriotic" (*moral'no-patrioticheskoe*), and "ethical-patriotic" (*nravstvenno-patrioticheskoe*) are used in Russian books much more often than "civic-patriotic" (*grazhdansko-patrioticheskoe*) or "patriotic" (*patrioticheskoe*) itself.

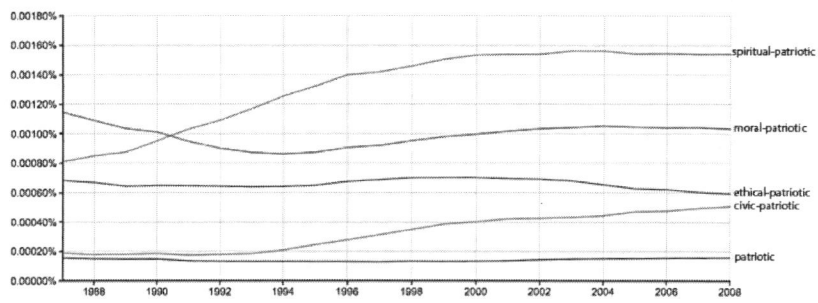

Figure 5.2 – Google Books Ngram Viewer distribution:
dukhovno-patrioticheskoe (spiritual-patriotic), *moral'no-patrioticheskoe* (moral-patriotic), *nravstvenno-patrioticheskoe* (ethical-patriotic), *grazhdansko-patrioticheskoe* (civic-patriotic), and *patrioticheskoe* (patriotic) in Russian books 1988–2008.

---

168 Robert Schatz, Ervin Staub, and Howard Lavine, "On the Varieties of National Attachment: Blind Versus Constructive Patriotism," *Political Psychology* 20, no. 1 (1999): 151–74.

One would assume that in using such adjectives, teachers, guidance counselors, and authors of the books want to stress the peaceful nature of patriotism. However, "spiritual," "moral," and "ethical" have different implications. They are used in the context of traditional Russian (that is, opposed to Western) values, as substitutes for a religious (mostly Orthodox) emphasis in patriotic education. The emergence and active use of these terms is associated with the rhetoric of Orthodox religiosity and traditional values, which has become a contextual antonym of civil rhetoric. According to a survey conducted by the Public Opinion Foundation,[169] 24 percent of Russians associate spirituality with faith in God, religiosity, and the Church; all other interpretations (morality, worldview, positive qualities of a person) have significantly fewer supporters. The growth of spirituality, according to respondents, contributes to the education of youth (10%) and religious education (9%).

The individual needs of faith, suppressed during the Soviet years, are an important catalyst for a massive religious renaissance,[170] as well as for the blending and growing together of the meanings of the religious, spiritual, moral, and ethical.[171] Forty-three percent of Russians believe that the life of contemporary Russian society is *less* spiritual or religious than it was during the Soviet era, when atheism was encouraged.[172] Being religious was almost forbidden

---

169 The survey of 1,500 Russians 18 years and older was conducted by the Public Opinion Foundation on June 15, 2014 in 100 settlements of 43 Russian regions (interview at the place of residence; statistical error does not exceed 3.6%). Source: "Votserkovlennost' pravoslavnykh," *fom.ru*, July 3, 2014, http://fom.ru/TSennosti/11587 (as of January 5, 2017).

170 Andrew Greeley, "A Religious Revival in Russia?", *Journal for the Scientific Study of Religion* 33, no. 3 (September, 1994): 253–72; Jennifer Wasmuth, "Russian Orthodoxy between State and Nation," in *Eastern Orthodox Encounters of Identity and Otherness*, ed. Andrii Krawchuk and Thomas Bremer (New York: Palgrave Macmillan US, 2014), 17–27.

171 While 68% of Russians consider themselves Orthodox, only 13% of the Orthodox can be called enchurched persons (*votserkovlënnyi*), those who attend church not less than once a month, regularly take communion, and pray. A large number of the Orthodox can be called half-enchurched (*poluvotserkovlënnyi*) persons, but their number is decreasing, while the number of poorly and very poorly enchurched (*slabo votserkovlënnyi*) people is increasing. Source: "Tsennosti: religioznost'," *fom.ru*, June 14, 2013, http://fom.ru/TSennosti/10953 (as of January 5, 2017).

172 "Rossiiane o dukhovnosti," *Fond Obschestvennoe Mnenie*, July 3, 2014, http://fom.ru/TSennosti/11589 (as of January 5, 2017).

then, yet many think that the spirituality of the Soviet country was deeper compared to that of today. Religiosity is associated not so much with faith in God and performing religious rituals, but with the revival of the values of conservatism and the fundamental conception of the Motherland, which are attributed to Soviet society. Alexander Agadjanian writes that as the Soviet society from the 1960s to the 1980s was largely isolated from the cultural turbulence that occurred in the West during the same period, "the Soviet moral system was much more traditional and conservative: it had substantially fewer opportunities for individual expression and permissiveness, a stronger collectivist emphasis and regulation, restrained sexual freedom, and an emphasis on family-oriented values and behavior."[173] One of the manifestations of spirituality in Soviet society was the development of patriotism and patriotic education.

Interview fragment
Faith in God and acceptance of spiritual values, a moral lifestyle, and ethical values are all elements of patriotism. All this, besides permitted faith in God, was in the Soviet years. The Orthodox Church is now being revived, and of course this helps in the education of children. But now it turns out that always, regardless of the state system, the Church was on the side of our society and helped in difficult times of war. The Church is probably one of the most patriotic institutions, and if we cannot entrust the upbringing of children to the school, then only in the Church can we trust, because these are our true Russian values.
   – Teacher of History and Social Science and deputy of extracurricular activity
   (woman, 53, Novgorod Oblast)

The relationship of faith, spirituality, and patriotism has a substantial stake in the rhetoric of the Russian Orthodox Church, with its keynotes of tradition, true values, and ideas of service.[174] As Boris Dubin points out, the process of searching for a collective identity, national solidarity symbols, and a Russian national idea was closely accompanied by speaking "of an Orthodox

---

173 Alexander Agadjanian, "Exploring Russian Religiosity as a Source of Morality Today," in *Multiple Moralities and Religions in Post-Soviet Russia*, ed. Jarrett Zigon (New York: Berghahn Books, 2011), 16–26. P. 17.
174 Richard Sakwa, "Christian Democracy in Russia," *Religion, State and Society* 20, no. 2 (1992); John Gordon Garrard and Carol Garrard, *Russian Orthodoxy Resurgent: Faith and Power in the New Russia* (Princeton: Princeton University Press, 2008).

rebirth of the country, on the one hand, and of transformation of Orthodoxy into a state religion, its 'statization,' on the other."[175]

From the beginning, the religiosity in the rhetoric of the Russian Orthodox Church was symbolically accompanied by spirituality; they were later joined by morality and ethical values in opposition to Western values. Religious spirituality spread through patriotism. One of the most influential political groups of the early 1990s, the Russian Christian Democratic Movement[176] (*Rossiiskoe Khristianskoe Demokraticheskoe Dvizhenie*), "argued that 'three fundamental principles: the primacy of spiritual values, enlightened patriotism and rejection of communist ideology' would guide the reawakening of spiritual consciousness and the renewal of Soviet society."[177] The Local Council of the Russian Orthodox Church stated in 1990 that for thousands of years, the Church educated the flock in the spirit of patriotism and peace. By definition of the Local Council, patriotism "reveals itself in a careful attitude toward the historical heritage of the Fatherland, in active citizenship, including concern for the joys and trials of the people, in zealous and conscientious work, in care about the moral health of society, and in the preservation of nature."[178]

Statements about patriotism became prevalent within the hierarchy of clergy, including at the highest level. Patriarch Aleksii II's famous quote from 2005 links patriotism to Orthodoxy:

> *Patriotism is, undoubtedly, relevant. It is a feeling that makes the people and each person responsible for the life of the country. Without patriotism there is no such responsibility. <...> A person without patriotism, in fact, has no country. A "man of the world" is the same as a homeless man. It seems to me that the feeling of love for one's own people is just as natural to a man as the feeling of love for God. <...>*

---

175 Boris Dubin, "Orthodoxy in a Social Context," *Russian Social Science Review* 39, no. 3 (1998): 40–45. P. 41.
176 Christian democracy is a political ideology, which combines traditional Christian (mostly Orthodox and Catholic) beliefs and democratic ideas. Political parties based on such an ideology exist in many countries, including Germany, Italy, Austria, Great Britain, Brazil, and Russia.
177 Zoe Katrina Knox, *Russian Society and the Orthodox Church: Religion in Russia after Communism* (New York: RoutledgeCurzon, 2005). P. 68.
178 "Osnovy sotsial'noi kontseptsii Russkoi Pravoslavnoi Tserkvi," *Pravmir.ru*, 2000, http://www.pravmir.ru/osnovyi-sotsialnoy-kontseptsii-russkoy-pravoslavnoy-tserkvi (as of January 10, 2017).

Patriotism in this sense is consonant with Orthodoxy. <...> I think today we have the main task for the patriots: the creation of our own country.[179]

Liubov Borusiak cites an interesting situation in which the Patriarch spoke about the Church's solidarity with the people in a patriotic situation:

> On June 21, the Russian team beat the Dutch team, which had not suffered a single defeat up until then. The next day, June 22, Patriarch Aleksii II found himself in a difficult position. On the one hand, the country was observing its Day of Memory and Mourning, and the Great War for the Fatherland is certainly a highly esteemed event in the country in terms of its value and significance. On the other hand, the Church could hardly stand on the sidelines with respect to the sensational victory that the Russian soccer players had won, especially a victory that did not take place sixty-seven years ago, like the beginning of the war, but literally on the eve of that observance. Since the Church is vitally involved in the interests and concerns of its flock, the head of the Orthodox Church simply could not fail to express these concerns. So he found himself in a difficult situation: what should he say about two such opposite events, when both are of such high value? How could he say something that would befit the one occasion and not say anything about the other? A compromise was found, a way to connect both events in a single statement: "Our mourning today, which is connected to the anniversary of the beginning of the Great War for the Fatherland, is mitigated by our shared joy because of the Russian team's victory yesterday," Aleksii II said in his address to the military personnel of the Moscow Military District, following the ceremony of the placing of the wreath on the Grave of the Unknown Soldier at the Kremlin wall."[180]

The Patriotic rhetoric of the Russian Orthodox Church has a pronounced political background. As Irina Papkova points out, the general framework of the political discourse of Russian Orthodoxy can be termed *pravoslavnaya derzhavnost'* ("Orthodox Powerhood"), an approach "oriented toward a strong Russia of Orthodox values whose strength is based on the renewal of Orthodox values in society. In this conception, the government must be Orthodox, not in any theocratic, formalistic sense but above all imbued with Orthodox spirituality

---

179 Valeriy Konovalov, "Patriarkh Aleksii: My prazdnuem spasenie naroda," *Trud, N 206,* November 3, 2005, http://www.trud.ru/article/03-11-2005/96041_patriarx_aleksij_m y_prazdnuem_spasenie_naroda.html (as of January 10, 2017).
180 Liubov Borusiak, "Soccer as a Catalyst of Patriotism," *Sociological Research* 48, no. 4 (2009): 57–81. P. 75.

and mentality."[181] The Russian Academy of Education and the Ministry of Education and Science have intensively cooperated with the Russian Orthodox Church, conducting joint activities such as the all-Russian competition in the field of pedagogy, "For the moral feat of the teacher." Part of this competition is dedicated to the spiritual, moral, civil, and patriotic education of children and youth.

However, despite the emphasis on spirituality and morality, the patriotic rhetoric of the Russian Orthodox Church does not exclude the military element of patriotic education; rather, it legitimizes their interconnections. Since the 1990s, the cooperation between the Russian Army and the Russian Orthodox Church has developed an intensive and showy character. Military units include chapels and temples, priests bless the military vehicles and even the missiles, and the priests participate in military parades and speak about patriotism and military-patriotic education.

Archpriest Mikhail, Abbot of the Patriarchal Monastery at the headquarters of the strategic missile forces, is quoted on the website defendingrussia.ru. Although this website covers news about the army, new Russian weapons, developments in the defense industry, and key events of the military and political agendas, interviews with the clergy are commonly included, too.

> *We are against the war, we don't want it. But we are ready for it and ready to defend our land boundaries, the longest in the world. We are opposed to an Arab-Chinese border passed along the Volga. We are totally opposed to war, but the good should also have good fists. And this is why we need Armed Forces able to resist evil.*[182]

Kathy Rousselet suggests that as the idea of Russia as a country in combat is at the heart of the teachings of the Church, the integration of the army and the Church looks rather harmonious and logical:

---

181 Irina Papkova, "The Freezing of Historical Memory? The Post-Soviet Russian Orthodox Church and the Council of 1917," in *Religion, Morality, and Community in Post-Soviet Societies*, ed. Mark Steinberg and Catherine Wanner (Bloomington and Indianapolis: Indiana University Press, 2008), 55–84. P. 69–70.

182 Aleksey Vladlenov, "Zachem nam parad Pobedy. Otvet sviaschennika," *Defendingrussia.ru*, May 7, 2016.

> The Russian army and the Church have signed several cooperation agreements and the authorities have authorized military chaplains. There is an ideological proximity between the Church and the army given that many former soldiers have joined monasteries. The religious dimension of patriotism is further supported by stories of divine miracles and God's intervention to help his people during moments of danger when Russia was involved in various wars. Religious patriotism is also nurtured by the idea that the tragic events experienced by the country during the twentieth century have to be interpreted in light of God's will. Believers had to endure a patriotic combat, both against violent atheism and Stalinist Terror, and the experience of crusading against Muslims in Afghanistan and in Chechnya.[183]

Teachers in contemporary Russian schools fully accept the religious context of a patriot's upbringing and understand moral and spiritual education as closer to a patriotic one than civic education. Even if the moral connotation is not emphasized and patriotic education is formed in a civic-patriotic or military-patriotic way, the religious and spiritual elements emerge in details such as artwork or biographies of military figures. For example, the manual "Spiritually-moral and patriotic education of youth"[184] offers scenarios for classes on the following topics: "Alexander Nevsky, Dmitry Donskoy, Dmitry Pozharsky as religious fighters (*ratobortsy*) of Russia in the 13th-17th centuries"; "The Holy Commander of the Russian Admiral Fyodor Ushakov"; and "The Orthodox traditions of the Russian army." Manuals on civic-patriotic education often include pictures of Orthodox religious symbols, even on their covers (Figure 5.3).

---

[183] Kathy Rousselet, "The Church in the Service of the Fatherland The Church in the Service of the Fatherland," *Europe-Asia Studies* 67, no. 1 (2015): 49–67. P. 52.
[184] Igor' Shilov and Anna Petii, *Dukhovno-nravstvennoe i patrioticheskoe vospitanie molodezhi na pravoslavnykh traditsiiakh rossiiskogo voinstva* (Volgograd: Korifei, 2011).

Figure 5.3 – The cover of the book "Civic-patriotic education in 6–7th grades. Russian statehood: Talks, class meetings, evening gatherings, celebrations, games"[185]
Despite the secular title of the book, its cover depicts an Orthodox church.

In most cases, these elements are associated with Orthodox religiosity; however, other religions are also considered to be involved in the patriotic education of schoolchildren. In the manual "Military-patriotic education in school," the author justifies the role of religion in patriotic education:

> *It should be noted that world history does not know non-religious peoples. The Orthodox Church has always reduced soldiers who defended their Homeland with their lives to the ranks of martyrs and saints. Famous spiritual leaders, like Sergius of Radonezh or Hermogenes, blessed warriors for their feats. <...> As for Islam, the Chairman of the Council of Muftis of Russia Ravil Gainutdin stated that in their activities they come from the words of the prophet Muhammad: "Love of the Homeland is a part of faith." <...> The attitude of the Russian Buddhists to military service can be*

---

185 Elena Tislenkova, *Grazhdansko-patrioticheskoe vospitanie v 6–7 klassakh* (Volgograd, 2007).

judged by the words of Hambo Lama Dam Aushev, who is the head of the traditional Buddhist Sanghas of Russia: "Military service should be regarded as a support of the country."[186]

Both meanings of patriotism, i.e. civil and spiritual (religious, moral, ethical), have a strange cohesion with military intention. Despite the fact that the words "military" and "spiritual," or "military" and "civilian," are oppositional in meaning, the context of patriotism unifies them in a solid and consistent cognitive structure. In any case, the military component prevails. Even when the words "patriotic education" appear in the titles of manuals (Table 5.1), both the content of the manuals and interpretations of the teachers show that these words nevertheless suggest military-patriotic education.

Table 5.1 – Distribution of the manuals on different meanings of patriotic education

	Military-patriotic	Spiritual-patriotic, Moral-patriotic, Ethical-patriotic	Civil-patriotic
Total Number of titles (1970–2016, N = 1,396)	454 (32.5%)	83 (5.9%)	154 (11.0%)
Distribution by period inside the group, %			
1970–1979	44.3	1.2	3.2
1980–1989	15.6	0	0
1990–1999	2.2	0	0
2000–2009	21.6	48.2	42.9
2010–2016	16.3	50.6	53.9
Total 1970–2016	100	100	100

Interview fragment

Military-patriotic always comes first. The military means glory. We have always had the glorious generals, and they showed us that the defense of the Fatherland is a sacred duty, and there is such a profession to defend the Motherland, and it is still all about war: the Great Patriotic War, the Afghan War, and so on. The war is when a man shows heroism and so on. It's all military-patriotic things. But we came to the civil-patriotic. It is a broader concept. This is a love of history, love for someone's land.

---

186 Vasilii Mikriukov, *Voenno-patrioticheskoe vospitanie v shkole: 1–11 klassy* (Moscow: VAKO, 2009). P. 16–17.

> *You should know your history. <...> Whatever it is, this is your homeland. And therefore, there is not only military duty, but love for the Homeland. Therefore, either civic, or patriotic, or together, it's all the same for us.*
> — History teacher and head of a school patriotic club (woman, 70, Pskov Oblast)

Teachers advocate the military element of patriotic education, stressing that it is very necessary to form the ability to defend the country in a hostile international environment. They also suggest that mixing military-patriotic education with Orthodox values helps to illuminate any possible undesirable consequences of militarism. An elementary school teacher in the Rostov region writes in her article titled "Spiritually-moral education of students in extracurricular activities," posted on a teaching web portal, that:

> *By spiritual-moral education, we mean the transmission of knowledge, shaping their [children's] morality on the basis of spirituality, which is traditional for our Fatherland; the formation of experience of their behavior on the basis of spiritual-moral values, developed by a Christian culture for two millennia. <...> The goal of teachers is instilling a sense of patriotism, active citizenship, belonging to the heroic history of the Russian state, readiness to serve the Fatherland, the formation of spiritual-moral landmarks based on traditional human and Christian values.*[187]

The interweaving of the military, spiritual, religious, and civic into a unified canvas of patriotic education is, on the one hand, a marker of time, showing the differences between the current model and the traditional Soviet one. On the other hand, these differences do not alter the semantic structure of patriotic education, nor do they change its tools and major agents. On the contrary, new agents find a place in the extant and well-established model of patriotic education. These agents are the adepts of the spiritual meanings of patriotic education, namely the Orthodox clergy.

---

187 Svetlana Kolesnichenko, "Dukhovno-nravstvennoe vospitanie obuchaiuschikhsia vo vneurochnoi deiatel'nosti," *1 Sentiabria*, 2012, https://festival.1september.ru/articles/607957 (as of January 10, 2017).

5.3 New Agents

According to the Church, the participation of religious agents in education is legitimized in the "Foundations of the Social Concept of the Russian Orthodox Church," a document adopted by the Jubilee Bishops' Council held in Moscow in August, 2000, to capture the basic context of the interaction of Church and society. The document states that "the patriotism of the Orthodox Christian should be active. It manifests itself in the defense of the Fatherland from the enemy, in the work for the good of the Motherland, as well as in the care about the arrangement of the people's life, including through the participation in public administration. The Christian is called to preserve and develop national culture and people's consciousness."[188]

Even before creating this document, Orthodox priests took an active part in school life, but the adoption of the "Foundations" meant legitimizing their actions at the highest level of Church bureaucracy. The participation of Orthodox priests in patriotic education has situational and organizational formats. The situational interaction of churches with schools has a quarter-century history, based on the personal initiative of the teachers, on their faith and desire to interact with the local priests. Despite the fact that clerical participation in patriotic education grows largely out of the political activity of the Orthodox Church, teachers believe that the involvement of the clergy in patriotism-building activities has significant advantages.

Interview fragment

Yes, our priest has some bureaucratic background and he is retired military, but I consider it only a benefit for the children. He has not just defended the Homeland, he came back from the war and built the church. He found the money, no matter, everybody knows that he played a role in the elections, and it seems he supports United Russia, but we all… I mean, he found money to rebuild the church, and now he heads services and raises children. We invite him to our lessons because he tells everything honestly and based on his experience. Children are very sensitive to a lie, so when the priest tells them that the good should be with fists, they see that these are not empty words. He can tell this, they [children] give him a right to criticize our state, and the fact that we are imposed upon by Western values. Now children hardly watch TV,

---

[188] "Osnovy sotsial'noi kontseptsii Russkoi Pravoslavnoi Tserkvi." https://mospat.ru/ru/documents/social-concepts/ii/ (as of January 5, 2017).

they surf the Internet and this is hardly controlled. And he has the credibility to tell them the right things, because he went through the war and is now engaged in the real thing.
– Literature teacher and deputy of extracurricular activity (woman, 58, Voronezh Oblast)

This is especially true for the local communities in regional settlements where the Orthodox Church is another center of social and cultural life.[189]

> **Box 5.3 – A message on the website of the Department for Charity and Social Service of the Moscow Diocese**
> On May 7, in the St. George gymnasium of the city of Egor'evsk in the school Museum of Military Glory, there was a lesson of courage. The priests of the Egor'evsk Beanery were invited, i.e. hegumen Theophan (Schelkunov), who is the Abbot of the Kazan' Church in the city of Egor'evsk, and hegumen Feofan (Kuznetsov), who is the Abbot of Vvedenskiy temple of the village Ryzhevo.
> The lesson was guided by History teacher Makarova and her student assistants. During the lesson, the children learned much about their Egor'evsk compatriots who fought on the fronts of the Great Patriotic War. Students talked about their relatives killed in that war.
> At the end of the lesson, the priests congratulated everyone on the coming holiday of the Victory. They wished the audience good health, happiness, excellent learning, and a peaceful sky over their heads. Hegumen Feofan (Kuznetsov) has donated to the school an album with reproductions of paintings on military themes.

---

189 Orthodox religious institutions are widespread in Russia. In 2015, there were 16,076 Orthodox religious organizations in the country (out of 27,496 organizations of all denominations), with 14,960 religious organizations functioning at a local level. This number corresponds to the number of settlements in Russia with a population of between 51 and 100,000 people. Source: RF Federal State Statistics Service. "Chislo religioznykh organizatsii, zaregistrirovannykh v Rossiiskoi Federatsii na 1 ianvaria 2015," *gks.ru*, n.d., http://www.gks.ru/bgd/regl/b15_11/IssWWW.exe/Stg/d01/11-03.htm (as of January 10, 2017).

Figure 5.4 – A photo from the website of the Department for Charity and Social Service of the Moscow Diocese
The lesson of courage in the Russian school: the teacher, the students, and the priests in the Room of Military Glory.[190]

Local dioceses support the organization of various events that, although formally dedicated to patriotic education, are contextually focused on the formation of the foundations of Orthodox culture.

> Box 5.4 – The message on the website of the Lyskovskaia Diocese (Nizhny Novgorod region) regarding the intellectual game "The spiritual basis of patriotism"[191] [abridged]
> On December 14, 2016, in the village of Vorotynets, an intellectual game called "The spiritual basis of patriotism" took place. The organizers were the Administration of the Vorotynsky municipal district, the "Vorotynskaya News," and the Lyskovskaia Diocese of the Russian Orthodox Church.
> The Council of Elders played the game. The Council included Archpriest Alexiy Melnikov, who is the Dean of the Tashinsky district of the Lyskovskaia Diocese; Archpriest

---

190 "Urok muzhestva," *Otdel po blagotvoritel'nosti i sotsial'nomu sluzheniiu moskovskoi eparkhii*, May 12, 2010, http://blago-mepar.ru/news/urok_muzhestva (as of January 10, 2017).
191 "14 Dekabria 2016 v Vorotyntse sostoialas' mezhraionnaia intellektual'naia igra 'Dukhovnye osnovy patriotizma,'" *Lyskovskaia Eparkhiia*, December 14, 2016, http://lyskovskaya-eparhya.ru/2016/12/14/14-desember-2016-v-vorotunce-sostoialas-meqeparhialnaia-igra-dyhovnue-osnovu-patriotizma/#more-67356 (as of January 10, 2017).

Ioann Lutiansky, who is the Dean of the Sechenovsky district of the Lyskovskaia Diocese; and Vladimir Akimov, the counselor of the Information-Diagnostic Chair of the Vorotynsky District Department of Education.

The young lords of thought, scholars of history, literature, and fundamentals of Orthodox culture were encouraged to correctly answer questions after one minute of discussion. The topics were known in advance: "Biblical winged words and expressions," "Holy Russian warriors," "The lives of the saints of the Lyskovskaia Diocese," and "The History of the Holy Trinity St. Macarius Monastery." It is our history, our culture, our traditions, and our Orthodox faith that form a very important contemporary concept, "the spiritual basis of patriotism."

The situational interaction of churches with schools is often developed further and works in an organizational format, i.e. the Orthodox patriotic clubs. These clubs operate in parishes, monasteries, or Sunday schools, and are commonly organized by Orthodox priests who have served in the military. Marlène Laruelle indicates that Orthodox patriotic clubs are one of the five categories of youth patriotic unions in Russia. These clubs "combine sports training, courses in morality, military history and initiations to Orthodoxy <…> and organizing cultural outings (Orthodox theatre and visits to monasteries)."[192] It is almost impossible to guess the total number of such clubs in Russia. The website pravoslavnyi.ru (*pravoslavnyi* means Orthodox) contains information on more than 500 such clubs, although in interviews conducted with priests, they speak of thousands of clubs.

Interview fragment
Who else but an Orthodox priest will talk to young people about famous Russian warriors like Alexander Nevsky, Dmitry Donskoy, and Fyodor Ushakov? They were all canonized by the Russian Orthodox Church because, in bloody battles, they defended not only their native borders, but also the Orthodox faith. School textbooks do not provide children with this truthful information because our school education is completely profane, it has no faith. Secular education is supposedly objective, but is it objective to hide the feelings and emotions of people who fought for the Orthodox faith? However, we have patriotic clubs at churches in the parishes, many of them across Russia, thousands of them. They teach the national history not in such a distorted way, and also develop the children physically. Sports don't save children from

---

192 P. 14.

drugs, from drinking—they need spirituality to be saved. Our clubs provide children with everything necessary; we provide a safe environment for their development.
— Orthodox priest, co-founder of a patriotic club (man, 52, Pskov Oblast)

Orthodox patriotic and military-patriotic clubs to engage both young and old are being established in parishes on the initiative of priests. As a rule, clubs have specializations that depend on the military or sporting past of their organizers. There are clubs specializing in hand-to-hand combat, combat Sambo, hiking, skydiving, boxing, and in Cossack training.

Interview fragment
For many years, the priests themselves, on their own initiative, have created the organizations for the upbringing of children in their parishes. There are many such organizations, thousands of such organizations around the country. In Ufa [the capital city of the Republic of Bashkortostan], there is the club "Alexander Nevsky," organized by a priest who is a former paratrooper. It teaches children morality, spirituality, and hand-to-hand combat. Many people ask how is it possible, the priest and hand-to-hand combat, and for children. But it's actually just an integrative development, both spiritual and physical.
— Orthodox priest, teacher in a patriotic club and Sunday school (man, 38, Novgorod Oblast)

Since the mid-2000s, separate clubs have united in associations, promoting cooperation not only among themselves but also with schools. For example, the *Stiag* ("Flag") Association unites about 60 Orthodox Patriotic clubs in the Central part of Russia,[193] and the *Vityaz'* ("Knight") Association, based at the Patriarchal Representation at St. John the Baptist in Moscow, has 44 regional branches, including the branch in Crimea.[194] This association even has an international status, with departments in Moldova, Serbia, Montenegro, Latvia, Estonia, and other countries.

The associations carry out their own military-sports competitions, and their content is not much different from the traditional patriotic *Zarnitsa* game. The visible difference is an articulated Orthodox message. For example, the *Stiag* Association holds an annual youth military-tactical game for the glory of

---

193 "Assotsiatsiia Stiag," http://stjag.ru.
194 "Assotsiatsiia Vitiazei," http://asvityazi.ru/?page_id=16.

the Holy Archangel Michael. Played for seven seasons, it usually takes place in the Church of Great Martyr St. Nikita in the Moscow region. Participants are divided into two teams and build field camps, receive laser tag weapons, and confront each other according to the rules.

Interview fragment
> This is our second year of participation in the games. The children from our club consider it an honor to participate in fights, albeit it is a game fight, but still it is a fight for our country. This year the teams arrived from Donetsk and Luhansk,[195] from the other cities of Russia. We had more than 10 teams. The children were in a combat environment, they had tents outdoors, and they had bonfires. We always have the traditional greeting to the teams, "Christ is risen!" And young people respond, "Truly He is risen!" The kids know the rules; their faith is in their souls, as well as their Homeland and awareness of the need to protect it. And they say, "I am happy to serve the Orthodox Fatherland!" This is our mission, as we are the Orthodox priests, and this mission does not depend on borders and distances. So this helps us all understand these games and activities.
> – Orthodox priest, teacher in a patriotic club (man, 50, Moscow Oblast)

The associations hold conferences of military-patriotic clubs, which involve representatives of the Russian Orthodox Church, government agencies, researchers, and university faculty. One of the largest conferences was held on December 5, 2016, at the State University of Management in celebration of the 75th anniversary of the Battle of Moscow.[196] The conference was held in order to discuss the possibilities of counteraction to the falsification of history of the Second World War. It was organized as a set of meetings and thematic round tables discussing topics such as "The current issues of organization of patriotic education in higher education," "The best practices of organization of patriotic

---

[195] The Donetsk People's Republic (DPR) and the Luhansk People's Republic (LPR) are self-declared states in the territory of Ukraine. They were proclaimed on the territory of the Donetsk and Luhansk regions in 2014, during mass protests against the new leadership that came to power as a result of Euromaidan (the 2014 Ukrainian revolution). Ukrainian authorities consider DPR and LPR as terrorist and separatist organizations.

[196] The Battle of Moscow was a strategically significant fight during World War II, known in Western military history as Operation Typhoon. It took place between October, 1941, and January, 1942, and became a symbol of Soviet resistance against the invading Axis forces.

clubs," and "Combating extremism and anti-social phenomena among students." Despite the secular nature of the topics, the initiative of this conference, as well as many other similar events, came from the clerical staff of the Russian Orthodox Church.

Surprisingly, in addition to the reproduction of "traditional Russian values," the clergy successfully performs patriotic education in such a way that it might answer an urgent request coming from the youth: a desire for coolness. The consumption of something that is interesting, cool, and new is known as a feature of childhood and adolescence.[197] The "secular" model of patriotic education uses this feature to promote patriotism through activities like the honoring of heroes, stressing the superiority of the country, or developing games with military equipment in Patriot Park. It is obvious that the conservative Russian Orthodox Church has fewer opportunities to meet this need. However, the military background as well as recent activities of priests, along with their participation in the everyday life of the school, allows them to be role models for the youth.

In conversations with schoolchildren, the priests turn to their army experience and tell children true stories about parachute jumping, overnight stays in the woods, and hand-to-hand combat competitions. These stories do not directly suggest any patriotic morality, but they always capture the attention of a younger audience because of the improbable compatibility of war and peace in the individual's life. The gender factor plays an important role, too, since priests, along with the Basic Military Training teachers, are in the male minority in the school educational process.

Interview fragment
Our school is patronized by priests who also bikers. For the kids, of course, they are like idols. On their motorcycles, they go all over Russia, and even abroad, and this is not just for fun. You know, for children it is very important that it is not just for fun. They have a mission, they take care of the graves of Russian soldiers killed in the Great

---

[197] See e.g.: Marcel Danesi, *Cool: The Signs and Meanings of Adolescence* (Toronto: University of Toronto Press, 1994); Shelagh Ferguson, "A Global Culture of Cool? Generation Y and Their Perception of Coolness," *Young Consumers* 12, no. 3 (August 30, 2011): 265–75.

Patriotic War. They perform the funeral rites on their graves, because they were buried without any rites during the war, of course. Our children, both boys and girls, help them to prepare for their trips. They come to school on the bikes, too. And then they tell their stories. These are real stories, you know, not like those written in the textbooks. I listen to them with pleasure, and children, they are so engaged! We always invite them [the priests] *for all of our holidays and for the lessons of courage. And for the children, they like a celebration in the flesh.*

– Literature teacher (woman, 40, Saint Petersburg)

Interestingly, the clerics themselves are aware of the young generation's demand for novelty and fun, and try to intentionally support it. During patriotic conversations, they often do not speak in high-flown language and a pathetic style, but use simple and sometimes humorous real-life examples. They organize trips and games for the children and involve teenagers in manual labor and volunteering. The clerics engage the youth not only in the life of the Church, but also in the life of the community.

Interview fragment

They called the family holiday the Day of Peter and Fevronia.[198] *They are saints, they are good. But let's just think about what we want to achieve by this holiday. Do we want it to compete with the holiday of St. Valentine's Day? Obviously we do. It is a Catholic holiday, it is not ours, we don't want the youth to celebrate it. We want our youth to make good families, strong families, of course. But should we pass this message in such a boring way? They will obviously prefer Valentine's Day. They say it is much cooler, and it obviously is for them.*

– Orthodox priest, teacher in a patriotic club (man, 40, Saint Petersburg)

Generally, in carrying out patriotic education, priests balance between the political ambitions of the Russian Orthodox Church and the real needs of the society and the young people in particular.

---

198 The Day of Family, Love, and Faithfulness (*Den' sem'i, liubvi i vernosti*), also known as The Day of Saints Peter and Fevronia (*Den' Sviatykh Petra i Fevron'i*), was introduced in Russia in 2008 and is celebrated every year on July 8. Saint Peter and Saint Fevronia, a husband and wife who died on the same day, are the Orthodox patrons of marriage. The Day of Saints Peter and Fevronia is promoted in Russian media as the "true" Russian holiday, opposed to St. Valentine's Day in the West. See: Geraldine Fagan, *Believing in Russia: Religious Policy After Communism* (New York: Routledge, 2013).

5.4 Conclusion

The contemporary model of patriotic education with its new objects, agents, and meanings shows that the basic Soviet model was not reorganized or significantly developed according to the new Russian realities. On the contrary, it has rooted and expanded in the society and obtained new adepts in different social groups. The format of patriotic upbringing in kindergartens repeats the rituals of military-patriotic education in the Soviet school. New meanings of citizenship introduced in the 1990s were almost completely blocked by the former pro-governmental sense of patriotism and spirituality. Largely through the rhetoric of the Russian Orthodox Church, spirituality and patriotism began to be associated with Orthodoxy. The clergy, many of whom are former members of the military, began to participate in patriotic education by participating in established model lessons of courage, patriotic clubs, and military games.

Kathy Rousselet and Marlène Laruelle, in their studies of the Orthodox patriotic clubs in Russia, come to a similar conclusion about their multidimensional ways of functioning. The clubs address different needs of the community (religious, moral, political, economic, and therapeutic) and very often criticize the state and the social and economic situation of Putin's Russia,[199] but their main message is the necessity of moralization of the country: "although morality is part of the Soviet heritage, it seeks to overturn its original foundations."[200] Research performed by Laruelle and Rousselet are in line with the interviews of teachers and priests taken for this monograph. The teachers positively evaluate the patriotic activities of the religious organizations, and children are happy to participate.

The existing format of patriotic education development does not bring anything truly new to the basic model, but highlights the traditional elements coming from Soviet times. Studies indicate that social reflection is not working in Russian society; it is substituted with nostalgia for the Soviet past. At the level of the Russian school system, this substitution manifests itself in the social support of the model of patriotic education, rooted in the Soviet era.

---

199 Rousselet, "The Church in the Service of the Fatherland"; Marlène Laruelle, "Patriotic Youth Clubs in Russia. Professional Niches, Cultural Capital and Narratives of Social Engagement," *Europe-Asia Studies* 67, no. 1 (2015): 8–27.

200 Rousselet, "The Church in the Service of the Fatherland The Church in the Service of the Fatherland." P. 66.

6. Conclusions: Social Roots of the Making of Citizens

This book is an attempt to study the field of patriotism formation in Russia, which is often neglected in political analysis. Employing Bourdieu's conception of habitus, I focus on the "deeply buried structures"[201] of the educational system and its main agents to frame a sociological answer to the question: Why is patriotic education in Russia revealing itself in a way that seems like a return to the Soviet past?

The contemporary school model of patriotic education rebuilt itself seemingly out of nowhere. Today, it claims to have an exclusive position in producing meanings and practices devoted to the creation of citizens. Using interviews with teachers, school administration, and local educational authorities, as well as historical and documental analysis, I attempt to show that the backgrounds of this astonishing phenomenon have a predominately social nature. The Soviet political ideas sprinkled throughout the educational system have ingrained deeply within the social structures of the society, and today, in the absence of a clear alternative for the implementation of teachers' attitudes, intentions, and values, they have manifested in the restoration of a basic model of patriotic education that is virtually the same as that of the Soviet era.

The essential difference between the model of patriotic education in contemporary Russia and its Soviet prototype is that there is no structured and pressing formal concept serving as its basis. In Soviet times, such a basis was firmly formed by communist ideology, providing clear frontiers for the proper education of citizens. Today, the official ideology, including the rules of patriotic education in Russia, is still under development, and the ways of its establishing are much more complex than a mere implementation of the authorities' agenda.

Nakedly ideological situations are occurring in Russia. For instance, the Union of Law Enforcement Veterans (*Sodruzhestvo veteranov*

---

201 Pierre Bourdieu, *The State Nobility: Elite Schools in the Field of Power* (Stanford: Stanford University Press, 1998). P. 1.

pravookhranitel'nykh organov) received state orders to lecture to youth organizations; their lectures consisted of a mix of the Dulles Plan,[202] the newest nationalist-oriented theories, and Orthodox patriotism.[203] A professor of Irkutsk State University was fired for "insufficiently patriotic views,"[204] and the Ministry of Education and Science condemned "anti-patriotic" statements by the Moscow State Institute of International Relations (*MGIMO*).[205] Figures of culture and art have raised concerns about the return of ideological censorship cloaked in lofty words like "patriotism," "homeland," and "morality."[206] The "foreign agents" law[207] has limited the educational, research, and cultural work of organizations with funding from abroad. In the Komi Republic, the local administration ordered the burning of publications issued by the Soros Foundation.[208] The politics of re-Stalinization acquire new, broader perspectives under the ongoing reassessment of the Soviet past.[209]

---

202 The Dulles Plan, a document reportedly authored by former CIA Director Allen Dulles, describes the US government's intentions to destroy the Soviet Union by the disruption of cultural heritage and national values of the Soviet people. Although widely cited in Russia over the last three decades, a verifiable original source for the document and its claims has never been found. See e.g.: Chaim Shinar, "Conspiracy Narratives in Russian Politics: From Stalin to Putin," November 4, 2016, https://ssrn.com/abstract=2864403 (as of January 31, 2017).

203 Anastasiia Yakoreva, "Stalin, plan Dallesa i sviataia Rus'. Chemu nauchit studentov vozhrozhdënnoe obshestvo 'Znanie,'" *Republic.ru*, February 6, 2016, https://republic.ru/posts/79147 (as of January 31, 2017).

204 "Prepodavatelia Irkutskogo Gosudarstvennogo Universiteta uvolili za nedostatochno patriotichnye vzgliady," *Mel.fm*, November 16, 2016, http://mel.fm/2016/11/16/no_patriot (as of January 31, 2017).

205 "V Minobrnauki osudili antipatriotichnye vysskazyvaniia studentki MGIMO," *Tass.ru*, October 25, 2016, http://tass.ru/obschestvo/3732855 (as of January 31, 2017).

206 See e.g.: Konstantin Raikin, "My kleveshim, donosim i opiat' hotim v kletku," *Meduza.io*, October 24, 2016, https://meduza.io/feature/2016/10/24/my-kleveschem-donosim-i-opyat-hotim-v-kletku (as of January 31, 2017); Andrey Zviagintsev, "Durnoi son goszakaza," *Kommersant*, October 26, 2016, http://www.kommersant.ru/doc/3126654 (as of January 31, 2017).

207 Russian Federal Law "On noncommercial organizations," No. 121-FZ adopted on July 20, 2012.

208 Anastasiia Efimova, "Zabrat' vse knigi da szhech'," *Vesti.ru*, January 16, 2016, http://www.vesti.ru/doc.html?id=2708265 (as of January 31, 2017).

209 Thomas Sherlock, "Russian Politics and the Soviet Past: Reassessing Stalin and Stalinism under Vladimir Putin," *Communist and Post-Communist Studies* 49, no. 1 (2016): 45–59.

It is hardly surprising that these episodes are alarming the liberal-oriented part of Russian society and some foreign observers as a possible return to the Soviet past. But still, these situations are a far cry from the all-encompassing and coherent system of ideological education and upbringing that formed Soviet citizens. These sporadic initiatives are unlikely to indicate a deliberate state policy aimed at ideologizing contemporary Russian society. On the contrary, they instead show that the authorities have little control over anything having to do with Russian values. They do not know their own people and, strictly speaking, they do not want to know them. The power system adapts to certain requests that may be made either in favor of the consolidation of an electoral majority that supports the regime, or to justify intensively corrupt government programs, but this is far from a focused and coherent ideological policy. History gives many examples of more rigorous and deliberate ideological strategies. There is no reason to suspect contemporary Russian authorities of a lower political professionalism than their predecessors – they simply have other goals for the development of a "kleptocratic regime,"[210] and they do not consider the common people a target worth investing in.

All of this explains why the current Concept and programs for patriotic education can be considered as a basis for the formation of patriotism only relatively. The adoption of such programs is meant to garner institutional support for the people's loyalty to the authorities; however, the real beneficiaries of the programs are not children or young people as future citizens, but certain social groups like pensioners, teachers, and the military. These groups are expected to vote *properly* in elections here and now. In addition, in most cases, the budgets of the federal and regional programs are managed by people who are close to power and thus loyal to it. This is the way to ensure the survival of the institution of the *kormushka* ("feeding trough").[211]

---

210 Karen Dawisha, *Putin's Kleptocracy: Who Owns Russia?* (New York: Simon & Schuster, 2015).

211 Although the *kormushka* is mostly considered another inheritance from Soviet times, it has deeper roots in Russian history. In general, it means some recurrent government investment in exchange for political loyalty. This term is broadly synonymous with the term "pork barrel legislation" used in the United States and other countries. See Stephen Lovell, "Power, Personalism, and Provisioning in Russian History," *Kritika: Explorations in Russian and Eurasian History* 9, no. 2 (2008): 373–88.

In this context, it would be an oversimplification to reduce the cause of patriotic education to the mere authoritarian ambitions of Russian leaders. Russian society has a specific social demand for the formation of certain political structures. At first glance, this demand seems to have been imposed upon society from above, but both society and the authorities take part in this game. Ideological trends and political appointments not only reflect positions of power, but inevitably meet the needs of the society.

This social demand for the formation of a certain political background is in most cases implicit. In the interviews for this book, none of the teachers denied the need for transparent education, rational critical thinking, and citizen engagement. However, this is the case when discursive practices are at odds with societal needs. Values and attitudes formed in the Soviet schools and pedagogical universities and broadcasted through the teachers' habitus require a different background for realization. This background, alas, cannot lead to results like transparency, rationality, and engagement.

What are the values and attitudes that have led to this situation? First, the teachers need an educational and moral charge to legitimize their low-paid work and increase their own professional value. Second, they require a clear methodological framework, not only for the core subjects of the school curriculum, but also for extracurricular activities. The need for methodological clarity is, on the one hand, inherited from the Soviet system of teachers' education, and on the other hand, it is an essential element of the teachers' routine and work organization, for, due to financial reasons, they are overworked. Third, teachers need the military element of patriotic education, as it is integral to their own perception of the concept. The military element of patriotism has been carefully preserved by teacher-enthusiasts and their supporters, for whom the memory of the Soviet Union's military achievements, especially in the Great Patriotic War, was a very important factor in their professional survival in the post-Soviet years.

These values, attitudes, and expectations make a civic or democratic direction of the school's extracurricular activity highly unlikely. Compared to education in the 1990s, today's schooling in Russia has greatly changed in spirit, and it is clear that the educational reforms initiated after the collapse of the Soviet Union in order to humanize, democratize, and decentralize schools in

Russia have failed. In 2015, a unified history textbook was introduced throughout the country; the Russian Movement of Schoolchildren and the *Yunarmiya* continue to perform robustly involving schools in an organized network; and in August, 2016, a new Minister of Education and Science, Olga Vasilyeva, was appointed. Before that appointment, her academic interests were devoted to studying the relationship between the Russian Orthodox Church and the Russian state; her accession to the position led to a new wave of debates about the nature of patriotic orientations in Russian education.[212] However, these activities, organizations, and appointments do not meet any significant protest. Teachers are only one of the social groups in Russian society, and the restoration of the Soviet model of patriotic education would not be possible if the broader social environment were different.

Jan Germen Janmaat and Nelli Piattoeva argue that recently emerged states, like Russia after the collapse of the USSR, are an "interesting arena in which to examine citizenship education."[213] I would add that recently emerged states are most of all an important area for an urgent but sophisticated implementation of citizenship education. Russia is an example of a failure of such attempts.

Today, Russia is no longer a recently emerged state, and the time for the formation of anything crucially new seems to be lost, while changes to the established model are much more difficult to implement. Are these changes possible, in principle? Constructive patriotism does not allow me to express pessimism in this matter. Since the ideology is not fully entrenched yet, there is hope for some progressive change.

In the absence of an ideological basis, the model of patriotic education works exactly like a social structure. It simultaneously comes from and supports the teachers' habitus, becoming an institutionalized construct and an inevitable part of the educational environment. However, to evaluate the political dimension of this model, we should look at the general results of patriotic education, and these results suggest that as a political structure, this model is inefficient.

---

212 "Patriotic Education," *Khodorkovsky.com*, August 31, 2016, https://www.khodorkovsky.com/patriotic-education (as of January 31, 2017).

213 Jan Germen Janmaat and Nelli Piattoeva, "Citizenship Education in Ukraine and Russia: Reconciling Nation-Building and Active Citizenship," *Comparative Education* 43, no. 4 (2007): 527–552. P. 527.

This can be judged according to the level of patriotism in the society.[214] The responses to the question, "Do you consider yourself a patriot of Russia?" consistently demonstrate a large number of patriotic citizens (Table 6.1).[215] However, the abrupt nature of patriotic identification is more significant than numbers and tendencies. The leaps in self-identification indicate that external events play a more valuable role than state policy in the formation of patriotism. The decrease in the number of those who identified as patriots in 2010 is likely connected to the economic crisis that started in 2008, and the increase in 2015 has clear connections to the 2014 annexation of Crimea.

Since patriotic education in Russia is practically separated from civic knowledge[216] and critical thinking, it is based solely on the emotional element, namely on fostering feelings of pride for the country and the passive hatred of enemies. The transformation of these passive emotions into the active position does not benefit anyone, including the authorities. The active position is much

---

[214] Of course, it would be incorrect to blame patriotic education in schools for the results of the national survey. It would also be incorrect to speak about any precise dependencies between the existing style of patriotic education and these data. And yet, some certain connections exist. The majority of Russians who expressed unconditional pride in being citizens of Russia (48%) were in the 18–24 age group, which means that they, at least for some time in their school lives, were exposed to the resurgent model of patriotic education. Source: "Patriotizm i gosudarstvo," *Levada.ru*, April 29, 2015, http://www.lev ada.ru/2015/04/29/patriotizm-i-gosudarstvo (as of January 31, 2017).

[215] Governmental programs provide frameworks for evaluation, which a priori demonstrate the great success of state institutions in this area. However, the measurement of patriotism, even when it is not prescribed by the state programs, is produced almost exclusively using direct questions. It is difficult to imagine that a person asked "Do you consider yourself a patriot?" would give a negative answer. However, such questions are rather commonly used by the largest Russian centers studying public opinion. From year to year, they reinforce the confidence of the authorities in the success of the chosen model of patriotic education.

[216] This strategy produces revealing results: 41% of Russians have never read the Constitution, 23% have read it but do not remember what they read, and 55% of respondents believe that under the Constitution, the President, not the people, is the source of power and sovereignty in Russia. Sources: "Den' Konstitutsii," *Levada.ru*, December 8, 2016, http://www.levada.ru/2016/12/08/den-konstitutsii (as of January 31, 2017); "Vlast' v Rossii: po Konstitutsii i po zhizni," *Wciom.ru*, December 11, 2014, http://wciom.ru/in dex.php?id=236&uid=115087 (as of January 31, 2017).

less controllable and does not allow for predicting the consequences of people's behavior. The passive position of the patriotically educated citizen ensures loyalty to the authorities and a lack of interest in community affairs.

Table 6.1 – The percentage of answers to the question, "Do you consider yourself a patriot of Russia?"[217]

	2000	2007	2010	2013	2015
Yes	77	78	70	69	78
No	16	12	19	19	11
Hard to say	7	9	11	13	11

The question arises: Can Russian patriotic education be considered as successful and effective when it involves jingoism and passive loyalty? An international comparison suggests that it cannot.[218] The World Values Survey (Wave 6: 2010–2014) allows a comparison of the attitudes of Russians with those of citizens of other countries, implementing different paradigms of civic education (USA), nation-building (Singapore), and patriotic education (China). According to the data, Russians have less pride in their nationality than Americans and Singaporeans (Table 6.2), and much less readiness to fight for their country than the Chinese (Table 6.3). According to the empirical data, even the most detailed and emphasized parts of Russian patriotic education – national pride and militarism – are ineffective.

Table 6.2 – The percentage of answers to the question, "How proud are you to be [nationality]?"[219]

	China	Russia	Singapore	USA
Very proud	21.7	28.7	46.8	58.2
Quite proud	56.5	47.8	42.4	29.9
Not very proud	8.7	14.4	9.1	6.2
Not at all proud	0.8	3.6	1.5	0.9
I am not [nationality]	0	0.4	0.2	3.4
No answer	12.3	0.4	0	1.4
Don't know	0	4.5	0	0

---

217 "Patriotizm i gosudarstvo," *Levada.ru*.
218 See Anna Sanina, "Patriotism of Russians and Patriotic Education in Modern Russia," *Sotsiologicheskie Issledovaniya*, no. 5 (2016): 44–53.
219 World Values Survey. Wave 6, http://www.worldvaluessurvey.org/WVSDocumentationWV6.jsp (as of January 31, 2017).

Table 6.3 – The percentage of answers to the question, "Of course, we all hope that there will not be another war, but if it were to come to that, would you be willing to fight for your country?"[220]

	China	Russia	Singapore	USA
Yes	73.5	52.0	57.8	58.6
No	19.8	21.8	18.5	39.7
No answer	3.5	2.9	0.1	1.7
Don't know	3.3	17.6	23.6	0

Despite the significant local and regional focus of patriotic education, Russians do not identify themselves with the local community. They are mostly uninterested in events at the local level, do not participate in daily activities to improve their local environment, and are not proud of their fellow citizens. Instead, they are ready to declare a general pride in the country: 85% of Russians agree with the statement, "For me, it is better to be a citizen of Russia than of any other country in the world," and 59% believe that "Russia is better than most other countries."[221] However, only 4% of Russians are proud of achievements in the educational sphere, 2% are proud of the healthcare system, 4% are proud of the economic successes, and only 9% of Russians are proud of their compatriots.[222]

According to the World Values Survey data, most citizens of the United States, China, and Singapore see themselves as part of the local community: 21.6–25% "definitely agree" with that statement, and 58.7–65.9% "agree." In contrast, Russian citizens often did not agree with this statement (24.4% "disagree" and 38.8% "definitely disagree") and are more likely see themselves "as a part of the (state) nation" (64.4%).[223] Such a priority in favor of belonging to the "entire state" but not to the local community demonstrates a low level of social responsibility in Russia. It is easy to express a sense of responsibility for what is happening in the country in general, but it is harder to take responsibility for what happens in one's own backyard.

---

220 Ibid.
221 "Gordost', patriotism i otvetstvennost'," Levada.ru, December 7, 2015, http://www.levada.ru/2015/12/07/gordost-patriotizm-i-otvetstvennost (as of January 31, 2017).
222 "Den' Narodnogo Edinstva i gordost' za stranu," Levada.ru, November 2, 2015, http://www.levada.ru/2015/11/02/den-narodnogo-edinstva-i-gordost-za-stranu/.
223 World Values Survey. Wave 6, http://www.worldvaluessurvey.org/WVSDocumentationWV6.jsp (as of January 31, 2017).

These are the consequences of and the reason for the successful reproduction of the model of patriotic education. They are also a testament to Russia's civilian inefficiency. George Schöpflin states that the implementation of communist ideology destroyed civil society and the ability of people to participate in their communities, forcing them to live in isolation and distrust.[224] It is hard to disagree with this logic, as it seems to be proved by the empirical reality. However, this style of living is not deliberate. There could be many reasons why it is still reproduced and maintained in Russian society, but the key to change is that it is principally against human and social nature.

Numerous social studies claim the necessity of trust, a protected social environment, and responsive communities in order for a human society to survive.[225] Trust, solidarity, and integration provide the basis for social order, cooperation, and cohesion required for a stable and routine social life. There is no reason to suggest that post-Soviet citizens experience universal human needs differently than other people – perhaps they have had little opportunity to reflect upon their own needs.

The problem of a pro-governmental and ideologically-based patriotic education exists not only in post-Soviet space; in many countries, much like in Russia, a political game for reproducing loyal citizens is played.[226] It is very important that this political game have working channels of communication and clarification. As I showed in Chapter 5, attempts to introduce a more liberal model of civic education had some success in the mid-1990s, but the *concerned social groups* who performed those attempts did not achieve that model's assimilation in society. That is why it so easily gave way to a moral

---

224 George Schöpflin, *Nations, Identity, Power* (London: Hurst & Company, 2000).
225 Some classical works on the subject are: Emile Durkheim, *Education and Sociology* (Glencoe, Ill: Free Press, 1956); Piotr Sztompka, *Trust: A Sociological Theory* (Cambridge: Cambridge University Press, 1999); Francis Fukuyama, *The Social Virtues and the Creation of Prosperity* (New York: Free Press, 1995).
226 See e.g.: Anzai, "Re-Examining Patriotism in Japanese Education: Analysis of Japanese Elementary School Moral Readers"; John R. Sala, "Can We Teach Patriotism?", *Improving College and University Teaching* 10, no. 1 (1962): 23–24; Kahne and Middaugh, "Is Patriotism Good for Democracy? A Study of High School Seniors' Patriotic Commitments"; Harry C. Boyte, "Civic Education and the New American Patriotism Post-9/11," *Cambridge Journal of Education* 33, no. 1 (2003): 85–100.

dimension of patriotic education, which flourishes today in tandem with militarism.

Those concerned social groups, commonly known as the liberal intelligentsia (*liberal'naya intelligentsiya*), educated intellectuals, or the creative class, are undoubtedly an unstudied phenomenon, and it is difficult to judge whether or not they constitute a more or less integrated community. In Russia, a certain number of people understand the danger of blind patriotism and appreciate the need for civic education and critical enlightenment. Nevertheless, they mostly exist outside the school environment and within the universities, research institutes, small businesses, and creative and innovative management. They are mostly concentrated in the big cities, especially in Moscow and Saint Petersburg, while the rural areas are characterized by more conservative and traditional nostalgic attitudes. The adherents of liberal and democratic values are in the geographical and numerical minority, but their weakness is not in numbers but in the tactics they chose to articulate their position.

After the collapse of the Soviet Union, a brand new liberal-oriented community began following the general tactics of the denial of patriotism. The liberal intelligentsia denied patriotism, together with Marxism-Leninism, government planning, and national ideology, in an absolutely categorical manner, without explanations as to what exactly was wrong with that system and why its revival should be avoided in the future. The tool of simple and catchy explanations is very important for spreading new ideas,[227] and ideas of democracy, liberalism, and civic education were really new in the New Russia.

The thoughts expressed in the liberal-oriented mass media, as well as in scholarly papers, do not reach the middle layers of Russian society, including teachers, school administrators, and local counselors. There is a problem with intergroup communication in Russia, in particular a problem of a lack of mechanisms to broadcast ideas which, although obvious to the liberal intelligentsia, are unclear to other groups in society.

The Internet, contrary to expectations, does not help. For some reason, those who understand the futility of jingoism and the mechanisms of its distri-

---

227 See Le Bon, *Psychology of Crowds*.

bution form conditionally closed online communities instead of raising awareness.[228] One of the common types of such communities is associated with political irony. In these communities, the manifestations of national chauvinism are subject to sophisticated criticism and ridicule, the meaning of which is not always clear to "ordinary" Russian citizens. For example, Russian writer and blogger Leonid Kaganov mocked the case of the "unpatriotic" math textbook (see Chapter 4) in a widely shared article loaded with irony and sarcasm. Stressing the absurdity of the situation, Kaganov wrote that he would create his own patriotic math textbook and obtain "money from the state order." Among the textbook's proposed problems are:

> *In a class of 57 children, one child is the daughter of a liberal. How many normal children are studying in the class?*
>
> *In the USSR, a loaf of bread cost 5 pennies [kopeks]. In the 1990s, it cost 1,000 rubles. How many times has [President Boris] Yeltsin ruined people's lives? (Don't use "inflation," "denomination," and other incomprehensible words in your explanation.)*
>
> *In the years of Stalinist repression, 3 million of our citizens were killed, but the enemy writer [Alexander] Solzhenitsyn thinks the number was 9 times higher. How many millions of our citizens did Solzhenitsyn bury alive?*
>
> *The Patriarch's prayer enhances the reliability of space rockets by 7 times, and the Metropolitan's prayer by 3 times. How much will the reliability of our space rockets increase if the Patriarch and the Metropolitan pray together?*[229]

This example is not unique. The Russian Internet is home to many communities that ironically share fanatically patriotic photos and news related to the conservative angles of nationhood, support of the state, Soviet history, and

---

228 I suggest that such communities be called "conditionally cognitively closed." Most of them are formally open to the public, but in order to participate, one should perceive the situation in the same ironical way as the other participants. See Anna Sanina, "Visual Political Irony in Russian New Media," *Discourse, Context & Media* 6 (2014): 11–21; Sanina, "Competing for a citizen: 'Visible' and 'invisible' forms of state identity in Russia"; Sanina, "'Whom Are You Kidding?' Visual Political Irony in Contemporary Russia."
229 Leonid Kaganov, "S Dnëm Znanii," September 1, 2016, https://lleo.me/dnevnik/2016/09/01.html (as of January 31, 2017).

militarism.[230] The purpose of these actions is to show that jingoism distorts the concept of patriotism to a comical degree and leads to the substitution of concepts, turning the philosophical concept of love of the Motherland into a subject of political manipulation.

Irony and satire, while amusing, are not the best way to make one's voice heard. The majority of Russians do not understand this kind of political sarcasm. Moreover, some of the jokes, particularly those associated with the Great Patriotic War, are genuinely experienced as sacrilege and a desecration of a family's tragic history. This only increases the gap in communication and culture between different strata of the Russian society, especially between a small number of pro-Western liberal intelligentsia and the mass of "ordinary Russians."

The cultural trauma[231] of the Soviet times cannot be treated quickly and intensively using in-group sarcasm. In a crisis, people prefer to rely on the most familiar attitudes and values, which historically seem to work better than any new, unknown, and unexplained concept or logic. These form a social background of revealing the model of patriotic education in contemporary Russia.

This book is a step forward in understanding that the problem of patriotism is not primarily political, but largely social. It has its roots in the social values, attitudes, and behavior of educational agents and the broader society. It demonstrates, among other things, the critical problem in communication between social groups. Its solution cannot come from somewhere outside, but should be elaborated within the society as a meaningful and reflexive community.

---

230 See e.g.: Illjustrirovannyj zhurnal 'Potsreotizm' [Illustrated Journal 'Potsreotizm'] http://potsreotizm.livejournal.com; Svobodnie novosti [Free News] http://vk.com/narod_protiv; Politicheskij jumor i ostrosjuzhetnaja satira [Political Humour and Extremely Topical Satire] https://www.facebook.com/PoliticanaRu; Sanina, "Competing for a citizen: 'Visible' and 'invisible' forms of state identity in Russia"; Sanina, "'Whom Are You Kidding?' Visual Political Irony in Contemporary Russia"; Sanina, "Visual Political Irony in Russian New Media."
231 Alexander et al., *Cultural Trauma and Collective Identity*.

Bibliography

Publications in English

Agadjanian, Alexander. "Exploring Russian Religiosity as a Source of Morality Today." In *Multiple Moralities and Religions in Post-Soviet*, edited by Jarrett Zigon, 16–26. New York: Berghahn Books, 2011.

Alexander, Jeffrey C., Ron Eyerman, Bernard Giesen, Neil Smelser, and Piotr Sztompka. *Cultural Trauma and Collective Identity*. California: University of California Press, 2004.

Allison, Clinton B., and Lloyd P. Williams. "Patriotism: Irrational and Rational." *The Educational Forum* 35, no. 2 (1971): 235–38.

Anzai, Shinobu. "Re-Examining Patriotism in Japanese Education: Analysis of Japanese Elementary School Moral Readers." *Educational Review* 67, no. 4 (2015): 436–58.

Baldwin, Rowenna Jane. "Rethinking Patriotic Education in the Russian Federation." University of Warwick, 2011.

Ben-Porath, Sigal. "Civic Virtue Out of Necessity: Patriotism and Democratic Education." *Theory and Research in Education* 5, no. 1 (2007): 41–59.

Blattberg, Charles. "We Are All Compatriots." In *Rooted Cosmopolitanism: Canada and the World*, edited by Will Kymlicka and Kathy Walker, 105–128. Vancouver: UBC Press, 2012.

Borusiak, Lyubov. "Soccer as a Catalyst of Patriotism." *Sociological Research* 48, no. 4 (2009): 57–81.

Bourdieu, Pierre. *Sociology in Question*. London: Sage, 1993.

———. *The Logic of Practice*. Stanford: Stanford University Press, 1990.

———. "Vive La Crise!: For Heterodoxy in Social Science." *Theory and Society* 17, no. 5 (1988): 773–87.

———. *Distinction: A Social Critique of the Judgement of Taste*. Cambridge: Harvard University Press, 1984.

———. *The State Nobility: Elite Schools in the Field of Power*. Stanford: Stanford University Press, 1998.

Boyte, Harry. "Civic Education and the New American Patriotism Post-9/11." *Cambridge Journal of Education* 33, no. 1 (2003): 85–100.

Chua, Shuyi et al. "Rethinking Critical Patriotism: A Case of Constructive Patriotism in Social Studies Teachers in Singapore." *Asia Pacific Journal of Education*, 2016.

Danesi, Marcel. *Cool: The Signs and Meanings of Adolescence*. Toronto: University of Toronto Press, 1994.

Daucé, Françoise, Marlène Laruelle, Anne Le Huérou, and Kathy Rousselet. "Introduction: What Does It Mean to Be a Patriot?" *Europe-Asia Studies* 67, no. 1 (2015): 1–7.

Dawisha, Karen. *Putin's Kleptocracy: Who Owns Russia?* New York: Simon & Schuster, 2015.

Dower, Nigel, and John Williams, eds. *Global Citizenship: A Critical Introduction.* New York: Routledge, 2002.

Dubin, Boris V. "Orthodoxy in a Social Context." *Russian Social Science Review* 39, no. 3 (1998): 40–45.

Durkheim, Emile. *Education and Sociology.* Glencoe, Ill: Free Press, 1956.

Fagan, Geraldine. *Believing in Russia: Religious Policy After Communism.* New York: Routledge, 2013.

Faraday, George. *Revolt of the Filmmakers: The Struggle for Artistic Autonomy and the Fall of the Soviet Film Industry.* Philadelphia: Pennsylvania State University Press, 2000.

Ferguson, Shelagh. "A Global Culture of Cool? Generation Y and Their Perception of Coolness." *Young Consumers* 12, no. 3 (2011): 265–75.

Fukuyama, Francis. *The Social Virtues and the Creation of Prosperity.* New York: Free Press, 1995.

Garrard, John Gordon, and Carol Garrard. *Russian Orthodoxy Resurgent: Faith and Power in the New Russia.* Princeton: Princeton University Press, 2008.

Goode, J. Paul. "Russian Patriotism without Patriots? Interviews (in Perm and Tyumen) Reveal the Limitations of Patriotic Education." *PONARS Eurasia Policy Memo*, no. 446 (2016): 1–8. http://www.ponarseurasia.org/memo/russian-patriotism-without-patriots.

Greeley, Andrew. "A Religious Revival in Russia?" *Journal for the Scientific Study of Religion* 33, no. 3 (1994): 253–72.

Hand, Michael, and Joanne Pearce. "Patriotism in British Schools: Principles, Practices and Press Hysteria." *Educational Philosophy and Theory* 41, no. 4 (2009): 453–65.

———. "Patriotism in British Schools: Teachers' and Students' Perspectives." *Educational Studies* 37, no. 4 (2011): 405–18.

Hannerz, Ulf. *Transnational Connections: Culture, People, Places.* London and New York: Routledge, 1996.

Haynes, Bruce. "History Teaching for Patriotic Citizenship in Australia." *Educational Philosophy and Theory* 41, no. 4 (2009): 424–40.

Hoffman, Lisa. "Autonomous Choices and Patriotic Professionalism: On Governmentality in Late-Socialist China." *Economy and Society* 35, no. 4 (2016): 550–70.

Hoffmann, David Lloyd. *Stalinist Values: The Cultural Norms of Soviet Modernity, 1917–1941.* Ithaca and London: Cornell University Press, 2003.

Janmaat, Jan Germen, and Nelli Piattoeva. "Citizenship Education in Ukraine and Russia: Reconciling Nation-Building and Active Citizenship." *Comparative Education* 43, no. 4 (2007): 527–552.

Jones, Alisa. "Changing the Past to Build the Future: History Education in Post-Mao China." University of Leeds, 2007.

Kahne, Joseph, and Ellen Middaugh. "Is Patriotism Good for Democracy? A Study of High School Seniors' Patriotic Commitments." *Phi Delta Kappan* 4 (2006): 600–607.

Kasamara, Valeria, and Anna Sorokina. "Post-Soviet Collective Memory: Russian Youths about Soviet Past." *Communist and Post-Communist Studies* 48, no. 2–3 (2015): 137–45.

Kenez, Peter. *The Birth of the Propaganda State: Soviet Methods of Mass Mobilization, 1917–1929.* Cambridge: Cambridge University Press, 1985.

Knox, Zoe Katrina. *Russian Society and the Orthodox Church: Religion in Russia after Communism.* New York: RoutledgeCurzon, 2005.

Kong, Lily, and Brenda S.a. Yeoh. "The Construction of National Identity through the Production of Ritual and Spectacle An Analysis of National Day Parades in Singapore." *Political Geography* 16, no. 3 (1997): 213–39.

Lane, Christel. "Legitimacy and Power in the Soviet Union Through Socialist Ritual." *British Journal of Political Science* 14, no. 2 (1984): 207.

Laruelle, Marlène. "Patriotic Youth Clubs in Russia. Professional Niches, Cultural Capital and Narratives of Social Engagement." *Europe-Asia Studies* 67, no. 1 (2015): 8–27.

———. *In the Name of the Nation.* New York: Palgrave Macmillan US, 2009.

———. "Rethinking Russian Nationalism: Historical Continuity, Political Diversity, and Docyrinal Fragmentation," in *Russian Nationalism and the National Reassertion of Russia*, ed. Marlène Laruelle (London: Routledge, 2009), 13–48.

Lassila, Jussi. *The Quest for an Ideal Youth in Putin's Russia II: The Search for Distinctive Conformism in the Political Communication of Nashi, 2005–2009.* Stuttgart: ibidem Press, 2014.

Le Bon, Gustave. *Psychology of Crowds.* Southampton, UK: Sparkling Books Ltd, 2009.

Lee, Lena, and Thomas Misco. "All for One or One for All: An Analysis of the Concepts of Patriotism and Others in Multicultural Korea Through Elementary Moral Education Textbooks." *Asia-Pacific Education Researcher* 23, no. 3 (2014): 727–34.

Lovell, Stephen. "Power, Personalism, and Provisioning in Russian History." *Kritika: Explorations in Russian and Eurasian History* 9, no. 2 (2008): 373–88.

Lucky, Michael. "Soviet Officer: A Credible Adversary." Maxwell Air Force Base, Alabama, 1986.

McConnell, Michael W. "Don't Neglect the Little Platoons." In *For Love of Country?*, edited by Joshua Cohen and Martha C. Nussbaum, 78–84. Boston: Beacon Press, 2002.

Nikolayenko, Olena. "Contextual Effects on Historical Memory: Soviet Nostalgia among Post-Soviet Adolescents." *Communist and Post-Communist Studies*, 2008, 243–59.

Nussbaum, Martha. "Patriotism and Cosmopolitanism." In *For Love of Country?*, edited by Joshua Cohen and Martha C. Nussbaum, 3–20. Boston: Beacon Press, 2002.

Oushakine, Sergei. *The Patriotism of Despair: Nation, War, and Loss in Russia.* New York: Cornell University Press, 2009.

Papkova, Irina. "The Freezing of Historical Memory? The Post-Soviet Russian Orthodox Church and the Council of 1917." In *Religion, Morality, and Community in Post-Soviet Societies*, edited by Mark Steinberg and Catherine Wanner, 55–84. Bloomington and Indianapolis: Indiana University Press, 2008.

Parker, C. S. "Symbolic versus Blind Patriotism: Distinction without Difference?" *Political Research Quarterly* 63, no. 1 (2010): 97–114.

"Patriotic Education." *Khodorkovsky.com*, August 31, 2016. https://www.khodorkovsky.com/patriotic-education/.

Rapoport, Anatoli. "Patriotic Education in Russia: Stylistic Move or a Sign of Substantive Counter-Reform?" *The Educational Forum* 73, no. 2 (2009): 141–52.

Reay, Diane. "'It's All Becoming a Habitus': Beyond the Habitual Use of Habitus in Educational Research." *British Journal of Sociology of Education* 25, no. 4 (2004): 431–44.

Rieber, Robert W., and Robert J. Kelly. "Substance and Shadow: Images of the Enemy." In *The Psychology of War and Peace: The Image of the Enemy*, edited by Robert W. Rieber, 3–40. New York, New York, USA: Plenum Press, 2001.

Rousselet, Kathy. "The Church in the Service of the Fatherland." *Europe-Asia Studies* 67, no. 1 (2015): 49–67.

Sakwa, Richard. "Christian Democracy in Russia." *Religion, State and Society* 20, no. 2 (1992).

Sala, John R. "Can We Teach Patriotism?" *Improving College and University Teaching* 10, no. 1 (1962): 23–24.

Sanina, Anna. "Citizenship and Civic Values in Modern Russia." In *Citizenship, Inclusion or Exclusion? A Contemporary Survey*, edited by S. J. Maldoran, 51–57. Oxford: Inter-Disciplinary Press, 2011.

———. "Competing for a Citizen: 'Visible' and 'Invisible' forms of State Identity in Russia." *Journal of Eurasian Studies* 3, no. 2 (2012): 126–46.

———. "'Whom Are You Kidding?' Visual Political Irony in Contemporary Russia." *Forum: Qualitative Social Research*, forthcoming (2017).

———. "Visual Political Irony in Russian New Media." *Discourse, Context & Media* 6 (2014): 11–21.

Schatz, Robert T., Ervin Staub, and Howard Lavine. "On the Varieties of National Attachment: Blind Versus Constructive Patriotism." *Political Psychology* 20, no. 1 (1999): 151–74.

Schöpflin, George. *Nations, Identity, Power*. London: Hurst & Company, 2000.

Sherlock, Thomas. "Russian Politics and the Soviet Past: Reassessing Stalin and Stalinism under Vladimir Putin." *Communist and Post-Communist Studies* 49, no. 1 (2016): 45–59.

Shinar, Chaim. "Conspiracy Narratives in Russian Politics: From Stalin to Putin," November 4, 2016. https://ssrn.com/abstract=2864403.

Sneider, Daniel. "Textbooks and Patriotic Education: Wartime Memory Formation in China and Japan." *Asia-Pacific Review* 20, no. 1 (2013): 35–54.

Sperling, Valerie. "Making the Public Patriotic: Militarism and Anti-Militarism in Russia." In *Russian Nationalism and the National Reassertion of Russia*, edited by Marlène Laruelle, 218–71. Routledge, 2009.

Szekely, Beatrice. "The New Soviet Educational Reform." *Comparative Education Review* 30, no. 3 (1986): 321–43.

Sztompka, Piotr. *Trust: A Sociological Theory*. Cambridge: Cambridge University Press, 1999.

"Teachers: OECD Data," 2013. https://data.oecd.org/eduresource/teachers.htm.

Tsyrlina-Spady, Tatyana, and Michael Lovorn. "A Curriculum of Ideology: Use and Abuse of Modern History Education in Russia and the United States." *International Dialogues on Education: Past and Present* 2, no. 2 (2015).

———. "Patriotism, History Teaching, and History Textbooks in Russia: What Was Old Is New Again." In *Globalisation, Ideology and Politics of Education Reforms*, 41–57. Cham: Springer International Publishing, 2015.

Tsyrlina-Spady, Tatyana, and Alan Stoskopf. "Russian History Textbooks in the Putin Era: Heroic Leaders Demand Loyal Citizens." In *Globalisation and Historiography of National Leaders: Symbolic Representations in School Textbooks*, edited by Joseph Zajda, Tatyana Tsyrlina-Spady, and Michael Lovorn, 15–33. Dordrecht: Springer, 2017.

Tumarkin, Nina. "Myth and Memory in Soviet Society." *Society* 24, no. 6 (1987): 69–72.

Waghid, Yusef. "Patriotism and Democratic Citizenship Education in South Africa: On the (Im)possibility of Reconciliation and Nation Building." *Educational Philosophy and Theory* 41, no. 4 (2009): 39–409.

Wang, Chee Keng John, Angeline Khoo, Chor Boon Goh, Steven Tan, and S. Gopinathan. "Patriotism and National Education: Perceptions of Trainee Teachers in Singapore." *Asia Pacific Journal of Education* 26, no. 1 (2006): 51–64.

Wasmuth, Jennifer. "Russian Orthodoxy between State and Nation." In *Eastern Orthodox Encounters of Identity and Otherness*, edited by Andrii Krawchuk and Thomas Bremer, 17–27. New York: Palgrave Macmillan US, 2014.

Wesson, Robert G. "The Military in Soviet Society." *The Russian Review* 30, no. 2 (1971): 139–45.

Westheimer, Joel. *Pledging Allegiance: The Politics of Patriotism in America's Schools*. New York and London: Teachers College Press, 2007.

White, Brent T. "Ritual, Emotion, and Political Belief: The Search for the Constitutional Limit to Patriotic Education in Public Schools." Arizona Legal Studies, 2009. http://ssrn.com/abstract=1344480.

Yurchak, Alexei. *Everything Was Forever, Until It Was No More: The Last Soviet Generation*. Princeton: Princeton University Press, 2006.

Zhiyuan, Tang. "Rethinking the Problem of Patriotic Education in the Subject of History in High Schools." *Chinese Education & Society* 32, no. 6 (1999): 78–81.

Publications in Russian

"Assotsiatsiia Stiag," n.d. http://stjag.ru.

"Assotsiatsiia Vitiazei," n.d. http://asvityazi.ru.

Abramov, Andrei. "Patrioticheskaia ideologiia v Rossii: etapy evoliutsii." In *Molodezhnaia politika, vospitatel'naia i patrioticheskaia rabota: praktika XXI veka*, edited by Mikhail Iudin, 6–14. Moscow: FGBOU VPO "RGUTiS," 2014.

Andreevskaia, Natalia. "Vospitatel'naia rabota na urokakh istorii." *Istoricheskii zhurnal*, no. 13 (1937): 89–95.

Balashov, Aleksey. "Rossiiskaja armiia: smena modeli." *Mir Rossii* 23, no. 4 (2014): 148–77.

Bikbulatova, Elena. "Proekt v detskom sadu 'Den' Pobedy'. Mladshaia gruppa." *Kladovaia razvlechenii*, 2016. http://kladraz.ru/blogs/elena-konstantinovna-bikbulatova/proekt-den-pobedy.html.

Boldyrev, Nikolai. *Vospitanie sovetskogo patriotizma u shkol'nikov*. Moscow: Pravda, 1949.

Chernykh, Alexander. "Prem'er kak primer." *Kommersant*, February 8, 2012. http://www.kommersant.ru/doc-rm/1868451.

RF Federal State Statistics Service. "Chislo religioznykh organizatsii, zaregistrirovannykh v Rossiiskoi Federatsii na 1 ianvaria 2015." *Gks.ru*, n.d. http://www.gks.ru/bgd/regl/b15_11/IssWWW.exe/Stg/d01/11-03.htm.

"Den' Konstitutsii." *Levada.ru*, December 8, 2016. http://www.levada.ru/2016/12/08/den-konstitutsii/.

"Den' Narodnogo Edinstva i gordost' za stranu." *Levada.ru*, November 2, 2015. http://www.levada.ru/2015/11/02/den-narodnogo-edinstva-i-gordost-za-stranu/.

"Detskaia organizatsiia Ritm imeni voina-internatsionalista Gennadiia Sergeevicha Boltneva," n.d. verhspas.68edu.ru/vospitanie/ritm.htm.

Efimova, Anastasiia. "Zabrat' vse knigi da szhech'." *Vesti.ru*, January 16, 2016. http://www.vesti.ru/doc.html?id=2708265.

Eliazberg, Nataliia, ed. *Grazhdanskoe obrazovaniie - pedagogicheskii, sotsial'nii i kul'turnii fenomen*. St. Petersburg: Soiuz, 2006.

Froumin, Isak. "Grazhdanskoe obrazovanie: spornye momenty i vozmozhnye tendentsii." *Direktor Shkoly* 5 (1997): 57–66.

Gofman, Alexander. "Sotsiologiia i grazhdanskaia religiia v Rossii." In *Sotsiologiia i sovremennaia Rossiia*, 84–107. Moscow: SU HSE, 2003.

Gokhberg, Leonid, Irina Zabaturina, and Natalia Kovaleva, eds. *Indicatory obrazovaniia: 2016 : Statisticheskii Sbornik*. Moscow: NRU HSE, 2016. https://www.hse.ru/data/2016/03/21/1128209800/Индикаторы образования 2016.pdf.

Golunov, Serguei. "Patrioticheskoe vospitanie v Rossii: za i protiv." *Voprosy Obrazovaniia* 3 (2012): 258–73. https://vo.hse.ru/2012--3/99472158.html.

"Gordost', Patriotism i otvetstvennost'." *Levada.ru*, December 7, 2015. http://www.levada.ru/2015/12/07/gordost-patriotizm-i-otvetstvennost/.

Gurevich, Vera. *Vladimir Putin. Roditeli. Druz'ia. Uchitelia.* 2nd ed. St. Petersburg: Izdatel'stvo Iuridicheskogo Instituta, 2004.

Idel'chik, Yakov. *Patrioticheskoe vospitanie shkol'nikov (Iz opyta)*. Minsk: Narodnaia asveta, 1968.

Ioffe, Andrei. "Sovremennye vyzovy i riski razvitiia grazhdanskogo obrazovaniia v sovremennoi Rossii." *Prepodavanie istorii i obschestvoznaniia v shkole* 9 (2006): 19–24.

Ivaniushina, Valeria, and Daniil Alexandrov. "Is there a differentiation of teachers in the Russian school system?" *Sotsiologicheskie Issledovaniya*, no. 9 (2016): 59–65.

Kaganov, Leonid. "S Dnëm znanii," September 1, 2016. https://lleo.me/dnevnik/2016/09/01.html.

Kaliukov, Evgenii. "V Rossiiskie shkoly postupit 7 mln uchebnikov Putina i Rotenberga po dzudo." *rbc.ru*, June 30, 2016. http://www.rbc.ru/society/30/06/2016/57752e6d9a79472c97f32963.

Kolesnichenko, Svetlana. "Dukhovno-nravstvennoe vospitanie obuchaiuschikhsia vo vneurochnoi deiatel'nosti." *1 sentiabria*, 2012. https://festival.1september.ru/articles/607957/.

Kondakova, Liudmila. "Klassnii chas na temu 'Krym - nash!'" *Mul'tiurok*, March 20, 2016. https://multiurok.ru/milakonda/files/klassnyi-chas-na-tiemu-krym-nash.html.

Konobulova, Raima. "Patrioticheskoe obuchenie i vospitanie na urokakh fiziki." *World of Teacher*, October 31, 2015. http://worldofteacher.com/9218-patrioticheskoe-obuchenie-i-vospitanie-na-urokah-fiziki.html.

Konovalov, Valeriy. "Patriarkh Aleksii: My prazdnuem spasenie naroda." *Trud, N 206*, November 3, 2005. http://www.trud.ru/article/03-11-2005/96041_patriarx_aleksij_my_prazdnuem_spasenie_naroda.html.

Kozenko, Andrei. "Patrioticheskoe vychitanie," April 8, 2014. https://www.znak.com/2014-04-08/pochemu_odin_iz_samyh_populyarnyh_uchebnikov_po_matematike_ne_proshel_gosudarstvennuyu_ekspertizu.

Kozhabaev, Kairzhan. "Patrioticheskoe vospitanie uchashchihsia na urokah matematiki i vo vneklassnoi rabote." *Matemetika v Shkole*, no. 1 (1978): 19–22.

Lebedeva, Ol'ga. "Patrioticheskoe vospitanie: vernopoddannicheskoe ili grazhdanskoe?" *Pedagogika* 9 (2003): 77–82.

Levanova, Elena, Svetlana Popova (Smolik), Margarita Prokokhina, Tat'iana Pushkariova, and Aleksei Korshunov. *Metodicheskie rekomendatsii dlia starshego vozhatogo*. Moscow: MPGU, 2015. https://рдш.рф/docs?page=2.

Levkin, Andrey. "Document kak dokument. Patriotism kak patriotizm." *Polit.ru*, 2015. http://polit.ru/article/2015/04/06/al060415.

Lunacharsky, Anatoly. *Moral' s marksistskoi tochki zreniia*. Sevastopol': Proletarii, 1925.

Magun, Vladimir, and Leokadiia Drobizheva, eds. *Grazhdanskie, etnicheskie i religioznye identichnosti v sovremennoi Rossii*. Moscow: Institute of Sociology of the Russian Academy of Sciences (ISRAS), 2006.

"Mamu Shkol'nitsy vozmutili absurdnye otvety na zadachki pro rubli i flomastery." *NGS. Novosti*, October 11, 2016.

Mikriukov, Vasilii. *Voenno-patrioticheskoe vospitanie v shkole: 1–11 klassy*. Moscow: VAKO, 2009.

Milovidov, Arsenii. *Kommunisticheskaiia nravstvennost' i voenno-patrioticheskoe vospitanie*. Moscow: Znanie, 1979.

"Na shkol'noi olimpiade vernyi otvet okazalsia matemticheski nepravil'nym. Zato patriotichnym." *Meduza*, October 11, 2016.

Nikiforova, Elena. "Voenno-patrioticheskoe vospitanie uchashchikhsia na urokakh matematiki." *1 Sentiabria*, 2005. http://festival.1september.ru/articles/212619/.

"O rossiiskom dvizhenii shkol'nikov." *Fond Obshchestvennoe Mnenie*, November 16, 2015. http://fom.ru/Obraz-zhizni/12394.

Omel'chenko, Elena, and Hilary Pilkington, eds. *S chego nachinaetsia Rodina: Molodezh' v labirintah patriotizma*. Ul'ianovsk: Ul'ianovskii State University, 2012.

"Osnovy sotsial'noi kontseptsii Russkoi Pravoslavnoi Tserkvi," *Pravmir.ru*, 2000, http://www.pravmir.ru/osnovyi-sotsialnoy-kontseptsii-russkoy-pravoslavnoy-tserkvi.

"Patriotizm i gosudarstvo." *Levada.ru*, April 29, 2015. http://www.levada.ru/2015/04/29/patriotizm-i-gosudarstvo/.

Popkov, Roman. "Yunarmiya Generala Shoigu." *Openrussia.org*, August 12, 2016. https://openrussia.org/media/140099.

"Prepodavatelia Irkutskogo Gosudarstvennogo universiteta uvolili za nedostatochno patriotichnye vzgliady." *Mel.fm*, November 16, 2016. http://mel.fm/2016/11/16/no_patriot.

Putin, Vladimir. "Beseda s finalistami konkursa 'Moi dom, moi gorod, moia strana.'" *Kremlin.ru*, June 5, 2003. http://www.kremlin.ru/events/president/transcripts/22021.

———. "Vstrecha s aktivom Kluba liderov." *Kremlin.ru*, February 3, 2016. http://kremlin.ru/events/president/news/51263.

Raikin, Konstantin. "My kleveshchem, donosim i opiat' khotim v kletku." *Meduza.io*, October 24, 2016. https://meduza.io/feature/2016/10/24/my-kleveschem-donosim-i-opyat-hotim-v-kletku.

"Rossiiane o dukhovnosti," *Fond Obschestvennoe Mnenie*, July 3, 2014. http://fom.ru/TSennosti/11589.

Samarina, Alexandra. "Patrioty dorogo stoiat." *Novaya Gazeta*, July 21, 2005. http://www.ng.ru/politics/2005-07-21/3_patrioty.html.

Sanina, Anna. "Patriotism of Russians and Patriotic Education in Modern Russia." *Sotsiologicheskie Issledovaniya*, no. 5 (2016): 44–53.

Shilov, Igor', and Anna Petii. *Dukhovno-nravstvennoe i patrioticheskoe vospitanie molodezhi na pravoslavnykh traditsiiakh rossiiskogo voinstva*. Volgograd: Korifei, 2011.

"Shoigu: osnovnaia zadacha Yunarmii - vospitat' patriotov RF, a ne voennykh," May 28, 2016. http://special.tass.ru/armiya-i-opk/3321648.

Simonenko, Boris. *Nachal'naia Voennaia Podgotovka*. Briansk: Poligram-Plus, 2011.

Somov, Vladimir. "Istoriia kak uchebnyi predmet v sovetskoi sisteme shkol'nogo vospitaniia vo vtoroi polovine 1930-kh godov." *Liudi i teksty. Istoricheskii al'manakh*, no. 6 (2014): 257–70.

"Stanislav Govorukhin predlozhil vossozdat' pionerskuiu organizatsiiu." *Novaya Gazeta*, February 16, 2012. https://www.novayagazeta.ru/news/2012/02/16/53966-stanislav-govoruhin-predlozhil-vossozdat-pionerskuyu-organizatsiyu.

Sungurov, Alexander. "Grazhdanskoe obrazovanie: v poiskakh optimal'noi modeli regional'nogo razvitiia." In *Sotsial'noe partnerstvo i razvitie institutov grazhdanskogo obschestva v regionakh i munitsipalitetakh: Praktika mezhsektornogo vzaimodeistviia*, 275–84. Moscow: Agentstvo Social'noi Informatsii, 2008.

Tislenkova, Elena. *Grazhdansko-patrioticheskoe vospitanie v 6–7 klassakh*. Volgograd, 2007.

"Tsennosti: religioznost'," *Fond Obshchestvennoe Mnenie*, June 14, 2013. http://fom.ru/TSennosti/10953.

Ul'ianova, Anna. *Detskie i shkol'nye gody Il'icha*. Moscow: Malysh, 1988.

"Urok Muzhestva." *Otdel po blagotvoritel'nosti i sotsial'nomu sluzheniiu Moskovskoi Eparkhii*, May 12, 2010. http://blago-mepar.ru/news/urok_muzhestva/.

"V Minobrnauki osudili antipatriotichnye vysskazyvaniia studentki MGIMO." *Tass.ru*, October 25, 2016. http://tass.ru/obschestvo/3732855.

Varlamov, Ilya. "Organizatorov 'Bessmertnogo Polka' ulichili v nabore massovki." *Livejournal.com*, May 7, 2016. http://varlamov.ru/1705935.html.

"V Rossii sozdano voenno-patrioticheskoe dvizhenie Yunarmiya." *Interfax*, August 3, 2016. http://www.interfax.ru/russia/521787.

"Velikaia Otechestvennaia voina v semeinoi istorii," *Fond Obshchestvennoe Mnenie*, May 6, 2015. http://fom.ru/Proshloe/12142.

Veksler, Igor', and Rimma Kharitonova, eds. *Vtoraia stupen' sovetskoi trudovoi shkoly. Organizatsiia. Soderzhanie. Metody*. Moscow, 1929.

"Vezhlivye liudi i kot." *Novii Krym*, December 3, 2014. http://www.newscrimea.ru/vezhlivye-lyudi-i-kot/.

"Vezhlivye liudi kak novyi obraz rossiiskoi armii." *RIA Novosti*, May 16, 2014. https://ria.ru/defense_safety/20140516/1007988002.html.

Vladlenov, Aleksey. "Zachem nam parad pobedy. Otvet sviaschennika."
Defendingrussia.ru, May 7, 2016.

"Vlast' v Rossii: po Konstitutsii i po zhizni." *Wciom.ru*, December 11, 2014.
http://wciom.ru/index.php?id=236&uid=115087.

Vorob'ëva, Natal'ia, and Ol'ga Sapozhnikova. *Formirovanie Patriotizma U Doshkol'nikov Na Primere Predstavlenii O Vooruzhënnyh Silah*. Moscow: Itellekt-Center, 2016.

"Voenno-patrioticheskoe dvizhenie Yunarmiya," 2016, http://www.youngarmiya.ru/2016/07/vse-otvety-o-yongarmiy.html.

"Votserkovlennost' Pravoslavnykh," *Fond Obshchestvennoe Mnenie*, July 3, 2014. http://fom.ru/TSennosti/11587.

Yakoreva, Anastasiia. "Stalin, plan Dallesa i sviataia Rus'. Chemu Nauchit Studentov vozhrozhdënnoe obshestvo 'Znanie.'" *Republic.ru*, February 6, 2016. https://republic.ru/posts/79147.

Zviagintsev, Andrey. "Durnoi son goszakaza." *Kommersant*, October 26, 2016. http://www.kommersant.ru/doc/3126654.

"Yunarmiya, Military-Patriotic Movement. Official Webpage," 2016, http://юн-армия.рф/about.

"14 Dekabria 2016 v Vorotyntse sostoialas' mezhraionnaia intellektual'naia igra 'Dukhovnye osnovy patriotizma,'" *Lyskovskaia Eparkhiia*, December 14, 2016, http://lyskovskaya-eparhya.ru/2016/12/14/14-desember-2016-v-vorotunce-sostoialas-meqeparhialnaia-igra-dyhovnue-osnovu-patriotizma/#more-67356.

Legislative acts in Russian

"Kotstitutsiia Rossiiskoi Federatsii (priniata na vsenarodnom golosovanii 12 dekabria 1993 goda)." http://base.garant.ru/10103000.

Ministerstvo Kultury SSSR, *Tipovoe polozhenie o muzee, rabotaiushchem na obshchestvennykh nachalakh, Postanovlenie ot 04/12/1978*. http://www.consultant.ru/cons/cgi/online.cgi?req=doc;base=ESU;n=21597#0.

Ministerstvo oborony RF i Ministerstvo obrazovaniia i nauki RF. *Ob utverzhdenii instruktsii ob organizatsii obucheniia grazhdan Rossiiskoi Federatsii nachal'nym znaniiam v oblasti oborony i ih podgotovki po osnovam voennoi sluzhby v obrazovatel'nykh uchrezhdeniiakh srednego (polnogo) obshhego obrazovaniia, Sovmestnyi prikaz № 96/134 ot 24/02/2010*. http://base.garant.ru/198025/#ixzz4SP3TqROw.

Ministerstvo obrazovaniia i nauki RF. *Primernyi stsenarii uroka dlia uchashchikhsia osnovnoi shkoly, posviashchennogo godovshhine priniatiia Kryma i Sevastopolia v sostav Rossiiskoi Federatsii*, минобрнауки.рф, 2015. Direct link: goo.gl/Uw1C3F.

Ministerstvo Obrazovaniia RF. *O kontseptsii modernizatsii rossiiskogo obrazovaniia na period do 2010, Prikaz № 393 ot 11/02/2002*. http://base.garant.ru/1588306/#block_1000#ixzz4Td8stAS3.

———. *Ob utverzhdenii federal'nogo komponenta gosudarstvennykh obrazovatel'nykh standartov nachal'nogo obshchego, osnovnogo obshchego i srednego (polnogo) obshchego obrazovaniia, Prikaz № 1089 ot 05/03/2004*. http://base.garant.ru/6150599/#ixzz4TdAFhG3P.

"O dniakh voinskoi slavy i pamiatnykh datakh Rossii, Federal'nyi zakon № 32-FZ ot 13/03/1995." http://base.garant.ru/1518352.

"O veteranakh, Federal'nyi zakon № 5-FZ ot 12/01/1995." http://base.garant.ru/10103548.

"O vnesenii izmenenii v otdel'nye zakonodatel'nye akty Rossiiskoi Federacii v chasti regulirovaniia deiatel'nosti nekommercheskikh organizatsii, vypolniaiushchikh funkcii inostrannogo agenta, Federal'nyi zakon № 80-FZ ot 20/07/2012." http://base.garant.ru/70204242.

"O voinskoi obiazannosti i voennoi sluzhbe, Federal'nyi zakon № 53-FZ ot 23/03/1998." http://base.garant.ru/178405.

"Ob obrazovanii v Rossiiskoi Federatsii, Federal'nyi zakon № 273-FZ ot 29/12/2012." http://base.garant.ru/70291362.

"Ob uvekovechenii Pobedy sovetskogo naroda v Velikoi Otechestvennoi Voine 1941–1945 godov, Federal'nyi zakon № 80-FZ ot 19/05/1995." http://base.garant.ru/1518946.

Pravitel'stvo RF. *O Gosudarstvennoi programme "Patrioticheskoe vospitanie grazhdan RF na 2001–2005 gody, Postanovlenie ot 02/10/2001, № 122."* http://base.garant.ru/1584972.

———. *O Gosudarstvennoi programme "Patrioticheskoe vospitanie grazhdan RF na 2006–2010 gody, Postanovlenie Pravitel'stva RF ot 07/11/2005, № 422."* http://base.garant.ru/188373.

———. *O Gosudarstvennoi programme "Patrioticheskoe vospitanie grazhdan RF na 2011–2015 gody, Postanovlenie Pravitel'stva RF ot 10/05/2010, № 795."* http://base.garant.ru/199483.

———. *O Gosudarstvennoi programme "Patrioticheskoe vospitanie grazhdan RF na 2016–2020 gody, Postanovlenie Pravitel'stva RF ot 10/05/2010, № 1493."* http://www.garant.ru/products/ipo/prime/doc/71196398.

President RF. *O sovershenstvovanii gosudarstvennoi politiki v oblasti patrioticheskogo vospitaniia, Ukaz № 1416 ot 20/10/2012.* http://base.garant.ru/70244894.

———. *O strategii natsional'noi bezopasnosti Rossiiskoi Federatsii, Ukaz № 683 ot 31/12/2015.* http://base.garant.ru/71296054.

"Ustav Obshcherossiiskoi obshchestvenno-gosudarstvennoi detsko-iunosheskoi organizatsii "Rossiiskoe dvizheniie shkol'nikov", priniatyi uchreditel'num s"ezdom Obshcherossiiskoi obshchestvenno-gosudarstvennoi detsko-iunosheskoi organizatsii "Rossiiskoe dvizheniie shkol'nikov", protokol № 1 ot 28/03/2016." http://www.dagminobr.ru/storage/files/rdsh/ustav.pdf.

SOVIET AND POST-SOVIET POLITICS AND SOCIETY

Edited by Dr. Andreas Umland

ISSN 1614-3515

1 Андреас Умланд (ред.)
Воплощение Европейской
конвенции по правам человека в
России
Философские, юридические и
эмпирические исследования
ISBN 3-89821-387-0

2 Christian Wipperfürth
Russland – ein vertrauenswürdiger
Partner?
Grundlagen, Hintergründe und Praxis
gegenwärtiger russischer Außenpolitik
Mit einem Vorwort von Heinz Timmermann
ISBN 3-89821-401-X

3 Manja Hussner
Die Übernahme internationalen Rechts
in die russische und deutsche
Rechtsordnung
Eine vergleichende Analyse zur
Völkerrechtsfreundlichkeit der Verfassungen
der Russländischen Föderation und der
Bundesrepublik Deutschland
Mit einem Vorwort von Rainer Arnold
ISBN 3-89821-438-9

4 Matthew Tejada
Bulgaria's Democratic Consolidation
and the Kozloduy Nuclear Power Plant
(KNPP)
The Unattainability of Closure
With a foreword by Richard J. Crampton
ISBN 3-89821-439-7

5 Марк Григорьевич Меерович
Квадратные метры, определяющие
сознание
Государственная жилищная политика в
СССР. 1921 – 1941 гг
ISBN 3-89821-474-5

6 Andrei P. Tsygankov, Pavel
A.Tsygankov (Eds.)
New Directions in Russian
International Studies
ISBN 3-89821-422-2

7 Марк Григорьевич Меерович
Как власть народ к труду приучала
Жилище в СССР – средство управления
людьми. 1917 – 1941 гг.
С предисловием Елены Осокиной
ISBN 3-89821-495-8

8 David J. Galbreath
Nation-Building and Minority Politics
in Post-Socialist States
Interests, Influence and Identities in Estonia
and Latvia
With a foreword by David J. Smith
ISBN 3-89821-467-2

9 Алексей Юрьевич Безугольный
Народы Кавказа в Вооруженных
силах СССР в годы Великой
Отечественной войны 1941-1945 гг.
С предисловием Николая Бугая
ISBN 3-89821-475-3

10 Вячеслав Лихачев и Владимир
Прибыловский (ред.)
Русское Национальное Единство,
1990-2000. В 2-х томах
ISBN 3-89821-523-7

11 Николай Бугай (ред.)
Народы стран Балтии в условиях
сталинизма (1940-е – 1950-е годы)
Документированная история
ISBN 3-89821-525-3

12 Ingmar Bredies (Hrsg.)
Zur Anatomie der Orange Revolution
in der Ukraine
Wechsel des Elitenregimes oder Triumph des
Parlamentarismus?
ISBN 3-89821-524-5

13 Anastasia V. Mitrofanova
The Politicization of Russian
Orthodoxy
Actors and Ideas
With a foreword by William C. Gay
ISBN 3-89821-481-8

14 Nathan D. Larson
    Alexander Solzhenitsyn and the
    Russo-Jewish Question
    ISBN 3-89821-483-4

15 Guido Houben
    Kulturpolitik und Ethnizität
    Staatliche Kunstförderung im Russland der
    neunziger Jahre
    Mit einem Vorwort von Gert Weisskirchen
    ISBN 3-89821-542-3

16 Leonid Luks
    Der russische „Sonderweg"?
    Aufsätze zur neuesten Geschichte Russlands
    im europäischen Kontext
    ISBN 3-89821-496-6

17 Евгений Мороз
    История «Мёртвой воды» – от
    страшной сказки к большой
    политике
    Политическое неоязычество в
    постсоветской России
    ISBN 3-89821-551-2

18 Александр Верховский и Галина
    Кожевникова (ред.)
    Этническая и религиозная
    интолерантность в российских СМИ
    Результаты мониторинга 2001-2004 гг.
    ISBN 3-89821-569-5

19 Christian Ganzer
    Sowjetisches Erbe und ukrainische
    Nation
    Das Museum der Geschichte des Zaporoger
    Kosakentums auf der Insel Chortycja
    Mit einem Vorwort von Frank Golczewski
    ISBN 3-89821-504-0

20 Эльза-Баир Гучинова
    Помнить нельзя забыть
    Антропология депортационной травмы
    калмыков
    С предисловием Кэролайн Хамфри
    ISBN 3-89821-506-7

21 Юлия Лидерман
    Мотивы «проверки» и «испытания»
    в постсоветской культуре
    Советское прошлое в российском
    кинематографе 1990-х годов
    С предисловием Евгения Марголита
    ISBN 3-89821-511-3

22 Tanya Lokshina, Ray Thomas, Mary
    Mayer (Eds.)
    The Imposition of a Fake Political
    Settlement in the Northern Caucasus
    The 2003 Chechen Presidential Election
    ISBN 3-89821-436-2

23 Timothy McCajor Hall, Rosie Read
    (Eds.)
    Changes in the Heart of Europe
    Recent Ethnographies of Czechs, Slovaks,
    Roma, and Sorbs
    With an afterword by Zdeněk Salzmann
    ISBN 3-89821-606-3

24 Christian Autengruber
    Die politischen Parteien in Bulgarien
    und Rumänien
    Eine vergleichende Analyse seit Beginn der
    90er Jahre
    Mit einem Vorwort von Dorothée de Nève
    ISBN 3-89821-476-1

25 Annette Freyberg-Inan with Radu
    Cristescu
    The Ghosts in Our Classrooms, or:
    John Dewey Meets Ceauşescu
    The Promise and the Failures of Civic
    Education in Romania
    ISBN 3-89821-416-8

26 John B. Dunlop
    The 2002 Dubrovka and 2004 Beslan
    Hostage Crises
    A Critique of Russian Counter-Terrorism
    With a foreword by Donald N. Jensen
    ISBN 3-89821-608-X

27 Peter Koller
    Das touristische Potenzial von
    Kam''janec'–Podil's'kyj
    Eine fremdenverkehrsgeographische
    Untersuchung der Zukunftsperspektiven und
    Maßnahmenplanung zur
    Destinationsentwicklung des „ukrainischen
    Rothenburg"
    Mit einem Vorwort von Kristiane Klemm
    ISBN 3-89821-640-3

28 Françoise Daucé, Elisabeth Sieca-
    Kozlowski (Eds.)
    Dedovshchina in the Post-Soviet
    Military
    Hazing of Russian Army Conscripts in a
    Comparative Perspective
    With a foreword by Dale Herspring
    ISBN 3-89821-616-0

29 Florian Strasser
    Zivilgesellschaftliche Einflüsse auf die
    Orange Revolution
    Die gewaltlose Massenbewegung und die
    ukrainische Wahlkrise 2004
    Mit einem Vorwort von Egbert Jahn
    ISBN 3-89821-648-9

30 Rebecca S. Katz
    The Georgian Regime Crisis of 2003-
    2004
    A Case Study in Post-Soviet Media
    Representation of Politics, Crime and
    Corruption
    ISBN 3-89821-413-3

31 Vladimir Kantor
    Willkür oder Freiheit
    Beiträge zur russischen Geschichtsphilosophie
    Ediert von Dagmar Herrmann sowie mit
    einem Vorwort versehen von Leonid Luks
    ISBN 3-89821-589-X

32 Laura A. Victoir
    The Russian Land Estate Today
    A Case Study of Cultural Politics in Post-
    Soviet Russia
    With a foreword by Priscilla Roosevelt
    ISBN 3-89821-426-5

33 Ivan Katchanovski
    Cleft Countries
    Regional Political Divisions and Cultures in
    Post-Soviet Ukraine and Moldova
    With a foreword by Francis Fukuyama
    ISBN 3-89821-558-X

34 Florian Mühlfried
    Postsowjetische Feiern
    Das Georgische Bankett im Wandel
    Mit einem Vorwort von Kevin Tuite
    ISBN 3-89821-601-2

35 Roger Griffin, Werner Loh, Andreas
    Umland (Eds.)
    Fascism Past and Present, West and
    East
    An International Debate on Concepts and
    Cases in the Comparative Study of the
    Extreme Right
    With an afterword by Walter Laqueur
    ISBN 3-89821-674-8

36 Sebastian Schlegel
    Der „Weiße Archipel"
    Sowjetische Atomstädte 1945-1991
    Mit einem Geleitwort von Thomas Bohn
    ISBN 3-89821-679-9

37 Vyacheslav Likhachev
    Political Anti-Semitism in Post-Soviet
    Russia
    Actors and Ideas in 1991-2003
    Edited and translated from Russian by Eugene
    Veklerov
    ISBN 3-89821-529-6

38 Josette Baer (Ed.)
    Preparing Liberty in Central Europe
    Political Texts from the Spring of Nations
    1848 to the Spring of Prague 1968
    With a foreword by Zdeněk V. David
    ISBN 3-89821-546-6

39 Михаил Лукьянов
    Российский консерватизм и
    реформа, 1907-1914
    С предисловием Марка Д. Стейнберга
    ISBN 3-89821-503-2

40 Nicola Melloni
    Market Without Economy
    The 1998 Russian Financial Crisis
    With a foreword by Eiji Furukawa
    ISBN 3-89821-407-9

41 Dmitrij Chmelnizki
    Die Architektur Stalins
    Bd. 1: Studien zu Ideologie und Stil
    Bd. 2: Bilddokumentation
    Mit einem Vorwort von Bruno Flierl
    ISBN 3-89821-515-6

42 Katja Yafimava
    Post-Soviet Russian-Belarussian
    Relationships
    The Role of Gas Transit Pipelines
    With a foreword by Jonathan P. Stern
    ISBN 3-89821-655-1

43 Boris Chavkin
    Verflechtungen der deutschen und
    russischen Zeitgeschichte
    Aufsätze und Archivfunde zu den
    Beziehungen Deutschlands und der
    Sowjetunion von 1917 bis 1991
    Ediert von Markus Edlinger sowie mit einem
    Vorwort versehen von Leonid Luks
    ISBN 3-89821-756-6

44 *Anastasija Grynenko in Zusammenarbeit mit Claudia Dathe*
    Die Terminologie des Gerichtswesens der Ukraine und Deutschlands im Vergleich
    Eine übersetzungswissenschaftliche Analyse juristischer Fachbegriffe im Deutschen, Ukrainischen und Russischen
    Mit einem Vorwort von Ulrich Hartmann
    ISBN 3-89821-691-8

45 *Anton Burkov*
    The Impact of the European Convention on Human Rights on Russian Law
    Legislation and Application in 1996-2006
    With a foreword by Françoise Hampson
    ISBN 978-3-89821-639-5

46 *Stina Torjesen, Indra Overland (Eds.)*
    International Election Observers in Post-Soviet Azerbaijan
    Geopolitical Pawns or Agents of Change?
    ISBN 978-3-89821-743-9

47 *Taras Kuzio*
    Ukraine – Crimea – Russia
    Triangle of Conflict
    ISBN 978-3-89821-761-3

48 *Claudia Šabić*
    "Ich erinnere mich nicht, aber L'viv!"
    Zur Funktion kultureller Faktoren für die Institutionalisierung und Entwicklung einer ukrainischen Region
    Mit einem Vorwort von Melanie Tatur
    ISBN 978-3-89821-752-1

49 *Marlies Bilz*
    Tatarstan in der Transformation
    Nationaler Diskurs und Politische Praxis 1988-1994
    Mit einem Vorwort von Frank Golczewski
    ISBN 978-3-89821-722-4

50 *Марлен Ларюэль (ред.)*
    Современные интерпретации русского национализма
    ISBN 978-3-89821-795-8

51 *Sonja Schüler*
    Die ethnische Dimension der Armut
    Roma im postsozialistischen Rumänien
    Mit einem Vorwort von Anton Sterbling
    ISBN 978-3-89821-776-7

52 *Галина Кожевникова*
    Радикальный национализм в России и противодействие ему
    Сборник докладов Центра «Сова» за 2004-2007 гг.
    С предисловием Александра Верховского
    ISBN 978-3-89821-721-7

53 *Галина Кожевникова и Владимир Прибыловский*
    Российская власть в биографиях I
    Высшие должностные лица РФ в 2004 г.
    ISBN 978-3-89821-796-5

54 *Галина Кожевникова и Владимир Прибыловский*
    Российская власть в биографиях II
    Члены Правительства РФ в 2004 г.
    ISBN 978-3-89821-797-2

55 *Галина Кожевникова и Владимир Прибыловский*
    Российская власть в биографиях III
    Руководители федеральных служб и агентств РФ в 2004 г.
    ISBN 978-3-89821-798-9

56 *Ileana Petroniu*
    Privatisierung in Transformationsökonomien
    Determinanten der Restrukturierungs-Bereitschaft am Beispiel Polens, Rumäniens und der Ukraine
    Mit einem Vorwort von Rainer W. Schäfer
    ISBN 978-3-89821-790-3

57 *Christian Wipperfürth*
    Russland und seine GUS-Nachbarn
    Hintergründe, aktuelle Entwicklungen und Konflikte in einer ressourcenreichen Region
    ISBN 978-3-89821-801-6

58 *Togzhan Kassenova*
    From Antagonism to Partnership
    The Uneasy Path of the U.S.-Russian Cooperative Threat Reduction
    With a foreword by Christoph Bluth
    ISBN 978-3-89821-707-1

59 *Alexander Höllwerth*
    Das sakrale eurasische Imperium des Aleksandr Dugin
    Eine Diskursanalyse zum postsowjetischen russischen Rechtsextremismus
    Mit einem Vorwort von Dirk Uffelmann
    ISBN 978-3-89821-813-9

60 Олег Рябов
    «Россия-Матушка»
    Национализм, гендер и война в России XX
    века
    С предисловием Елены Гощило
    ISBN 978-3-89821-487-2

61 Ivan Maistrenko
    Borot'bism
    A Chapter in the History of the Ukrainian
    Revolution
    With a new introduction by Chris Ford
    Translated by George S. N. Luckyj with the
    assistance of Ivan L. Rudnytsky
    ISBN 978-3-89821-697-5

62 Maryna Romanets
    Anamorphosic Texts and
    Reconfigured Visions
    Improvised Traditions in Contemporary
    Ukrainian and Irish Literature
    ISBN 978-3-89821-576-3

63 Paul D'Anieri and Taras Kuzio (Eds.)
    Aspects of the Orange Revolution I
    Democratization and Elections in Post-
    Communist Ukraine
    ISBN 978-3-89821-698-2

64 Bohdan Harasymiw in collaboration
    with Oleh S. Ilnytzkyj (Eds.)
    Aspects of the Orange Revolution II
    Information and Manipulation Strategies in
    the 2004 Ukrainian Presidential Elections
    ISBN 978-3-89821-699-9

65 Ingmar Bredies, Andreas Umland and
    Valentin Yakushik (Eds.)
    Aspects of the Orange Revolution III
    The Context and Dynamics of the 2004
    Ukrainian Presidential Elections
    ISBN 978-3-89821-803-0

66 Ingmar Bredies, Andreas Umland and
    Valentin Yakushik (Eds.)
    Aspects of the Orange Revolution IV
    Foreign Assistance and Civic Action in the
    2004 Ukrainian Presidential Elections
    ISBN 978-3-89821-808-5

67 Ingmar Bredies, Andreas Umland and
    Valentin Yakushik (Eds.)
    Aspects of the Orange Revolution V
    Institutional Observation Reports on the 2004
    Ukrainian Presidential Elections
    ISBN 978-3-89821-809-2

68 Taras Kuzio (Ed.)
    Aspects of the Orange Revolution VI
    Post-Communist Democratic Revolutions in
    Comparative Perspective
    ISBN 978-3-89821-820-7

69 Tim Bohse
    Autoritarismus statt Selbstverwaltung
    Die Transformation der kommunalen Politik
    in der Stadt Kaliningrad 1990-2005
    Mit einem Geleitwort von Stefan Troebst
    ISBN 978-3-89821-782-8

70 David Rupp
    Die Rußländische Föderation und die
    russischsprachige Minderheit in
    Lettland
    Eine Fallstudie zur Anwaltspolitik Moskaus
    gegenüber den russophonen Minderheiten im
    „Nahen Ausland" von 1991 bis 2002
    Mit einem Vorwort von Helmut Wagner
    ISBN 978-3-89821-778-1

71 Taras Kuzio
    Theoretical and Comparative
    Perspectives on Nationalism
    New Directions in Cross-Cultural and Post-
    Communist Studies
    With a foreword by Paul Robert Magocsi
    ISBN 978-3-89821-815-3

72 Christine Teichmann
    Die Hochschultransformation im
    heutigen Osteuropa
    Kontinuität und Wandel bei der Entwicklung
    des postkommunistischen Universitätswesens
    Mit einem Vorwort von Oskar Anweiler
    ISBN 978-3-89821-842-9

73 Julia Kusznir
    Der politische Einfluss von
    Wirtschaftseliten in russischen
    Regionen
    Eine Analyse am Beispiel der Erdöl- und
    Erdgasindustrie, 1992-2005
    Mit einem Vorwort von Wolfgang Eichwede
    ISBN 978-3-89821-821-4

74 Alena Vysotskaya
    Russland, Belarus und die EU-
    Osterweiterung
    Zur Minderheitenfrage und zum Problem der
    Freizügigkeit des Personenverkehrs
    Mit einem Vorwort von Katlijn Malfliet
    ISBN 978-3-89821-822-1

75 Heiko Pleines (Hrsg.)
    Corporate Governance in post-
    sozialistischen Volkswirtschaften
    ISBN 978-3-89821-766-8

76 Stefan Ihrig
    Wer sind die Moldawier?
    Rumänismus versus Moldowanismus in
    Historiographie und Schulbüchern der
    Republik Moldova, 1991-2006
    Mit einem Vorwort von Holm Sundhaussen
    ISBN 978-3-89821-466-7

77 Galina Kozhevnikova in collaboration
    with Alexander Verkhovsky and
    Eugene Veklerov
    Ultra-Nationalism and Hate Crimes in
    Contemporary Russia
    The 2004-2006 Annual Reports of Moscow's
    SOVA Center
    With a foreword by Stephen D. Shenfield
    ISBN 978-3-89821-868-9

78 Florian Küchler
    The Role of the European Union in
    Moldova's Transnistria Conflict
    With a foreword by Christopher Hill
    ISBN 978-3-89821-850-4

79 Bernd Rechel
    The Long Way Back to Europe
    Minority Protection in Bulgaria
    With a foreword by Richard Crampton
    ISBN 978-3-89821-863-4

80 Peter W. Rodgers
    Nation, Region and History in Post-
    Communist Transitions
    Identity Politics in Ukraine, 1991-2006
    With a foreword by Vera Tolz
    ISBN 978-3-89821-903-7

81 Stephanie Solywoda
    The Life and Work of
    Semen L. Frank
    A Study of Russian Religious Philosophy
    With a foreword by Philip Walters
    ISBN 978-3-89821-457-5

82 Vera Sokolova
    Cultural Politics of Ethnicity
    Discourses on Roma in Communist
    Czechoslovakia
    ISBN 978-3-89821-864-1

83 Natalya Shevchik Ketenci
    Kazakhstani Enterprises in Transition
    The Role of Historical Regional Development
    in Kazakhstan's Post-Soviet Economic
    Transformation
    ISBN 978-3-89821-831-3

84 Martin Malek, Anna Schor-
    Tschudnowskaja (Hrsg.)
    Europa im Tschetschenienkrieg
    Zwischen politischer Ohnmacht und
    Gleichgültigkeit
    Mit einem Vorwort von Lipchan Basajewa
    ISBN 978-3-89821-676-0

85 Stefan Meister
    Das postsowjetische Universitätswesen
    zwischen nationalem und
    internationalem Wandel
    Die Entwicklung der regionalen Hochschule
    in Russland als Gradmesser der
    Systemtransformation
    Mit einem Vorwort von Joan DeBardeleben
    ISBN 978-3-89821-891-7

86 Konstantin Sheiko in collaboration
    with Stephen Brown
    Nationalist Imaginings of the
    Russian Past
    Anatolii Fomenko and the Rise of Alternative
    History in Post-Communist Russia
    With a foreword by Donald Ostrowski
    ISBN 978-3-89821-915-0

87 Sabine Jenni
    Wie stark ist das „Einige Russland"?
    Zur Parteibindung der Eliten und zum
    Wahlerfolg der Machtpartei
    im Dezember 2007
    Mit einem Vorwort von Klaus Armingeon
    ISBN 978-3-89821-961-7

88 Thomas Borén
    Meeting-Places of Transformation
    Urban Identity, Spatial Representations and
    Local Politics in Post-Soviet St Petersburg
    ISBN 978-3-89821-739-2

89 Aygul Ashirova
    Stalinismus und Stalin-Kult in
    Zentralasien
    Turkmenistan 1924-1953
    Mit einem Vorwort von Leonid Luks
    ISBN 978-3-89821-987-7

90 Leonid Luks
Freiheit oder imperiale Größe?
Essays zu einem russischen Dilemma
ISBN 978-3-8382-0011-8

91 Christopher Gilley
The 'Change of Signposts' in the Ukrainian Emigration
A Contribution to the History of Sovietophilism in the 1920s
With a foreword by Frank Golczewski
ISBN 978-3-89821-965-5

92 Philipp Casula, Jeronim Perovic (Eds.)
Identities and Politics During the Putin Presidency
The Discursive Foundations of Russia's Stability
With a foreword by Heiko Haumann
ISBN 978-3-8382-0015-6

93 Marcel Viëtor
Europa und die Frage nach seinen Grenzen im Osten
Zur Konstruktion ‚europäischer Identität' in Geschichte und Gegenwart
Mit einem Vorwort von Albrecht Lehmann
ISBN 978-3-8382-0045-3

94 Ben Hellman, Andrei Rogachevskii
Filming the Unfilmable
Casper Wrede's 'One Day in the Life of Ivan Denisovich'
Second, Revised and Expanded Edition
ISBN 978-3-8382-0044-6

95 Eva Fuchslocher
Vaterland, Sprache, Glaube
Orthodoxie und Nationenbildung am Beispiel Georgiens
Mit einem Vorwort von Christina von Braun
ISBN 978-3-89821-884-9

96 Vladimir Kantor
Das Westlertum und der Weg Russlands
Zur Entwicklung der russischen Literatur und Philosophie
Ediert von Dagmar Herrmann
Mit einem Beitrag von Nikolaus Lobkowicz
ISBN 978-3-8382-0102-3

97 Kamran Musayev
Die postsowjetische Transformation im Baltikum und Südkaukasus
Eine vergleichende Untersuchung der politischen Entwicklung Lettlands und Aserbaidschans 1985-2009
Mit einem Vorwort von Leonid Luks
Ediert von Sandro Henschel
ISBN 978-3-8382-0103-0

98 Tatiana Zhurzhenko
Borderlands into Bordered Lands
Geopolitics of Identity in Post-Soviet Ukraine
With a foreword by Dieter Segert
ISBN 978-3-8382-0042-2

99 Кирилл Галушко, Лидия Смола (ред.)
Пределы падения – варианты украинского будущего
Аналитико-прогностические исследования
ISBN 978-3-8382-0148-1

100 Michael Minkenberg (ed.)
Historical Legacies and the Radical Right in Post-Cold War Central and Eastern Europe
With an afterword by Sabrina P. Ramet
ISBN 978-3-8382-0124-5

101 David-Emil Wickström
Rocking St. Petersburg
Transcultural Flows and Identity Politics in the St. Petersburg Popular Music Scene
With a foreword by Yngvar B. Steinholt
Second, Revised and Expanded Edition
ISBN 978-3-8382-0100-9

102 Eva Zabka
Eine neue „Zeit der Wirren"?
Der spät- und postsowjetische Systemwandel 1985-2000 im Spiegel russischer gesellschaftspolitischer Diskurse
Mit einem Vorwort von Margareta Mommsen
ISBN 978-3-8382-0161-0

103 Ulrike Ziemer
Ethnic Belonging, Gender and Cultural Practices
Youth Identitites in Contemporary Russia
With a foreword by Anoop Nayak
ISBN 978-3-8382-0152-8

104 Ksenia Chepikova
‚Einiges Russland' - eine zweite
KPdSU?
Aspekte der Identitätskonstruktion einer
postsowjetischen „Partei der Macht"
Mit einem Vorwort von Torsten Oppelland
ISBN 978-3-8382-0311-9

105 Леонид Люкс
Западничество или евразийство?
Демократия или идеократия?
Сборник статей об исторических дилеммах
России
С предисловием Владимира Кантора
ISBN 978-3-8382-0211-2

106 Anna Dost
Das russische Verfassungsrecht auf dem
Weg zum Föderalismus und zurück
Zum Konflikt von Rechtsnormen und
-wirklichkeit in der Russländischen Föderation
von 1991 bis 2009
Mit einem Vorwort von Alexander Blankenagel
ISBN 978-3-8382-0292-1

107 Philipp Herzog
Sozialistische Völkerfreundschaft,
nationaler Widerstand oder harmloser
Zeitvertreib?
Zur politischen Funktion der Volkskunst
im sowjetischen Estland
Mit einem Vorwort von Andreas Kappeler
ISBN 978-3-8382-0216-7

108 Marlène Laruelle (ed.)
Russian Nationalism, Foreign Policy,
and Identity Debates in Putin's Russia
New Ideological Patterns after the Orange
Revolution
ISBN 978-3-8382-0325-6

109 Michail Logvinov
Russlands Kampf gegen den
internationalen Terrorismus
Eine kritische Bestandsaufnahme des
Bekämpfungsansatzes
Mit einem Geleitwort von
Hans-Henning Schröder
und einem Vorwort von Eckhard Jesse
ISBN 978-3-8382-0329-4

110 John B. Dunlop
The Moscow Bombings
of September 1999
Examinations of Russian Terrorist Attacks
at the Onset of Vladimir Putin's Rule
Second, Revised and Expanded Edition
ISBN 978-3-8382-0388-1

111 Андрей А. Ковалёв
Свидетельство из-за кулис
российской политики I
Можно ли делать добро из зла?
(Воспоминания и размышления о
последних советских и первых
послесоветских годах)
With a foreword by Peter Reddaway
ISBN 978-3-8382-0302-7

112 Андрей А. Ковалёв
Свидетельство из-за кулис
российской политики II
Угроза для себя и окружающих
(Наблюдения и предостережения
относительно происходящего после 2000 г.)
ISBN 978-3-8382-0303-4

113 Bernd Kappenberg
Zeichen setzen für Europa
Der Gebrauch europäischer lateinischer
Sonderzeichen in der deutschen Öffentlichkeit
Mit einem Vorwort von Peter Schlobinski
ISBN 978-3-89821-749-1

114 Ivo Mijnssen
The Quest for an Ideal Youth in
Putin's Russia I
Back to Our Future! History, Modernity, and
Patriotism according to Nashi, 2005-2013
With a foreword by Jeronim Perović
Second, Revised and Expanded Edition
ISBN 978-3-8382-0368-3

115 Jussi Lassila
The Quest for an Ideal Youth in
Putin's Russia II
The Search for Distinctive Conformism in the
Political Communication of Nashi, 2005-2009
With a foreword by Kirill Postoutenko
Second, Revised and Expanded Edition
ISBN 978-3-8382-0415-4

116 Valerio Trabandt
Neue Nachbarn, gute Nachbarschaft?
Die EU als internationaler Akteur am Beispiel
ihrer Demokratieförderung in Belarus und der
Ukraine 2004-2009
Mit einem Vorwort von Jutta Joachim
ISBN 978-3-8382-0437-6

117 Fabian Pfeiffer
Estlands Außen- und Sicherheitspolitik I
Der estnische Atlantizismus nach der
wiedererlangten Unabhängigkeit 1991-2004
Mit einem Vorwort von Helmut Hubel
ISBN 978-3-8382-0127-6

118 Jana Podßuweit
Estlands Außen- und Sicherheitspolitik II
Handlungsoptionen eines Kleinstaates im
Rahmen seiner EU-Mitgliedschaft (2004-2008)
Mit einem Vorwort von Helmut Hubel
ISBN 978-3-8382-0440-6

119 Karin Pointner
Estlands Außen- und Sicherheitspolitik III
Eine gedächtnispolitische Analyse estnischer
Entwicklungskooperation 2006-2010
Mit einem Vorwort von Karin Liebhart
ISBN 978-3-8382-0435-2

120 Ruslana Vovk
Die Offenheit der ukrainischen
Verfassung für das Völkerrecht und
die europäische Integration
Mit einem Vorwort von Alexander
Blankenagel
ISBN 978-3-8382-0481-9

121 Mykhaylo Banakh
Die Relevanz der Zivilgesellschaft
bei den postkommunistischen
Transformationsprozessen in mittel-
und osteuropäischen Ländern
Das Beispiel der spät- und postsowjetischen
Ukraine 1986-2009
Mit einem Vorwort von Gerhard Simon
ISBN 978-3-8382-0499-4

122 Michael Moser
Language Policy and the Discourse on
Languages in Ukraine under President
Viktor Yanukovych (25 February
2010–28 October 2012)
ISBN 978-3-8382-0497-0 (Paperback edition)
ISBN 978-3-8382-0507-6 (Hardcover edition)

123 Nicole Krome
Russischer Netzwerkkapitalismus
Restrukturierungsprozesse in der
Russischen Föderation am Beispiel des
Luftfahrtunternehmens "Aviastar"
Mit einem Vorwort von Petra Stykow
ISBN 978-3-8382-0534-2

124 David R. Marples
'Our Glorious Past'
Lukashenka's Belarus and
the Great Patriotic War
ISBN 978-3-8382-0574-8 (Paperback edition)
ISBN 978-3-8382-0675-2 (Hardcover edition)

125 Ulf Walther
Russlands "neuer Adel"
Die Macht des Geheimdienstes von
Gorbatschow bis Putin
Mit einem Vorwort von Hans-Georg Wieck
ISBN 978-3-8382-0584-7

126 Simon Geissbühler (Hrsg.)
Kiew – Revolution 3.0
Der Euromaidan 2013/14 und die
Zukunftsperspektiven der Ukraine
ISBN 978-3-8382-0581-6 (Paperback edition)
ISBN 978-3-8382-0681-3 (Hardcover edition)

127 Andrey Makarychev
Russia and the EU
in a Multipolar World
Discourses, Identities, Norms
With a foreword by Klaus Segbers
ISBN 978-3-8382-0629-5

128 Roland Scharff
Kasachstan als postsowjetischer
Wohlfahrtsstaat
Die Transformation des sozialen
Schutzsystems
Mit einem Vorwort von Joachim Ahrens
ISBN 978-3-8382-0622-6

129 Katja Grupp
Bild Lücke Deutschland
Kaliningrader Studierende sprechen über
Deutschland
Mit einem Vorwort von Martin Schulz
ISBN 978-3-8382-0552-6

130 Konstantin Sheiko, Stephen Brown
History as Therapy
Alternative History and Nationalist
Imaginings in Russia, 1991-2014
ISBN 978-3-8382-0665-3

131 Elisa Kriza
Alexander Solzhenitsyn: Cold War
Icon, Gulag Author, Russian
Nationalist?
A Study of the Western Reception of his
Literary Writings, Historical Interpretations,
and Political Ideas
With a foreword by Andrei Rogatchevski
ISBN 978-3-8382-0589-2 (Paperback edition)
ISBN 978-3-8382-0690-5 (Hardcover edition)

132 Serghei Golunov
     The Elephant in the Room
     Corruption and Cheating in Russian
     Universities
     ISBN 978-3-8382-0570-0

133 Manja Hussner, Rainer Arnold (Hgg.)
     Verfassungsgerichtsbarkeit in
     Zentralasien I
     Sammlung von Verfassungstexten
     ISBN 978-3-8382-0595-3

134 Nikolay Mitrokhin
     Die "Russische Partei"
     Die Bewegung der russischen Nationalisten in
     der UdSSR 1953-1985
     Aus dem Russischen übertragen von einem
     Übersetzerteam unter der Leitung von Larisa Schippel
     ISBN 978-3-8382-0024-8

135 Manja Hussner, Rainer Arnold (Hgg.)
     Verfassungsgerichtsbarkeit in
     Zentralasien II
     Sammlung von Verfassungstexten
     ISBN 978-3-8382-0597-7

136 Manfred Zeller
     Das sowjetische Fieber
     Fußballfans im poststalinistischen
     Vielvölkerreich
     Mit einem Vorwort von Nikolaus Katzer
     ISBN 978-3-8382-0757-5

137 Kristin Schreiter
     Stellung und Entwicklungspotential
     zivilgesellschaftlicher Gruppen in
     Russland
     Menschenrechtsorganisationen im Vergleich
     ISBN 978-3-8382-0673-8

138 David R. Marples, Frederick V. Mills
     (eds.)
     Ukraine's Euromaidan
     Analyses of a Civil Revolution
     ISBN 978-3-8382-0660-8

139 Bernd Kappenberg
     Setting Signs for Europe
     Why Diacritics Matter for
     European Integration
     With a foreword by Peter Schlobinski
     ISBN 978-3-8382-0663-9

140 René Lenz
     Internationalisierung, Kooperation
     und Transfer
     Externe bildungspolitische Akteure in der
     Russischen Föderation
     Mit einem Vorwort von Frank Ettrich
     ISBN 978-3-8382-0751-3

141 Juri Plusnin, Yana Zausaeva, Natalia
     Zhidkevich, Artemy Pozanenko
     Wandering Workers
     Mores, Behavior, Way of Life, and Political
     Status of Domestic Russian Labor Migrants
     Translated by Julia Kazantseva
     ISBN 978-3-8382-0653-0

142 David J. Smith (eds.)
     Latvia – A Work in Progress?
     100 Years of State- and Nation-Building
     ISBN 978-3-8382-0648-6

143 Инна Чувычкина (ред.)
     Экспортные нефте- и газопроводы
     на постсоветском пространстве
     Анализ трубопроводной политики в свете
     теории международных отношений
     ISBN 978-3-8382-0822-0

144 Johann Zajaczkowski
     Russland – eine pragmatische
     Großmacht?
     Eine rollentheoretische Untersuchung
     russischer Außenpolitik am Beispiel der
     Zusammenarbeit mit den USA nach 9/11 und
     des Georgienkrieges von 2008
     Mit einem Vorwort von Siegfried Schieder
     ISBN 978-3-8382-0837-4

145 Boris Popivanov
     Changing Images of the Left in
     Bulgaria
     The Challenge of Post-Communism in the
     Early 21st Century
     ISBN 978-3-8382-0667-7

146 Lenka Krátká
     A History of the Czechoslovak Ocean
     Shipping Company 1948-1989
     How a Small, Landlocked Country Ran
     Maritime Business During the Cold War
     ISBN 978-3-8382-0666-0

147 Alexander Sergunin
     Explaining Russian Foreign Policy
     Behavior
     Theory and Practice
     ISBN 978-3-8382-0752-0

148   Darya Malyutina
       Migrant Friendships in
       a Super-Diverse City
       Russian-Speakers and their Social
       Relationships in London in the 21st Century
       With a foreword by Claire Dwyer
       ISBN 978-3-8382-0652-3

149   Alexander Sergunin, Valery Konyshev
       Russia in the Arctic
       Hard or Soft Power?
       ISBN 978-3-8382-0753-7

150   John J. Maresca
       Helsinki Revisited
       A Key U.S. Negotiator's Memoirs
       on the Development of the CSCE into the
       OSCE
       With a foreword by Hafiz Pashayev
       ISBN 978-3-8382-0852-7

151   Jardar Østbø
       The New Third Rome
       Readings of a Russian Nationalist Myth
       With a foreword by Pål Kolstø
       ISBN 978-3-8382-0870-1

152   Simon Kordonsky
       Socio-Economic Foundations of the
       Russian Post-Soviet Regime
       The Resource-Based Economy and Estate-
       Based Social Structure of Contemporary
       Russia
       With a foreword by Svetlana Barsukova
       ISBN 978-3-8382-0775-9

153   Duncan Leitch
       Assisting Reform in Post-Communist
       Ukraine 2000–2012
       The Illusions of Donors and the Disillusion of
       Beneficiaries
       With a foreword by Kataryna Wolczuk
       ISBN 978-3-8382-0844-2

154   Abel Polese
       Limits of a Post-Soviet State
       How Informality Replaces, Renegotiates, and
       Reshapes Governance in Contemporary
       Ukraine
       With a foreword by Colin Williams
       ISBN 978-3-8382-0845-9

155   Mikhail Suslov (ed.)
       Digital Orthodoxy in the Post-Soviet
       World
       The Russian Orthodox Church and Web 2.0
       With a foreword by Father Cyril Hovorun
       ISBN 978-3-8382-0871-8

156   Leonid Luks
       Zwei „Sonderwege"? Russisch-
       deutsche Parallelen und Kontraste
       (1917-2014)
       Vergleichende Essays
       ISBN 978-3-8382-0823-7

157   Vladimir V. Karacharovskiy, Ovsey I.
       Shkaratan, Gordey A. Yastrebov
       Towards a New Russian Work Culture
       Can Western Companies and Expatriates
       Change Russian Society?
       With a foreword by Elena N. Danilova
       Translated by Julia Kazantseva
       ISBN 978-3-8382-0902-9

158   Edmund Griffiths
       Aleksandr Prokhanov and Post-Soviet
       Esotericism
       ISBN 978-3-8382-0903-6

159   Timm Beichelt, Susann Worschech
       (eds.)
       Transnational Ukraine?
       Networks and Ties that Influence(d)
       Contemporary Ukraine
       ISBN 978-3-8382-0944-9

160   Mieste Hotopp-Riecke
       Die Tataren der Krim zwischen
       Assimilation und Selbstbehauptung
       Der Aufbau des krimtatarischen
       Bildungswesens nach Deportation und
       Heimkehr (1990-2005)
       Mit einem Vorwort von Swetlana
       Czerwonnaja
       ISBN 978-3-89821-940-2

161   Olga Bertelsen (ed.)
       Revolution and War in
       Contemporary Ukraine
       The Challenge of Change
       ISBN 978-3-8382-1016-2

162   Natalya Ryabinska
       Ukraine's Post-Communist
       Mass Media
       Between Capture and Commercialization
       With a foreword by Marta Dyczok
       ISBN 978-3-8382-1011-7

163 *Alexandra Cotofana,*
James M. Nyce (eds.)
Religion and Magic in Socialist and
Post-Socialist Contexts I
Historic and Ethnographic Case Studies of
Orthodoxy, Heterodoxy, and Alternative
Spirituality
With a foreword by Patrick L. Michelson
ISBN 978-3-8382-0989-0

164 *Nozima Akhrarkhodjaeva*
The Instrumentalisation of Mass
Media in Electoral Authoritarian
Regimes
Evidence from Russia's Presidential Election
Campaigns of 2000 and 2008
ISBN 978-3-8382-1013-1

165 *Yulia Krasheninnikova*
Informal Healthcare in Contemporary
Russia
Sociographic Essays on the Post-Soviet
Infrastructure for Alternative Healing
Practices
ISBN 978-3-8382-0970-8

166 *Peter Kaiser*
Das Schachbrett der Macht
Die Handlungsspielräume eines sowjetischen
Funktionärs unter Stalin am Beispiel des
Generalsekretärs des Komsomol
Aleksandr Kosarev (1929-1938)
Mit einem Vorwort von Dietmar Neutatz
ISBN 978-3-8382-1052-0

167 *Oksana Kim*
The Effects and Implications of
Kazakhstan's Adoption of
International Financial Reporting
Standards
A Resource Dependence Perspective
With a foreword by Svetlana Vlady
ISBN 978-3-8382-0987-6

168 *Anna Sanina*
Patriotic Education in
Contemporary Russia
Sociological Studies in the Making of the
Post-Soviet Citizen
With a foreword by Anna Oldfield
ISBN 978-3-8382-0993-7

169 *Rudolf Wolters*
Spezialist in Sibirien
Faksimile der 1933 erschienenen
ersten Ausgabe
Mit einem Vorwort von Dmitrij Chmelnizki
ISBN 978-3-8382-0515-1